PRAISE FOR *PREACH*

"Feel called to preach on justice t[opics but worried] about backlash from a divided congregation in a divided culture. Schade comes to the rescue. Her sermon-dialogue-sermon approach is a practical, pastoral way to get the prophetic conversation rolling. A must read!"
   —**O. Wesley Allen, Jr., Lois Craddock Perkins Professor of Homiletics, Perkins School of Theology, Southern Methodist University**

"This book is one of the most helpful resources to teach and learn how preachers give prophetic voices to controversial justice issues in the midst of socially and politically divided times. Based on her rich experience of preaching ministry, rigorous scholarly and scientific research, and pastoral sensibility, Dr. Schade provides the reader with practical wisdom for prophetic preaching."
   —**Eunjoo Kim, Iliff School of Theology**

"In these turbulent political times, Dr. Leah Schade offers a hopeful and realistic roadmap for preaching to listeners with diverse opinions. Concrete examples for a process beyond the Sunday sermon provide opportunities for growth and healing. This is a much-needed book at a critical juncture in the Church—not just for leaders but for the laity as well."
   —**Rev. Angela Zimmann, vice president of institutional advancement and adjunct professor of homiletics, United Lutheran Seminary**

"The past generation of scholarship in homiletics has been leading to *Preaching in the Purple Zone*. Field tested and theologically grounded, Schade provides a truly conversational blueprint for preachers who want to preach about difficult social justice issues *with* their congregations rather than simply *to* their congregations. In our contentious cultural moment, this book is a gift to preachers, congregations, and the world."
   —**Richard Voelz, assistant professor of preaching and worship, Union Presbyterian Seminary**

"How can preachers engage diverse congregations in difficult moral conversations that often have political implications? And how can preachers preach sermons that capture the complexities of those conversations while nudging participants forward toward new and better moral understandings and social commitments? These are the core questions answered in this well-researched, clearly written, and wise book. Strongly recommended."
   —**John S. McClure, Charles G. Finney Professor of Preaching and Worship, Vanderbilt Divinity School**

"Rooted in Jesus' ability to stimulate dialogue, Schade's book provides preachers with a scholarly approach to prophetic proclamation and practical direction to engage worshippers in faithfully deliberating the issues of the day. *Preaching in the Purple Zone* echoes de Tocqueville's respect for the role of religion in civic life."

—**Gregg Kauffman, ELCA pastor,
Kettering Foundation Research Associate**

"There's nothing sophomoric about Leah Schade's sophomore contribution in homiletics. Drawing its wisdom from her preaching, classroom, and community activism expertise, *Preaching in the Purple Zone* refreshingly offers controversy-averse pastors a quantitatively researched, timely guide for decentering the progressive versus conservative (idolatry of perspective) battle in theologically constructive ways. Schade's skill building 'five paths' preaching methodology invites preachers into prophetically conscious sermon preparation and urges them to reconceive preaching as a biblical, theological, co-creative task—one that shifts preaching's objective from, as she rightly puts it, 'simply opening minds and hearts, to moving hands and feet in tangible ways.'"

—**Kenyatta R. Gilbert, professor of homiletics,
Howard University School of Divinity**

"Leah D. Schade has dedicated herself as a pastor and theologian to bringing the social gospel of Christianity into congregational dialogue, and she is realistic about doing so in our polarizing and messy culture. With her commanding knowledge of homiletic literature and years of experience as a Lutheran pastor, and having surveyed over twelve hundred preachers and done training with the National Issues Forum, Schade presents a comprehensive sermon-dialogue-sermon process that can bring a congregation into respectful learning and a more consequential practice of relevant discipleship. I plan to use this book as a peer-learning resource for Roman Catholic preachers who value Catholic social teaching but seriously wonder how to preach on potentially threatening issues such as racism or health care at the end of life."

—**Gregory Heille, professor of preaching and evangelization,
Aquinas Institute of Theology, St. Louis**

"Leah Shade's *Preaching in the Purple Zone* should be required reading for pastors who preach to congregations that include both conservative and liberal listeners, seeking a way to address difficult, controversial issues. This book is a clear, profound, and practical homiletical resource for our current culture of animosity and incivility. Shade identifies fears that 'muzzle' prophetic preach-

ing, chief among them the objection that our preaching is 'too political.' She offers a biblical, theological, homiletical rationale for prophetic preaching that shifts the focus from the lone voice of the preacher to a shared conversation in the congregation. She outlines a process of deliberative dialogue by which both preacher and congregation can grow together in engaging tough topics. The book includes sample sermons and detailed guidelines for addressing current issues. My advice: buy, read, and use this book!"
—**Alyce McKenzie, director of the Center for Preaching Excellence, Perkins School of Theology, Southern Methodist University**

"Here are three reasons why preachers need to read Dr. Leah Schade's *Preaching in the Purple Zone*: (1) Know you're not alone. Based on her extensive surveys and interviews, Dr. Schade proves you're not alone in your concerns about prophetic preaching or weathering their potential consequences. (2) Craft prophetic sermons wisely and pastorally. Apply these sage, practical suggestions and real-life examples to develop your purple-zone sermons in concert with those who will hear them. (3) Know what to do afterward. After the sermon you'll have the steps you need to continue to develop relationships with your listeners—whether they agree with the sermon or not—to proclaim the Gospel together. Thanks to this book you'll be able to preach your purple zone sermons with deeper theological and biblical craftsmanship, purpose, and care."
—**Lisa Cressman, author of** *Backstory Preaching: Integrating Life, Spirituality and Craft*

"If you are looking for a recitation of preaching techniques, this is not the book! If you crave insight and guidance for leading a faith community in this fractured and fractious time, you'll find it in these pages. Leah Schade offers guidance that will lead you deep into the issues that divide our civic and faith communities to discover common values, commitments, and shared work centered in Christ crucified and risen for the life of the world. By weaving preaching carefully into the fabric of the community's life together, Leah provides theologically rooted, eminently practical, and effective guidance that brings together prophetic and pastoral roles into one public ministry. Those who follow her guidance will find both roles deepened in their own ministries and will see their faith community knit together in new and life-giving ways that empower preacher and community together to share the new, abundant, and lasting life of Christ with the world with vigor and grace."
—**Bishop William O. Gafkjen, Indiana-Kentucky Synod, Evangelical Lutheran Church in America**

"What an invaluable and timely book! *Preaching in the Purple Zone* addresses head-on the many significant divides we face in church and world and posits a way forward for preaching that is marked by genuine dialog, deep engagement with the scriptures and one another, and a pastoral commitment to tackling divisive issues with openness and humility. Leah Schade helpfully models what she proposes by her ongoing use of actual sermons and conversations around controversial issues she and her students have engaged with[. Ultimately this book is about more than preaching; it is about how the church can prophetically model an alternative way to live together in the midst of a seriously polarized nation and world."

—**Leonora Tubbs Tisdale, Clement Muehl Professor of Homiletics Emerita, Yale Divinity School**

"*Preaching in the Purple Zone* is *the* preaching book for the times in which we live. Almost every preacher has red and blue voters in their pews—sometimes on the same row. Learning ways to preach in these conflicting times is a skill richly needed, and Leah Schade has the lessons for us in this exciting and intriguing book. It's going to be on my preaching resource shelf from now on."

—**Karyn L. Wiseman, United Lutheran Seminary**

"In this season of our life as a church and a nation, the capacity to reach a broad spectrum of political and theological views is being put to the test. In *Preaching in the Purple Zone*, Dr. Schade helps us address the emergent, often 'messy,' matters and wide-ranging opinions within our faith communities with grace and integrity. *Preaching in the Purple Zone* is an excellent guide that helps clergy courageously and respectfully engage with their congregations to discover and sometimes create an intersection of common values while faithfully preaching the gospel."

—**Cynthia Fierro Harvey, Bishop, Louisiana Conference of The United Methodist Church**

"When 'red' and 'blue' convictions meet, is an outcome other than purplish bruises all around even possible? 'Yes!' says Leah Schade. The purple zone, where blue meets red in deliberative dialogue, is a place for royal celebrations of life-changing truth proclaimed with never-ending love. Preachers and parishioners alike will find here a marvelous roadmap for honest interaction that produces light and hope for the journey ahead."

—**Brad A. Binau, Trinity Lutheran Seminary at Capital University**

Preaching in the Purple Zone

Ministry in the Red-Blue Divide

Leah D. Schade

ROWMAN & LITTLEFIELD
Lanham • Boulder • New York • London

Published by Rowman & Littlefield
An imprint of The Rowman & Littlefield Publishing Group, Inc.
4501 Forbes Boulevard, Suite 200, Lanham, Maryland 20706
www.rowman.com

6 Tinworth Street, London SE11 5AL, United Kingdom

Copyright © 2019 by The Rowman & Littlefield Publishing Group, Inc.

All rights reserved. No part of this book may be reproduced in any form or by any electronic or mechanical means, including information storage and retrieval systems, without written permission from the publisher, except by a reviewer who may quote passages in a review.

British Library Cataloguing in Publication Information Available

Library of Congress Cataloging-in-Publication Data

Names: Schade, Leah D., author.
Title: Preaching in the purple zone : ministry in the red-blue divide / Leah Schade.
Description: Lanham : Rowman & Littlefield, [2019] | Includes bibliographical references and index.
Identifiers: LCCN 2018058284 (print) | LCCN 2019000091 (ebook) | ISBN 9781538119891 (ebook) | ISBN 9781538119877 (cloth : alk. paper) | ISBN 9781538119884 (pbk. : alk. paper)
Subjects: LCSH: Preaching—Political aspects—United States. | Topical preaching—United States—Case studies. | Christianity and politics—United States. | Social justice—Sermons.
Classification: LCC BV4211.3 (ebook) | LCC BV4211.3 .S3456 2019 (print) | DDC 251—dc23
LC record available at https://lccn.loc.gov/2018058284

∞™ The paper used in this publication meets the minimum requirements of American National Standard for Information Sciences—Permanence of Paper for Printed Library Materials, ANSI/NISO Z39.48-1992.

Printed in the United States of America

Contents

Acknowledgments		*ix*
Foreword		*xiii*
	Ronald J. Allen	
Introduction		*1*
1	Preaching about Controversial Justice Issues: Tracing the Contours of the Purple Zone	13
2	Beyond "Political": Reframing Our Understanding of Politics and Preaching	29
3	Homiletical Foundations for Purple Zone Preaching	47
4	Five Paths of Prophetic Preaching in the Purple Zone	59
5	Preparing for the Sermon-Dialogue-Sermon Process	73
6	Preaching Sermon 1: Prophetic Invitation to Dialogue	85
7	Deliberative Dialogue in the Purple Zone	97
8	Preaching Sermon 2: Communal Prophetic Proclamation	119
9	Case Studies from the Purple Zone, Part 1: Immigration	141
10	Case Studies, Part 2: Four Journeys into the Purple Zone	159
11	Building Bridges in the Purple Zone: Where Do We Go from Here?	181

Appendix A: Sample Newsletter Article Announcing Deliberative Dialogue   201

Appendix B: Options for Planning One, Two, or Three Sessions for the Deliberative Dialogue   203

Appendix C: "Cheat Sheet" Questions for Facilitating Deliberative Dialogue   207

Notes   209

Selected Bibliography   221

Scripture Index   225

Index   227

About the Author   243

Acknowledgments

This book is a nexus of the work, input, ministries, feedback, and mentoring of literally thousands of people. From the congregations where these Purple Zone sermons were preached, to the 1,200 preachers who filled out the survey, to the institutions that supported the scholarship for this work, to a host of individuals who gave me feedback, advice, and encouragement—this book stands on the shoulders of a "great cloud of witnesses."

The education I received from the faculty at the Lutheran Theological Seminary at Philadelphia (now United Lutheran Seminary) gave me the theological and theoretical foundations I needed for understanding the Purple Zone. I'm especially grateful to Katie Day, who has guided and encouraged me for more than two decades. Angela Zimmann has also been an enthusiastic supporter of my work as we've developed parallel courses and shared insights on preaching in a divided culture.

The three congregations I have served as pastor—Reformation Lutheran in Media, Pennsylvania; Spirit and Truth Worship Center in Yeadon, Pennsylvania; and United in Christ Lutheran Church in Lewisburg, Pennsylvania—each showed me a different shade of the Purple Zone and how to effectively minister therein. The congregation in which my family and I are now members, Gethsemane Lutheran in Lexington, Kentucky, is also a Purple Zone church, and I am thankful to them and to Pastor Laura Altmann for their willingness to engage difficult conversations with me in order to learn and grow.

I am also grateful to the clergy groups and individual colleagues whose questions, discussions, and feedback on my work contributed to this project. The Upper Susquehanna Synod of the Evangelical Lutheran Church in America (ELCA) is where this project found its genesis, and I am grateful to former Bishop Robert Driesen, current Bishop Barbara Collins, my colleagues in the Buffalo Valley Conference (especially Bill Henderson), and those who attended the 2016 Bishops Retreat who were all among the early sounding boards for this project. The Isaiah 1:17 Justice Team of the Indiana-Kentucky Synod of the ELCA has been enthusiastic in learning about and experimenting with the sermon-dialogue-sermon method. I am blessed to work with this dedicated group of pastors and parishioners who are committed to prophetic preaching and ministry. Thanks also to Bishop William Gafkjen who has welcomed my teaching ministry in the Indiana-Kentucky Synod.

Three seminaries have given me the opportunity to teach courses related to the Purple Zone and the sermon-dialogue-sermon method. Brad Binau, former dean, invited me to teach for Trinity Lutheran Seminary in Ohio. Alyce McKenzie, director of the Center for Preaching Excellence at Perkins School of Theology in Dallas, invited me to teach a cohort of early-career pastors in Louisiana. And Lexington Theological Seminary (LTS), where I teach preaching and worship, allowed me to design both an elective and a webinar about preaching in the Purple Zone.

The faculty and staff at LTS have been overwhelmingly supportive of my scholarship and teaching. President Charisse Gillett, Vice President for Academic Affairs and Dean Loida Martell, and my colleagues Drs. Emily Askew, Barbara Blodgett, and Jerry Sumney, each gave helpful feedback on this project.

The deliberative dialogue method I use in this book and in my teaching has been developed by the Charles F. Kettering Foundation and the National Issues Forum Institute. I am deeply appreciative of my colleagues in the faith-based research exchange group and to Ekaterina Lukianova, program officer, and John Dedrick, vice president and program director, for convening us. I am also indebted to Gregg Kaufman for his partnership, sharing of resources for deliberative dialogue, and encouragement.

Several colleagues were early testers of the questionnaire, "Preaching about Controversial Justice Issues," and gave important feedback as I developed the instrument. Those individuals were Kris Bentley, Erin Cash, Chris Cash, and Michael Dubsky. Kenneth Inskeep, executive for research and evaluation at the ELCA, provided key advice for improving the survey.

I am especially thankful to Richard Weis, dean emeritus at Lexington Theological Seminary, who enabled me to conduct the research for this project through the seminary's channels, painstakingly explained how to create an effective survey, and mentored me through the early stages of presenting the results of the research to a wider audience.

To the hundreds of people who took the time to complete the survey, "Preaching about Controversial Justice Issues"—my deepest thanks. Your honesty, forthrightness, and willingness to share your experiences with preaching about issues of public concern have provided a wealth of information and data that have already made an important contribution to the academy. The data will be the source of many other projects going forward that I hope will be worthwhile to preachers and the church in the United States and beyond.

Many colleagues within the Academy of Homiletics gave helpful feedback and advice as this project began to take shape. The Preaching and Culture Workgroup convened by Eunjoo Mary Kim workshopped early drafts of chapters with me. Wes Allen offered helpful advice for content and chapter structure. Aimee Moiso and Ellen Ott Marshall alerted me to the emerging field of inquiry around the "theology of conflict" and provided me with helpful resources. I'm especially grateful to Ron Allen, who has championed this project from the beginning and shared important resources, as well as his own scholarship, that have shaped this book in indelible ways.

Four friends were kind enough to read the early drafts of the manuscript. With their "eagle eyes" they offered invaluable editorial critique, corrections, and suggestions for improving the book. Daryl and Shea Emowrey, Karleen Jung, Richard Voelz—I am grateful to each of you.

I'm thankful to my editor, Rolf Janke and his team at Rowman & Littlefield, who believed in this project and worked to usher this book through the process, from proposal to end product.

My parents, Carl and Peggy Jacobs, didn't know it at the time, but they were raising me to be prepared for the Purple Zone by teaching me critical thinking skills, engaging all manner of political topics with me growing up, and steeping me in the life of the church. My in-laws, Jim and Carolyn Schade, have been an unwavering source of support for more than half my life, and I am grateful for all they have done for our family these many years.

To my husband, Jim, and our children, Rachel and Benjamin—thank you for your understanding as I worked on this book. Not only do you keep me laughing to lighten my serious work, you have accompanied me every step along the way. As I've answered God's call, you've had to adjust to four moves, different schools, and leaving behind the friends and churches you've loved. But you have always put your best foot forward and trusted in God. I am grateful to God for the three of you, that you have so willingly accompanied me and rallied around me on this journey.

This book would not have been possible without the hard work of my students and pastoral colleagues who were the "guinea pigs" for testing the sermon-dialogue-sermon method. While space limitations meant that not everyone's work could be included, the case studies and reflections of many appear in this book. I am grateful to each of them for their willingness to learn, experiment, and give feedback to me on the process. Those individuals are David Allred, Imro Anys, Brooke Baker, Kelly Berne, Cody Blust,

Colleen Bookter, Evan Cameron, Julie Cory, Daryl Emowrey, Laura Ferree, Ken Greble, Dan Gutman, Branden Hunt, Karleen Jung, TJ Lynch, Rachel McConnell-Switzer, Ian McMichael, Lucas McSurley, Anders Nilsen, Kevin O'Bryan, Jenny Perkins, Tiffanie Postel, Andrew Potsko, JoAnne Pounds, Amanda Price, Julia Puac-Romero, Adele Rapelye, Joel Rothe, Joanna Samuelson, Allison Sauls, Andrew Shue, Leslie Stephens, Marissa Teauseau, Michael Wright, and Ali Young.

This book is dedicated to all of you, and to every minister who strives to preach the gospel and minister to the church in the Purple Zone.

Foreword

Ronald J. Allen

During election season, television and computer news put maps of the United States on the screen picturing blue states and red states. In blue states, most people support values and policies associated with the Democratic party and vote for those candidates. In red states, most people support the values and policies of the Republican party and vote for that party's candidates.* The blue and red designations often signal not only immediate political interests but also much larger worldviews that include such things as the makeup of community, attitudes toward others, civil rights, sexuality and gender, social responsibility in areas ranging from education to health care, distribution of material resources, ecology, and relationships with other countries.

Critical discussion with thoughtful comparison and contrast among proposals is supposed to be the heart of the democratic process. Yet parties and candidates today frequently attack not only the policies but also the people in the other party in terms that go beyond the unflattering and caricature to the extremes of disrespect. The result is that where politics is concerned, people are often polarized. Politicians in each party make their pitches in openly partisan terms to the party's base and to independent or undecided voters. They rally the members of the base to reinforce their values and commitments and while strategizing how to get and keep a grip on power. Today's political leaders can typically assume that their audience already sees the world the way they do. The leader's task, then, is to simply to motivate the base.

---

*Of course, there are exceptions. A Democrat can be elected in a red state. A blue state can have some values and practices that are similar to those of the Republican party. And, of course, states can change colors from election to election.

Preachers, especially in congregations in the historic Eurocentric denominations, are usually in very different situations.* While there are occasional blue and red congregations in the historic churches, Leah Schade insightfully notes that most such congregations nowadays are "purple" in the sense that they contain both blue (Democratic) and red (Republican) members. In today's highly politicized and polarized climate, some listeners in the purple zone want the preacher to pass the hand of divine blessing over their politics, while others want the preacher to avoid politics altogether, while still others would like for the preacher to bless their particular political interests while remaining silent on others.

The purple zone is a minefield of explosive possibilities for the preacher. Yet, the preacher is called to help congregations in the purple zone interpret the whole of life from a theological perspective. A practical question is, What can ministers do to encourage people in the purple zone to come together in mutual search for adequate interpretations of God's presence and purposes, and how to respond appropriately?

In this groundbreaking book, Professor Leah Schade invites preachers and congregations into a process of deliberative dialogue that seeks to respect all voices and positions in the theological conversation. The preacher is less the singular oracle of God whose sermon settles all theological issues, and more the one who convenes a sacred conversation in search of the best understanding of God's purposes and how to respond at the present moment. The congregation becomes a preaching community in the prophetic mode.

The heart of the book is the sermon-dialogue-sermon method. Instead of preachers offering the final word on a text or topic in a single sermon, they initiate a process of congregational conversation after the sermon in which people actually speak with one another and with the preacher about the topic in a context of respect and mutual exchange. Preachers begin the process with a sermon called a "Prophetic Invitation to Dialogue" indicating why the issue at hand is important to the preacher, the congregation, and the world, and why dialogue about the issue is needed. After the initial sermon, members of the congregation meet to consider what is important to them about the issue and how they relate to it personally. The group considers the issue critically,

---

*By historic churches, I have in mind churches that were once "mainline," but which have declined in both size and cultural influence. The historic denominations include churches like the Christian Church (Disciples of Christ), Episcopal Church, Evangelical Lutheran Church in America, Presbyterian Church U.S.A., United Church of Christ, United Methodist Church. At the same time the public presence of the historic churches is fading, more independent, community, and typically evangelical congregations have gained numbers and cultural influence. Some of the latter congregations are expressly red, equating red values and policies with the divine will. Many urban areas contain occasional congregations that are blue in similar theological and political ways. Preachers in these red and blue congregations can operate more like politicians in political parties. My impression is that many African American congregations are open to public advocacy in the pulpit.

naming interpretive possibilities and indicating the pros and cons of each possibility. They identify common themes and shared values that emerge in the conversation, including flagging points of disagreement. The dialogue concludes with pondering next steps toward taking action on the issue in their particular congregational context.

The preacher then returns to the study in order to reflect on the dialogue. What insights came out? What did the preacher learn as she or he facilitated and participated in the dialogue? What questions are still open and need to be addressed? Professor Schade calls the follow-up sermon the "Communal Prophetic Proclamation." In this approach, the preacher is not a lonely voice railing against the system. The congregation becomes a prophetic community as it wrestles with how to understand and respond to significant issues.

The author reminds preachers that while this model deepens congregational interaction around sensitive and significant issues, a single episode of this process will not resolve all issues for all people. Preachers and congregations may need to think in incremental steps in addressing important matters and return to issues again . . . and again . . . over time.

The book is richly illustrated with case studies from real congregations that show the sermon-dialogue-sermon method in operation. The case studies suggest that congregations following this approach not only buy into the process but are deeply affected by it, as they do not simply receive the predigested thoughts of the preacher in a single sermon but must think carefully in community toward what they really believe. Even when the process does not result in a unified congregational perspective, it nevertheless creates a climate of mutual understanding and patience with one another.

This book calls for nothing less than a change in the preaching culture of the congregation as it envisions preaching as a community vocation. In this, it reclaims some of the communal identity of the biblical world while placing the process of preaching in the growing stream of rediscovery of community so characteristic of the postmodern world.

Many ministers in the historic churches today seek to be countercultural. I regard *Preaching in the Purple Zone* as a deeply countercultural work. In a culture that reduces public discourse to sound bites, slogans, and tweets—often shot at one another like bullets from a gun—this book calls for respectful dialogue with others. All partners in the conversation seek to understand how others see the world, and why, and what is at stake for them. Rather than promote a particular agenda, the preacher in the purple zone seeks for the community to come together in search of God's purposes for the *common* good. This volume then offers an alternative to the culture of rhetorical violence so common in public life today. Indeed, the capacity for respectful dialogue around important issues may be one of the greatest gifts of the church to the world today.

Introduction

THE RED-BLUE DIVIDE

*J*ust before the 2012 presidential election in the United States, CNN posted to its website an article by John Blake titled, "Do You Believe in a Red State Jesus or a Blue State Jesus?" The question assumes a false dichotomy, but the author's observation about that year's election was just as applicable for the 2016 presidential campaign:

> Here's a presidential election prediction you can bet on. Right after the winner is announced, somebody somewhere in America will fall on their knees and pray, "Thank you Jesus." And somebody somewhere else will moan, "Help us Jesus." But what Jesus will they be praying to: a red state Jesus or a blue state Jesus?[1]

Blake went on to explain that both faith and elections are about choices, and that those choices are informed by how one views Jesus. It may be tempting to assume that liberals "see Jesus as a champion of the poor who would support raising taxes on the wealthy, while some conservatives think Jesus would be more concerned with opposing abortion and same-sex marriage," Blake observed. But Christians are more nuanced in their beliefs. And Jesus cannot so easily be co-opted into a political position. "Perhaps most Christians follow not one Jesus, but many—including a bit of a red state Jesus and a bit of a blue state Jesus," the author surmises.

Blake's article includes a quiz that reinforces this red-blue dichotomy. Only two choices are offered for each of the ten questions aimed to help voters see where they fall on the red-state-blue-state-Jesus scale. Thus, despite the author's premise, the quiz reinforces the fact that many people often categorize themselves along these ideological lines. Of course, none of us lives in a truly "red" or "blue" state. The colors run together in our families, our houses of worship, our schools, our places of employment, and even within our own hearts and minds. Of course, there are also many other colors beyond red and blue (an environmentalist, for example, might consider themselves blue-green). Thus, the red-blue divide is, admittedly, an artificial one. Nevertheless, the image of the contrasting colors denotes the divisiveness we experience in political discourse in this country. And the blending of those colors gives us the Purple Zone—the place where the boundaries of red and blue merge, mix, and produce another shade altogether.

For the purposes of this book, I have chosen to use the red-blue descriptor for the current political dichotomy as dictated by our two-party system. The Purple Zone is where clergy find themselves as they are ministering, preaching, and teaching to divided congregations in the midst of the politically contested red-blue ideologies of their parishioners and the wider society. My question is, How might preachers approach the homiletic task of addressing controversial justice issues in such a fractured and deeply divided sociopolitical culture? How can we engage the red-blue divide within our congregations and communities to find and navigate the Purple Zone? Before I can answer such questions, I will share how I developed my approach and some of my own experiences around ministering in the Purple Zone.

MY EXPERIENCE IN THE PURPLE ZONE

If you are a clergyperson, you have likely felt the tension of divisiveness manifesting itself in your own congregation. Of course, this political animosity didn't start with the 2016 or 2012 elections. Our country's history has been marked with periods of deep divides during the Civil War, the Vietnam Era, and the Civil Rights Movement, for example. In fact, the challenge of addressing controversial issues from the pulpit is one that pastors have faced since the very beginnings of the church when early Christians debated about the inclusion of Gentiles within the faith community. Since that time, the church has experienced both major splits and minor splinters, from the Protestant Reformation to the local church breaking up over seemingly minor disputes. In my time as an ordained pastor, however, I have observed a deterioration of civil relationships and an alarming rise in animosity over the past twenty years that warrants attention.

As a parish pastor, preaching in the red-blue divide was a challenge I faced repeatedly while serving in three different ministry settings over the years. My commitment to raising a prophetic voice about social justice issues sometimes put me at odds with congregants who did not share my views or commitments. Thus, I have had to learn some of my lessons about preaching in the Purple Zone the hard way.

Full disclosure: I preach and write as a cisgender, heterosexual, temporarily-abled, married female in my mid-forties who benefits from the privilege of my white race, middle-class upbringing, marital status, functioning body, and level of education. While I was raised as a Republican in central Pennsylvania, I registered to vote as a Democrat in college. As a Master of Divinity student at the Lutheran Theological Seminary at Philadelphia, and then as an ordained Lutheran (ELCA) pastor, I began serious and ongoing work to understand the intersections of race, gender, sexuality, socioeconomics, and religion. My pastoral experience has included ministries in suburban (mainly white and middle- to upper-class), urban (mainly African American working-class), and rural (mainly white working class) settings. Thus, I've ministered in congregations that have spanned the spectrum of the Purple Zone, with staunch "red" conservatives as well as bright "blue" progressives. So I have had my feet in both the red and blue camps for many decades.

As a PhD student, I studied the additional layer of ecological theology among those intersections. This led me to become an environmental activist and community organizer during my ministry. It was in writing my first book, *Creation-Crisis Preaching: Ecology, Theology, and the Pulpit*, that I discovered that most clergy and congregations are neither equipped nor eager to undertake discussions about controversial topics such as climate change.[2] That is what led me to begin the work of trying to understand why clergy are hesitant to preach about justice issues, and what would be most helpful for them in this task. Today, as a professor of preaching and worship at Lexington Theological Seminary within the Disciples of Christ–Christian Church tradition (a mainline Protestant denomination), I teach my students that the challenge of addressing controversial justice issues from the pulpit, while fraught with risks, also offers opportunities to proclaim the gospel and build profound experiences of community.

So, as a pastor of three very different churches whose parishioners have spanned the Purple Zone, and now as a seminary professor of students from different denominations and across the political spectrum, I have learned some important lessons. What I have learned is that no matter where I locate myself in the political, theological, and cultural constellation, I must meet people where they are, listen to them with respect, and—within the congregation— be their pastor. I must be genuinely interested in them, curious about who they are and how they've come to believe what they do, and care for them with the love of Christ so that a relationship of trust is built between us.

At the same time, I take very seriously the call to exercise the prophetic voice in the pulpit and in the public square, trusting that God's got my back when I face forward into an issue that I or my faith community discerns needs to be addressed. As I'll share in this book, I have made mistakes and missteps, but I try not to make the same mistake twice. Those mistakes have taught me valuable lessons about what *not* to do in the Purple Zone, and how to be a better pastor in the long run. Along the way, I have become very interested in how other preachers navigate the dilemma of prophetic preaching in a time of corrosively divisive politics as well. The dilemma is accurately described by a colleague of mine in a clergy study group:

> On the one hand, I don't want to alienate my parishioners by saying something in a sermon that might anger them. But I also feel like I'm abdicating my pastoral and homiletical authority by not saying anything at all. At the same time, I can't pretend that I'm in some kind of middle position on this issue, because even after looking at this from many angles, I have definite thoughts about this topic. I know I need to at least speak to it in my sermon, but I don't know how to do it without stepping on a landmine.

Does this sound familiar? If you're a pastor, perhaps you've thought or felt the same thing at some point. If you're a parishioner, perhaps you've observed these same dynamics pulling at the pastor of your own congregation. For some, the color purple is not just the blending of red and blue perspectives, but a reminder of the bruising one may suffer when stepping into that place of controversy and divisiveness.

NOT A NEW DILEMMA, BUT MORE URGENT

Several scholars have made similar observations about the dilemma faced by clergy when deciding how, or even if, they will broach a difficult topic within a sermon. Nearly twenty years ago, sociologist of religion and seminary professor Katie Day observed that religious voices that had historically been heard in public debates over issues such as slavery, civil rights, and the Vietnam War had become more reticent to advocate for progressive social change. "[I]n more recent years a faith perspective has rarely been heard in the social struggles over current issues such as welfare reform, military interventions [or] gun control . . . Despite denominational policy statements on these issues, advocacy is seldom seen or heard beyond the staff of the Washington offices of the mainline Protestant groups."[3] She did note that these kinds of issues are "messy," and that churchgoers recognize the existence of a wide range of opinions on these matters within their faith community. Thus, the hesitancy to enter this messiness has resulted in "the disengagement of the church and its individual members from public deliberation," she lamented, noting that, "we have lost the capacity to talk to each other in significant ways."[4]

In a 2004 essay, homiletician David Buttrick also bemoaned the reticence of preachers to speak to the injustices of the day. "Do our pulpits address such issues?" he asked. "Generally, no. But preaching that does not build concern for the human common good is downright unsatisfactory, if not wicked. How has the pulpit tumbled into irrelevancy? How has the pulpit lost 'public voice'?"[5]

Leonora Tubbs Tisdale wrote a book called *Prophetic Preaching: A Pastoral Approach* in which she asked similar questions: "Where have all the prophets gone? Why do churches and pastors so often seem to shy away from prophetic witness? . . . Why do we avoid speaking truth in love regarding some of the burning issues of our day? And why are we often fearful of what becoming prophetic witnesses will mean for our lives?"[6]

In light of these urgent questions, it is worth taking some time to consider *why* people get so contentious when talking about controversial issues. Ronald J. Allen, John S. McClure, and O. Wesley Allen observe that

> the early twenty-first century is a season of fractiousness, especially in politics and in matters of social and economic policy, in which people often segregate into groups that engage one another not through respectful listening to others but through polemic, sound bite, caricature, manipulation, and even misrepresentation. Churches sometimes intensify such polarization with rhetorics of superiority, exclusivism, and separation.[7]

Ron Allen further explains the realities of *polarization* as people withdraw into "gated enclaves of closed perspectives, and regard others with suspicion and even hostility. Polarized groups tend to see the world in binary terms of us and them, right and wrong, and seek to dominate the social world. They seldom take the perspectives of others into account, and typically claim to have *the* answers for the larger world."[8] Whether the issue is immigration or health care, land use or gun control, the current state of our body politic is such that "counter-perspectives and resistance to the group often reinforce the commitment of group members to their polarizing ideology. Polarizing groups sometimes reject a proposal from a rival group simply because the proposal originated in that outside source, and with no reference to the strengths and weaknesses of the proposal itself."[9]

Preaching in a fraught time is, of course, nothing new. Every generation finds itself in a unique confluence of cultural, political, societal, and economic forces that call for preachers to draw on all of their skills, training, and gifts of the Holy Spirit in order to create sermons that are relevant, timely, and effective. This moment in our nation's and, indeed, our planet's history, however, is particularly overwrought. With any of these issues there is much at stake: incredible amounts of wealth, questions of power and equality, personal and community identity, the ecological conditions that support life itself, and the very real beings (human and otherwise) affected by these issues all have a stake in our conversations, decisions, policies, and actions.

Because of the intense and complex overlay of competing interests, we find ourselves, in Jesus' words, "a house divided against itself" (Matthew 12:25). And, indeed, the *oikos*—meaning "house" in Greek—of our society, and even Earth itself, is crumbling, flooding, and burning all around us. Some of us may have enough temporary wealth, power, and privilege to cocoon ourselves in little enclaves longer than our poorer sisters and brothers. But the frantic grasps to protect this illusory wealth only hasten the speed at which the ensuing economic and ecological domino effect will collapse the collective house of this planet.

It is "for such a time as this" (Esther 4:14) that preachers are called to summon their courage to address the vital issues of our time by attending faithfully to God's Word. We must give due diligence to studying the topic at hand, listening intently to our parishioners, attuning to the guidance of the Holy Spirit, and "speaking truth in love" in ways that "enable congregations to genuinely hear and respond to that Word."[10] In the midst of this red-blue divide, our job as preachers is to find a way to courageously step into the Purple Zone—where the colors red and blue combine into various shades of purple. We are called to listen with hospitality, engage with integrity and prayer, and learn with intellectual rigor in order to speak God's Word that addresses the powers, casts out demons, and proclaims the crucified and risen Christ.

My research has shown, however, that despite their deep sense of call, pastors do not feel adequately trained or prepared to enter the Purple Zone. More often than not, preachers choose to avoid controversial issues rather than open themselves and their congregations to the inherent risks involved in such an undertaking. Moreover, some doubt whether such preaching can even make a difference in the lives of parishioners or the larger community.

THE PURPLE ZONE: WHERE ANGELS—
AND PASTORS—FEAR TO TREAD

In *Prophetic Preaching,* Tisdale suggests a myriad of reasons why pastors resist preaching about justice issues and offers practical suggestions and strategies for ways to be both pastoral and prophetic in their preaching. My project builds on her work. In 2017, I designed a research questionnaire to ascertain if, why, and how theologically trained, ordained preachers in mainline Protestant traditions choose to address controversial issues in their sermons. Just over 1,200 clergy responded to the survey. The results provide a snapshot of how a sampling of mainline Protestant clergy self-reported with regard to their attitudes toward preaching about controversial issues at that particular time. The questionnaire asked what topics they are willing to address, their reasons for addressing controversial issues (or not), and their concerns about consequences of prophetic preaching in their congregations. I'll be drawing on those data to help us better understand what it looks like to preach in the Purple Zone and to point out new directions for preaching prophetically in courageous, yet nonpartisan ways.

A significant finding from the survey is that many pastors do not feel equipped to undertake this task of preaching in the Purple Zone. Knowing their own political stance on the issues and how it likely conflicts with those in the pew, a significant number of preachers do not feel prepared to navigate this challenging homiletical task. According to the survey, nearly half (46%) of the pastors surveyed did not feel adequately trained in seminary or divinity school for preaching about controversial issues. Are they picking up skills in post-seminary classes, courses, or workshops? Only a third said yes (32%).

In any case, a significant majority of those surveyed indicated a desire for further training or guidance on how to preach about controversial issues. Eighty-four percent (84%) indicated they would appreciate having resources to use either in their congregations or with clergy study groups for how to talk about controversial issues within the church. Seventy-five percent (75%) indicated they would be interested in taking a continuing education class or attending a workshop. Seventy-nine percent (79%) said that they would appreciate learning ways to be trained in how to facilitate dialogue with their congregations about controversial issues in the church.

This feedback indicates that there is a need for new approaches, innovative ideas, and practical suggestions for addressing issues of public concern in congregations. What are clergy looking for? In their own words:

"Ways to make it less threatening to members."
"Thoughtful questions to invite people into conversation."
"Tools and encouragement."

In other words, clergy are eager for training, continuing education, reading materials, and support networks to aid them as they preach and minister in the Purple Zone. *Preaching in the Purple Zone* is a resource for helping the church understand the challenges facing parish pastors, while encouraging and equipping preachers to address the vital justice issues of our time. This book will help pastors and congregations rethink the task of addressing controversial justice issues using a method I have developed called the *sermon-dialogue-sermon process*. The chapters will provide both theoretical grounding and practical instruction for navigating the hazards of prophetic preaching with tested strategies and prudent tactics grounded in biblical and theological foundations.

Key to this endeavor is using a method of civil discourse called *deliberative dialogue* for finding common values among politically diverse parishioners. This book will provide instruction on using the sermon-dialogue-sermon process I have developed that will expand the preacher's—and the congregation's—level of engagement on justice issues beyond the single sermon. I wrote *Preaching in the Purple Zone* to guide clergy to respectfully engage with their congregations in deliberation about "hot topics," find the common values that bind them together, and respond faithfully to God's Word.

In workshops and seminars, seminary courses, as well as individual consultations with parish pastors, I have introduced nearly one hundred clergy, seminary students, and laity to the sermon-dialogue-sermon method I have developed. Thirty of the students and clergy received intensive instruction in the method. Based on their feedback, I have found that preachers emerge with new insights and healthier relationships not only within the church, but for civic and public discourse in our communities and our country. This book distills the training I have developed so that more people will have access to the tools and explanation of the process for entering the Purple Zone.

STEPS FOR ENTERING THE PURPLE ZONE

Chapter 1 explores why preachers are reticent to engage controversial issues in preaching and forthrightly names what's at stake for clergy, congregations, the larger church, and society. Results from my 2017 survey of preachers show the difficult challenges that clergy face when preaching about controversial justice issues. I'll establish what I mean by the word "justice," and use the work of Leonora Tubbs Tisdale in *Prophetic Preaching* as a springboard into this project.

In chapter 2 we'll explore what people mean when they say that a sermon is "too political." Using the categories of principles, emotions, and relationships, I'll deconstruct the term "politics" and reframe it within the larger context of public theology informed by Richard Niebuhr's *Christ and Culture*. This chapter will look specifically at the tension around the notion of the separation of church and state as well as the Lutheran doctrine of the "two kingdoms." We'll then discuss how to find alternative language for the word "politics," noting that Jesus himself was a "political" preacher, in that he addressed issues of public concern and directly addressed the powers and principalities. Chapter 2 concludes with a suggestion proposed by Richard Voelz to reclaim the image of the preacher-as-teacher and offers tips on how to prepare a congregation for a prophetic sermon.

Chapter 3 explores the question, "What is prophetic preaching?" with the help of reflections from various homileticians. The word "prophet" comes from the Greek word meaning "spokesperson." When used to describe a certain kind of preaching, it generally refers to a sermon that addresses the structural, social, or systemic issues affecting individuals, communities, or society at large. After examining the homiletical precedent for preaching in dialogue with different voices, we'll trace the historical and ethical movement in homiletics from authoritative to inductive to conversational preaching. This last is the mode of preaching best suited for the Purple Zone because it welcomes conversation as the community discerns the theological, scriptural, traditional, and experiential implications of engaging issues of public concern. As we will see, it is conversational preaching that enables the prophetic word to be heard and integrated into the lives of the listeners and the larger congregation.

In chapter 4, I offer my "Five Paths of Prophetic Preaching," and make the case that there are many entry points for addressing controversial issues in the pulpit. The key to Purple Zone preaching, however, is approaching both scripture and the sermon itself with a "dialogical lens" for interpreting scripture informed by a public theology for preaching. It is preaching that stands at the crossroads of church and society, finding ways to create dialogue through listening, understanding, discernment, and finding common values. A selection of sermon excerpts will show how this dialogical lens can be applied for preaching a variety of scripture passages.

Chapter 5 will help the preacher and congregation prepare for the sermon-dialogue-sermon process. To help us set the stage, we turn to the figure of Lydia of Thyatira whose story in Acts gives us a model for how we might prepare ourselves for entering the Purple Zone. In this chapter we'll go through the practical steps of determining the timeline for the sermon-dialogue-sermon process, and how to choose a topic to address. This will include taking a "temperature reading" of the congregation's tolerance of conflict, as well as how they might respond to a particular issue depending on context. I'll provide some advice on choosing a "cool," "warm," or "hot" topic, as well as address the way a congregation's "theology of conflict" can impact the choice of a topic. The chapter concludes with suggestions on preaching a "topical sermon," drawing on the work of Ronald Allen.

In chapter 6, I introduce the sermon-dialogue-sermon method beginning with the first sermon, the Prophetic Invitation to Dialogue. Rather than a once-and-done approach to addressing social issues, this method requires the preacher to think expansively and more long-term in their preparation and planning. In this chapter, I explain how to preach a sermon introducing a controversial justice issue for the congregation to engage in dialogue. In this sermon, instead of taking a stand on an issue, the preacher acknowledges its complexity, considers many voices and perspectives, and frames it within a scriptural and theological context. Listeners are invited to participate in a deliberative dialogue about the topic, assured that the Holy Spirit's gift of discernment is part of this process within the Body of Christ. This chapter includes several sermon excerpts to illustrate how this prophetic invitation approach can be applied for various scripture passages and within different contexts.

Chapter 7 is about the process of deliberative dialogue developed by the Charles F. Kettering Foundation and the National Issues Forums Institute (NIFI). Deliberative dialogue involves small groups of diverse individuals in face-to-face roundtable discussions using nonpartisan issue guides available from the NIFI. Moderated by a facilitator, participants begin with ground rules for how they will conduct themselves in the dialogue. They then share what is at stake for them in this topic and how it has touched them personally. Next, they weigh the pros and cons of three different approaches to the issue. Together they then discern what common values emerge. These values provide a basis for "next steps," such as continued dialogue or specific actions to engage the issue within the congregation or ministry setting. In this chapter, step-by-step instructions for the process help the reader to host a deliberative dialogue in their own congregation. A few examples of how deliberative dialogue has been used in different churches are included.

Chapter 8 explains the follow-up sermon after the deliberative dialogue, the Communal Prophetic Proclamation. This sermon is informed by the "collaborative/conversational" form described in John McClure's *The Roundtable Pulpit*. By incorporating aspects of the deliberative dialogue and highlighting different perspectives that were explored, the sermon lifts up the shared values discerned by the group as well as possible next steps the congregation could take to move forward on the issue. In this sermon, the preacher's prophetic witness arises from the dialogue, rather than from her or his own position on the issue. This sermon emphasizes God's presence in the midst of the complexity and the Spirit's guidance within the dialogue. This enables the congregation to see beyond partisanship in order to move into more genuine community. Thus, the culture of the church begins to transform from that of either divisiveness or avoidance, to one of healthy conversation and faithful engagement with the issues that concern the common good. Two sermon excerpts round out the chapter by showing examples of Communal Prophetic Proclamation.

Chapters 9 and 10 include case studies of the sermon-dialogue-sermon process, along with sermon excerpts and descriptions of the situations in which each sermon was preached. These examples are drawn from preachers I have trained in this process through the courses I have taught. Chapter 9 will show how four different preachers approached the same topic—immigration. In chapter 10, the case studies include health care, end-of-life issues, climate change, and food insecurity.

The final chapter summarizes the insights gained from the sermon-dialogue-sermon process and frames them within the image of bridge-building and the "prophetic care" concept developed by the late Dale P. Andrews. This chapter also includes a section on what to do when the sermon-dialogue-sermon method fails. Despite our best efforts, some congregational systems are unable to engage difficult topics and conversations in a healthy way. I will offer suggestions for picking up the pieces when bridges collapse so that both pastor and congregation can take steps toward recovery. I will also show how the bridge between the red-blue divide can also lead to even more connections and possibilities for healing and growth beyond the single congregation.

NOTE FOR LAITY AND THOSE NOT IN A CHURCH CONTEXT

While the whole book will be helpful for clergy and preachers, it is also written with a broader audience in mind. All but four of the chapters (3, 4, 6, and 8, which focus on the preacher's process) can be useful for laity and those outside of the church looking to engage with religious partners in crossing the red-blue divide. Not only does the book provide insights into the factors that have led to our current state of divisiveness, but it also offers case studies and practical ideas for how to be the church (or engage with church folk) within the Purple Zone. If you are a member of a congregation, chapters 1, 2, 5, 7, 9, 10, and 11 will be useful for discussion groups and for ways to be supportive of your pastor as she or he preaches in the Purple Zone. To aid in these discussions, you can find a study guide with questions to help you enter the Purple Zone in your own congregation at www.thepurplezone.net.

WELCOME TO THE PURPLE ZONE!

Preaching in the Purple Zone is primarily about working with one's community through preaching and dialogue to answer God's call to be a prophetic witness. While there are obvious hazards in attending to this call, it need not necessarily lead to the rupturing of relationships. Based on my research and teaching thus far, the sermon-dialogue-sermon method is an effective and potentially powerful tool for entering the Purple Zone. My hope for you as you read this book is that you will emerge with new insights for civic and public discourse and healthier relationships not only within your church, but in your community and our country as a whole.

As I tell students who I have trained in the sermon-dialogue-sermon method, you are being equipped to be the "white blood cells" in the Body of Christ to help create a healthier church. White cells, or leukocytes, are part of the immune system and help protect the body. Their function is to counteract foreign substances and diseases and eliminate pathogens that threaten the body. There will always be pathogens and "free radicals" floating around, but if the body is healthy enough, it can neutralize the toxicity. Relating this concept to the church, when we equip congregations with the skills of deliberative dialogue, and preachers with the tools for Purple Zone preaching, we can create more of those "leukocytes" in churches and communities. This, in turn, can help our congregations to be healthier "bodies" with stronger relationships ready to engage in God's work in the world.

Most importantly, I hope that through the guidance of the Holy Spirit, the death and resurrection of Jesus Christ, and the love of God, you will find powerful resources within yourself and your congregation that can be activated in the Purple Zone. Together, we are sustained by this divine love, knowing that "there is no fear in love. But perfect love drives out fear" (1 John 4:18a).

• 1 •

Preaching about Controversial Justice Issues

Tracing the Contours of the Purple Zone

If you are a pastor, what gives you pause when you consider taking a prophetic stance on a contemporary issue in a sermon? Do you worry about being "too political"? Perhaps you have concerns about angering parishioners who disagree with your prophetic critique? Maybe you worry that preaching a sermon about a public issue could cause discord and division in your congregation? Or perhaps your congregation actually welcomes your sermons that engage contemporary issues?

If you are a parishioner, how do you feel about your preacher addressing a "political" issue in their sermon? Are you in a congregation that has been wracked by controversy in the past and hope that your pastor does not open Pandora's box again? Do you worry about being "preached at" and made to feel guilty for your political position if it differs from your pastor's? Or perhaps you look forward to the sermons where your pastor gives you biblical and theological guidance for thinking about contemporary topics?

Whether you are a clergyperson or a member of a congregation, the question of addressing social issues in a sermon is fraught with both risk and opportunity. Tackling justice issues in the pulpit can provide the preacher and congregation with a chance to apply scripture to topics that relate to our daily lives, our social institutions, and our community's well-being. But there are also many reasons preachers hold back on their prophetic voice, such as concern about angering those who disagree with their stance or alienating those who believe that politics do not belong in a worship service.

Whatever your stance is on these questions, the Bible shows us that the presence of the prophetic word is woven throughout the history of God's people. The word "prophet" literally means "one who comes before another to speak," based on the Greek word *prophetes*, from *pro* meaning "before" and *phenai* meaning "speak." The prophet speaks on behalf of and before God and God's people, particularly those who are most vulnerable to the systems and leaders that abuse their power. While there is no singular definition of "prophetic preaching," we can say that a sermon in this mode expresses God's care and concern for those who are oppressed, abused, or victimized; announces God's judgment of the people or systems wielding and abusing power; and proclaims a new future for reordering the community according to God's standards of justice.

If you're among those who are torn between wanting to answer the call to be prophetic while also worrying about the negative outcomes of such a sermon, you're not alone in your fears and concerns. Or if you're a parishioner concerned about how your congregation engages (or doesn't engage) social issues, know that you are not alone either. In this chapter we'll look at research to help us understand why clergy are hesitant to address issues of public concern in their preaching. With these data in hand, we'll begin to discern what we need in order to create a "Purple Zone Homiletic" to engage congregations in a healthy, nonpartisan way on the important issues of our time.

"PREACHING ABOUT CONTROVERSIAL JUSTICE ISSUES" SURVEY

Just after the 2016 presidential election, I conducted a survey of mainline Protestant clergy in the United States to assess how preachers were approaching their sermons during this divisive time in our nation's history. Using a social scientific approach, I designed and conducted a sixty-question online survey via SurveyMonkey (https://www.surveymonkey.com) entitled "Preaching about Controversial Justice Issues" which ran for six consecutive weeks beginning in January 2017. I received responses from 1,205 participants in forty-five states with an almost equal number of male and female respondents, well over the 1,051 responses needed for a statistically accurate sampling.[1] The survey explored a range of topics, including:

- The difference the 2016 presidential election has made in preachers' willingness to address controversial issues in the pulpit.
- Topics clergy intended to address in the six months following the presidential inauguration as compared to the topics they engaged prior to the election.
- Reasons clergy list for either engaging controversial topics in their sermons or avoiding them.

- What kind of training and support pastors are seeking to foster healthy dialogue about public issues in their congregations.

The survey was designed in response to the work of Leonora Tubbs Tisdale in her book *Prophetic Preaching: A Pastoral Approach*. Tisdale lists several theories as to why pastors resist preaching about justice issues:

1. An inherited model of biblical interpretation that marginalizes the prophetic dimensions of scripture.
2. Pastoral concern for parishioners.
3. Fear of conflict.
4. Fear of dividing a congregation.
5. Fear of being disliked, rejected, or made to pay a price for prophetic witness.
6. Feelings of inadequacy in addressing prophetic concerns.
7. Discouragement that our own prophetic witness is not making a difference.[2]

I designed my questionnaire not only to test her theories but also to identify possible patterns and trends in preaching about contemporary issues. The survey also gathered demographic information which reveals the complexity that things like gender identity and sexuality, race, economics, geographic locations, and political leanings of clergy and parishioners alike bring to the task of preaching about justice issues.[3]

What Is "Justice"?

Before we go further, I need to clarify what I mean when I use the word "justice." Duncan Forrester stated that because of the variety of social, cultural, and religious stances in the public realm, "nobody knows what justice is."[4] I agree with this observation, so it's important to make some distinctions and explain how I'm using that word. In this book, I am referring to *social justice*, which theologian Richard McBrien describes as "dedicated to the reordering of society, to the changing of institutions, systems, and patterns of behavior which deny people their basic human rights and which thereby destabilize society."[5]

I'm also distinguishing between *individual morality* and *social justice*. Individual morality pertains to proper behavior of persons. Social justice, on the other hand, is concerned with the ethics of systems, institutions, and society at large rather than individuals alone. Justice has to do with the conditions that enable fairness in society.

I chose McBrien's definition of social justice because it fits best with the biblical concepts of *mishpat* and *tsĕdaqah*, the Hebrew words for *justice* and *righteousness*, respectively. In the Bible, notions of justice have less to do with individual rights and more to do with the good of the entire community. Daniel Maguire states that "justice is the love language of the Bible."[6] Consider, for example, the numerous times that the pairing of these words *mishpat* and *tsĕdaqah* are found in the First Testament. In Jeremiah 22:3, for instance, God speaks through the prophet, saying, "Act with justice and righteousness, and deliver from the hand of the oppressor anyone who has been robbed. And do no wrong or violence to the alien, the orphan, and the widow, or shed innocent blood in this place." Similarly, Psalm 112 states that the "upright will be blessed" because of being righteous and "conducting their affairs with justice." Specifically, "They have distributed freely, they have given to the poor; their righteousness endures forever; their horn is exalted in honor" (v. 9). As well, Isaiah 1:17 encourages the faithful to "learn to do good; seek justice, rescue the oppressed, defend the orphan, plead for the widow." While these may seem like pleas to individuals to live in this way, the prophets and psalmist are addressing whole communities, saying "we" must do these things together.

Moreover, the foundational story of God's justice in the Bible is God's liberation of the slaves from Egypt in Exodus. The saga of Israel's release from bondage establishes the core narrative that slavery has no place in God's beloved community, and as such, is always overturned by God as an action of God's eternal love for humankind. It follows, then, that "(t)he entire history of Israel under God is subordinated to one purpose—righteousness expressed in justice," according to James Luther Mays.[7] He observes that in scripture, "When someone cries out for justice, all hear in that word a claim that something has gone wrong in the relation between a society and its members."[8] That claim, then, insists that justice is theological, moral, and attainable for the community.

In fact, Mays goes as far as to say that "righteousness expressed in justice is the indispensable qualification for worship—no justice, no acceptable public religion."[9] In other words, because the heart of worship is a community gathered to encounter God's presence, and God desires God's beloved community to have righteousness expressed in justice, our worship itself is impacted in a negative way if we fail to engage these issues. This is an important rejoinder to those who claim that justice issues have no place in worship (and the sermon therein). This is not to say that worship is invalid if the participants are unjust, but to note that the relationship between worship and justice is so strong that God longs to gather us in and then send us out with the goal of working toward justice and righteousness. In this way, when we encounter injustice in the world, we return to worship and preaching to encounter the God who overcomes that injustice.

Another way to think about biblical justice is as *neighborliness*, a term suggested by Walter Brueggemann. He describes justice as "the maintenance of neighborliness that permits all members of the community to flourish without the distortion or subversion of economic leverage."[10] He points out that in the Bible, the monarchical notion of justice was that of the legitimate accumulation and concentration of wealth, while the prophets of Israel asserted that justice is *covenantal*. That is, God's covenant, or promise, made with the people of Israel meant that they (and we) must be concerned with the well-being of *all* neighbors, especially the poor, the widow, the orphan, the foreigner, and those on the margins. Giving, sharing, and caring in generous ways creates well-being for all parties. "Righteousness, the practice of generative neighborliness, recognizes an alliance of haves and have-nots that focuses not upon generous charity but upon justice."[11]

Hence, justice has a strong theological component. Quite simply, the very being of God is justice. The manifestation of God's love is the creation of just and equal relationships, particularly as it pertains to those who are excluded, abused, impoverished, and vulnerable. Because justice is essential to the character of God, justice is thus demanded of God's people, especially those in power. Justice is associated with the basic requirements of life in the community and necessitates rectifying gross social inequalities of the disadvantaged. Most importantly, justice puts an end to the conditions that produce the injustice.[12] Thus, preaching about justice as a manifestation of God's love reorients us away from the therapeutic, "touchy-feely," spiritualized understanding of love to a love that changes the oppressive structures humans create.

It is for this reason that Duncan Forrester insists that religion can be helpful in formulating just policies that protect those most vulnerable, hold those most powerful accountable, and contribute to the common good. This is not to say that justice replaces or is qualitatively better than individual morality. In fact, both personal responsibility *and* public policy are needed to create the conditions for a fair society. But to lay the blame of society's ills solely on individuals is to ignore the responsibility of institutions and those who wield power and influence over the systems that undergird our social structures. Moreover, such ignorance enables those who abuse their power to continue unchecked in this affront to God's intention for individuals, families, communities, and the Earth itself.

Preaching in the Purple Zone, then, takes biblical justice as a basic premise, because it is the grounding orientation for all relationships—between people and God, between people and the natural world, and among people themselves. Doing ministry in the red-blue divide spurs us to ask questions about *neighbor-love*, as Cynthia Moe-Lobeda calls it.[13] Those questions include:

- Who has power and who does not?
- Who benefits, and who does not, from the way things are?
- Whose voices are heard and whose are ignored?
- Who counts in decision-making and who does not?

These are questions that every preacher must decide how to engage—or even *if* they will engage them. Whether or not clergy do address these justice issues, the reasons for their decisions, and the implications for their vocations, their congregations, and the larger church are all of interest to me. These are what I set out to explore in my survey.

"Prophetic Preaching" versus "Preaching about Controversial Justice Issues"

Before we look at the responses to the questionnaire, I need to point out the distinction between Tisdale's focus on *prophetic preaching,* and my survey which asked about *controversial justice issues in preaching*. While I will discuss the different understandings of prophetic preaching in more detail in chapter 3, for now we can say that a prophetic sermon critiques the present reality of injustice and provides an alternative vision of God's future. However, my survey did not ask preachers whether they engage in *prophetic* preaching, because definitions of the term "prophetic" do vary. Thus, it would have been difficult to account for respondents' subjective opinions about whether or not their preaching was "prophetic."[14]

Instead, the questionnaire explored how preachers deal with *controversial justice issues*. For the purposes of this survey, I defined a *controversial justice issue* as having the following characteristics (which were shared with participants as they began the questionnaire):

- A controversial justice issue affects people and communities at multiple levels (personal, familial, institutional, governmental, societal, global).
- Decisions made about this issue at any level have an impact on other levels.
- There is a wide range of opinions about how best to deal with the issue.
- Emotions about the issue tend to be very strong for some people.
- There are a variety of factors involved in explaining why the issue is a "problem."
- There is a great deal at stake for certain parties depending on how decisions are made at the personal, familial, institutional, business,

governmental, economic, policy, and global levels, and the power differentials therein.
- There is usually a perceived debate about "rights" versus "responsibilities."
- The issue is in some realm of public debate and has some bearing on politics and public policy.

Of course, what is considered a controversial topic depends on the congregation, as well as the context of the time and place in which the sermon is preached. A contentious issue for one church might not be controversial at all in another. For example, preaching about caring for God's Creation by addressing climate change might not be controversial in Church A, a fairly progressive church. But in Church B located in the heart of a community whose parishioners work in the fossil fuel industry, such a sermon may be taboo. By the same token, a sermon about welcoming immigrants might be met with negative pushback in Church A because of tense relations among residents and new arrivals. But in Church B that has voted to "nest" an immigrant worshipping community, such a sermon wouldn't be controversial at all. Thus, what is controversial is a matter of perspective and context.

There is also a difference between merely mentioning controversial issues in a sermon and engaging in actual *prophetic* preaching. One can speak *about* a social justice issue without saying anything prophetic. Yet, as Tisdale notes, just naming a hot topic in the pulpit can sometimes elicit negative pushback. In some contexts, it takes prophetic courage just to mention a controversial issue in a sermon.

For example, a colleague of mine reported that he once touched on the topic of gun violence in a sermon as part of a list of other issues that have our country in turmoil. The following Sunday, a parishioner confronted him just as he was ready to enter the sanctuary to begin the worship service and told him he should *never* talk about that issue again in the pulpit. The fact that the parishioner had laid in wait and ambushed the pastor, instead of asking to talk with him at a reasonable time and place, indicates the reactiveness of some folks when it comes to certain issues.

This anecdote is not an isolated event. Through the information I gathered from the survey, as well as in conversations with colleagues and in class discussions with students, I have learned that the experience of being confronted by parishioners angered by sermons that delve into "political" issues is something that many have experienced. The data collected in this survey help to quantify attitudes, opinions, and behaviors of clergy engaging in preaching about "hot button" topics. This, in turn, provides some clues as to what might be helpful for those pastors looking to engage difficult issues while still maintaining their pastoral relationships.

20   Preaching in the Purple Zone

Anger, Fear, and Consequences of Preaching About "Hot Topics"

While there are numerous questions to pursue from the survey responses, for this project I examined the following data points:[15]

- The number of respondents who indicated willingness to preach about controversial justice issues.
- Reasons respondents listed for avoiding controversial justice issues in their sermons.
- Negative responses clergy have received in response to such sermons.

In one question, I asked respondents to indicate how frequently they preach on controversial political or justice issues (see table 1.1). The data indicate that nearly half of mainline Protestant clergy preach on controversial justice issues at least a few times a year, and that one-third of them intentionally tackle such topics in their sermons on a regular basis.[16] This means that, by their own admission at the time of the survey, <u>nearly a quarter of mainline Protestant preachers in the United States rarely—or never—preach about controversial justice issues.</u>[17]

One caveat: 89 percent of respondents self-identified as white/Caucasian in this survey. Thus, the data perhaps reflect the attitudes of *white* mainline Protestant preachers rather than clergy of color.[18] This is a research question that deserves further study. However, the predominance of white respondents is actually in line with the percentage of white clergy serving congregations in mainline Protestant churches (78.3%, according to the National Congregations Surveys for 1998, 2006–2007, and 2012 combined). Thus, the data set does not necessarily negate potential insights from the survey. Regardless of

Table 1.1. **Frequency of Preaching on Controversial Political or Justice Issues**

Please indicate which of the following statements is most true for you

Answer Options	Response Percent	Response Count (Out of 731*)
I generally do not preach on controversial political or justice issues.	6.8	50
I only preach on controversial political or justice issues on rare occasions.	16.3	119
I sometimes preach on controversial political or justice issues (at least a few times a year).	46.9	343
I intentionally preach on or reference controversial political or justice issues on a regular basis (at least once a month).	30.0	219

*Confidence level = 90%; margin of error = 3%.

the racial/ethnic dynamics of the congregation, most preachers likely would be able to relate to some of the experiences described by the pastors in the questionnaire. Additionally, nearly every pastor can name at least one or two "hot topics" they would be hesitant to address in the pulpit. The reasons for this avoidance are many and varied.

Reasons Why Preachers Avoid Controversial Justice Issues

The questions in my survey were designed to compare Tisdale's theories about why preachers avoid prophetic sermons with actual clergy responses about their reticence to preach about controversial justice issues. In her list, reason 1 (an inherited model of biblical interpretation that marginalizes the prophetic dimensions of scripture) has to do with principles and intellectual justifications. Reason 6 (feelings of inadequacy in addressing prophetic concerns) and reason 7 (discouragement that our own prophetic witness is not making a difference) have to do with personal feelings of inadequacy and effectiveness. While my survey contained questions to explore these reasons (which will be addressed in a later work), I am concentrating on reasons 2–5 because they involve the *emotional* component of actual fears and concerns about consequences that can occur as a result of prophetic preaching. Again, those reasons are:

2. Pastoral concern for parishioners.
3. Fear of conflict.
4. Fear of dividing a congregation.
5. Fear of being disliked, rejected, or made to pay a price for prophetic witness.

To test these reasons, I created a survey question in which respondents were given a set of eight scenarios and asked to indicate which ones make them hesitant to preach about controversial issues. In table 1.2, the responses are ranked from highest to lowest according to the percentage of respondents indicating "very much" or "somewhat." It appears that for more than half of the pastors surveyed, the reasons for not addressing issues of public concern boil down to four main concerns:

A. Fear about hurting or dividing their congregation.
B. Fear about compromising their ability to effectively minister in their church.
C. Fear about receiving negative pushback for being "too political."
D. Fear about loss—loss of members, money, and their own positions.

While these fears are not exact correlations with Tisdale's list, they do corroborate reasons 2–5 (pastoral concern for parishioners, fear of conflict, fear of dividing a congregation, fear of being disliked or made to pay a price). However, the fear listed in B—compromising one's ability to effectively minister in one's congregation—is one not named in Tisdale's list.[19] I believe this concern needs to be added to the list of reasons why preachers avoid prophetic preaching, especially since it ranked second in the survey. As we will see, these fears are not unfounded. The negative fallout that can result from preaching about controversial justice issues can affect a clergyperson's relationships with their parishioners, relationships among members of the church, and even the pastor's own position within the congregation.

Table 1.2. Reasons Clergy Hesitate to Preach about Controversial Justice Issues

Please indicate to what extent each of the following makes you hesitant to preach about controversial justice issues

Answer Options	Response Percent (Very Much/ Somewhat)	Response Count (Out of 761*)
Concern about creating controversy and conflict within the membership	68	518
Concern that the fallout from preaching on a controversial justice issue might negatively affect my ability to pastor in this congregation	60	454
Concern that people may see me as too political if I preach about this	55	418
Strong possibility of receiving negative pushback if I preach about controversial justice issues	54	414
Concern that some people might withdraw their membership if I preach about certain controversial issues	35	269
Concern that some people might withhold their financial giving to the church if I preach about controversial issues	33	250
Concern that certain people might refuse to speak to me if I preach about controversial justice issues	27	208
I have experienced negative responses or pushback to sermons in which I have engaged controversial issues in the past and do not want to take that risk again	27	206
Concern about being asked to leave the church if I preach about controversial issues	21	163

*Confidence level 90%; margin of error 3%.

Fears That Muzzle the Preacher's Prophetic Voice

These fears were brought into sharp relief in August of 2017 when I wrote a blog piece urging preachers to address the events in Charlottesville, Virginia, in their sermons. On August 12, 2017, neo-Nazis, white nationalists, and members of the Ku Klux Klan descended on the city to protest the planned removal of Confederate statues. Their violent rally resulted in numerous injuries and the death of one counterprotester, Heather Heyer. This event brought the realities of white privilege, white supremacy, anti-Semitism, and racism to the fore in our nation. My article called for clergy to preach about these issues in the days after the rally.[20] However, a colleague responded by sharing with me the realities of his church context that silenced his prophetic voice:

> I sit in the middle of a town that time forgot. I'm a "blue dot" in a "red" church. My job depends on my ability to preach and teach the congregation in a way they can accept, and any controversial topics could negatively affect my position. I need my job. But I feel like a coward because I'm not able to be as prophetic as I want. The previous attempts by another minister were met with so much backlash that I'm scared to even "go there" with them.

This pastor is not alone in the concern that addressing controversial justice issues in the pulpit can have serious consequences. In other words, these are not unfounded fears. The blowback is real and has concrete effects on clergy and their congregations. The responses in table 1.3 indicate that the majority of clergy have received negative pushback of one kind or another when they have preached about controversial justice issues in the past. As you can see, the pushback against sermons that address controversial issues takes many forms. Anger expressed indirectly or directly, drops in attendance, withdrawal of membership and financial support, and threats to the pastor's job are all ways in which clergy have experienced negative responses from parishioners after such sermons.

In their own words, some respondents shared about the kinds of things they have experienced when they have preached about controversial justice issues:

- "I have lost members over the past two years due to preaching about race. There's only so many losses a small congregation can handle."
- "I have concern that my [senior pastor] might berate me or make me apologize for what I've preached."

- "I have received threats in the past and worry that they might be acted upon if I continued to speak as freely as I would like."
- "I am in the midst of leaving my congregation because they did push back saying I was too political. I chose to leave to avoid causing more issues. I would rather leave than stay and be afraid to speak what I feel God is calling us to do."

Threats, intimidation, withholding of relational and financial support—it's no wonder some clergy in certain congregations are afraid to preach about justice issues.

Table 1.3. Types of Negative Responses Clergy Experience When Preaching about Controversial Justice Issues

I have experienced the following negative responses when I've preached about controversial justice issues in the past (check all that apply)

Answer Options	Response Percent	Response Count (Out of 761*)
Some people reported to me that one or more individuals in the congregation were angry as a result of the sermon.	58.6	446
I received angry words, letters, or other forms of negative pushback after I preached the sermon.	51.0	388
One or more individuals stopped attending worship services for a while after I preached the sermon.	50.1	381
One or more individuals refused to speak to me for a time after I preached the sermon.	34.6	263
One or more individuals withdrew their membership from the congregation after I preached the sermon.	26.5	202
One or more individuals threatened to or actually did withhold their financial giving to the church if I preached anymore controversial sermons.	22.9	174
A controversy and/or conflict arose within the church after I preached the sermon.	17.0	129
One or more individuals threatened to call for or actually called for my resignation from the church as a result of a sermon I preached or because my preaching was seen as too controversial.	8.4	64
I was asked to resign my position as a result of a sermon I preached or because my preaching was deemed too controversial.	2.5	19
I actually left the congregation or was let go by the church as a result of my preaching about a controversial issue(s).	2.5	19
None of the above	21.0	160
Other	9.3	71

*Confidence level 90%; margin of error 3%.

This is not to say that there aren't justifiable reasons to be cautious when approaching contemporary issues in sermons, and we'll discuss those in the chapters ahead. But many of the pastors in the survey also recognized that despite the personal risk and fears about negative pushback, the call to preach prophetically about justice issues outweighs the feelings of trepidation. The pastors in this survey who indicated that they do, in fact, address controversial topics when necessary and appropriate indicated numerous reasons for this willingness.

Reasons Why Clergy Choose to Preach about Controversial Justice Issues

In one question, respondents were given eleven reasons for why they might choose to preach about controversial issues and were asked to indicate how much they agreed or disagreed with each statement. Table 1.4 shows how they responded. These responses indicate that the overwhelming majority of clergy appear to justify their decision to address social issues in the pulpit by drawing authority from Jesus, scripture, and their own sense of discernment. They also take into consideration the contemporary issues of the day, including those at the national and local level. Also important is their understanding of their call to preach prophetically and engage in public theology.

"WISE AS SERPENTS, GENTLE AS DOVES"

Given a preacher's desire to proclaim God's justice while also maintaining positive pastoral relationships with their congregation, is there a way to "thread the needle," so to speak? Can clergy preach prophetically without endangering their positions of trust and rupturing their pastoral relationships with parishioners? Is there a way for preachers to avoid the extremes of quietism on the one hand or opting for martyrdom on the other? I believe there is. As I will discuss in the chapters ahead, addressing controversial justice issues in a prophetic yet pastoral way is often a matter of making strategic and tactical decisions about when and how to do so. We must be "wise as serpents and gentle as doves," so to speak (Matthew 10:16).

In this book, I will introduce a strategy called the *sermon-dialogue-sermon* method that uses the process of *deliberative dialogue*—in tandem with prophetic preaching—to facilitate healthy conversation in congregations about the important public issues of our time.[21] I have taught several courses to equip both seminary students and practicing clergy in this sermon-dialogue-sermon method with encouraging results. Feedback from those who have

Table 1.4. Reasons Preachers Give for Addressing Controversial Political and Social Issues

Please indicate the importance of each of the following reasons for why preachers SHOULD address controversial political/social issues in their sermons

Answer Options	Somewhat or Strongly Agree (699 Total Responses*)	Percentage	Rating Average
Jesus spoke about justice issues, so preachers have a mandate to do the same.	664	94	4.56
The church has a responsibility to address controversial issues because it has a contribution to make to the public discourse informed by scripture, theology, and moral/ethical discernment.	626	94	4.55
The Bible speaks about controversial issues, so preachers are authorized to address them as well.	624	93	4.46
If I as a preacher feel called or discern a need to speak about an issue, it's acceptable to address it in a sermon.	621	93	4.44
What's going on in current events often influences or is incorporated into my preaching.	619	93	4.39
When there is a NATIONAL OR GLOBAL issue that needs a moral, biblical, or theological perspective, it's acceptable to speak about the issue from the pulpit.	613	92	4.38
When there's a LOCAL OR STATE issue that needs a moral, biblical, or theological perspective, it's acceptable to speak about the issue from the pulpit.	600	89	4.35
There is great potential for growth and discernment among church members when we tackle controversial issues in a helpful way.	594	89	4.36
People are looking for a place to talk about these issues, and the church is an ideal setting.	494	74	3.96
If I am asked by my bishop or ecclesial leader or larger church body to preach about an issue, it's acceptable to address it in a sermon.	434	65	3.81
Only if the lectionary readings specifically address the issue is it acceptable to preach about it.	164	25	2.36

*Confidence level 90%; margin of error 3%.

worked with this method in their own congregations indicates that the sermon-dialogue-sermon process can be an effective strategy for entering the Purple Zone. By utilizing specific sermonic tools and exercising skills in facilitating deliberative dialogue, it is possible to navigate the political red-blue divide in congregations and emerge with strengthened relationships and healthier faith communities.

From immigration to climate change, from mental health to food insecurity, from gender-based violence to economic sustainability, *Preaching in the Purple Zone* seeks to frame our responses to these and other issues as a people of faith in Christ Jesus. Whether you are a preacher, a lay person, or an active citizen in your community seeking to work with religious folk on these issues, my aim is to show how the sermon-dialogue-sermon method can help the church reclaim its prophetic voice, amplify that voice in the community, and work for the *mishpat* and *tsĕdaqah*—justice and righteousness—that are God's intention for human society.

• 2 •

Beyond "Political"

Reframing Our Understanding of Politics and Preaching

In chapter 1, we looked at results from a survey I conducted with mainline Protestant clergy called "Preaching about Controversial Issues." Throughout the survey, participants noted that one of the main reasons they avoid preaching in the prophetic mode is that they fear listeners will accuse them of being "too political." No matter how gently preachers trod the ground of contemporary justice issues in their sermons, it's likely that someone at some point will react with that dreaded accusation. But what do people actually mean when they say a preacher is "too political"? Scratch beneath the surface, and you'll find that "political" is really a code word for other underlying concerns.

In this chapter, we'll lift the lid on the term "political" and examine the emotional, relational, and principled reasons people resist sermons that address contemporary issues. Beginning with principles, we'll turn to H. Richard Niebuhr's *Christ and Culture* which provides some helpful categories for understanding some of the underlying tenets that inform people's reactions to hearing social issues addressed in church. More specifically, we'll examine the oft-cited principle of the separation of church and state as rationale for pastors to keep quiet on issues of public concern. Then we'll discuss some of the emotional and relational dynamics and the importance of cultivating trust with one's listeners.

UNPACKING "TOO POLITICAL"

What parishioners mean by the phrase "too political" depends, of course, on the person making the accusation, their theology, ecclesiology, personal politics, and their relationship with the preacher. When people resist a justice sermon, we need to understand the feelings, relationships, and underlying ideologies that inform people's reasons for accusing a preacher of being too political. In other words, the reasons for negative reactions generally fall under one or more of three categories: *emotions, relationships,* and *principles.*

In my Purple Zone classes and workshops, I ask people to surmise what folks *really* mean when they accuse the preacher of being "too political." They are able to come up with a list of subtexts quite easily. Consider these responses and whether they are *emotional, relational, principled,* or some *combination* of the three:

- You're making me uncomfortable.
- I don't agree with your position.
- You're crossing "church-and-state" boundaries that I think should stay in place.
- Don't challenge my comfort zone.
- You're taking sides when you should remain neutral.
- You're challenging me (and the media that informs my position), and I don't appreciate it.
- I come to church to escape or get a break from the world, not to further engage.
- This is too complicated to talk about or hear preached.
- It's too difficult for me to think about this.

You can probably see that for many of these reasons, there is a combination of categories. For example, "You're taking sides when you should remain neutral" can be informed by certain principles the person has. Perhaps they hold strictly to the tenet of the separation of church and state (which we'll discuss further on). The preacher's willingness to cross this divide can cause the parishioner to be reactive. But their reaction may also be fueled by an emotional component. The person may feel angry that their position is being challenged, for example. At the same time, if the preacher has taken a position that does not align with the parishioner's political orientation, she or he may feel hurt that their pastor cannot join them in their position on the issue. This means that, at least for this parishioner, there is a now a wedge in the pastoral relationship. This, in turn, can lead to feelings of alienation, hurt, and the potential for anger, which can further rupture the relationship between the clergyperson and the parishioner. You can see how quickly the situation can spiral downward.

Let's take a more in-depth look at these three categories of resistance, starting with principles. To help us understand some of the underlying assumptions people have about politics and the church, we turn to H. Richard

Niebuhr. His seminal work, *Christ and Culture,* provides a helpful (if somewhat oversimplified) typology of the different ways in which Christians see the relationship between the church and society.¹ These five types can give us insight into the principles that undergird some people's resistance to sermons that engage in social or cultural critique.

Understanding Principles: H. Richard Niebuhr's Christ and Culture

While acknowledging that religion is a subset of culture, Niebuhr saw Christ as one who stands over, under, and against culture and religion. There is a relationship between how culture shapes Christianity, as well as how Christianity has shaped and continues to form the culture. It is out of this tension that Niebuhr developed five typologies to help us think about the relational continuum between the two.

- *Christ against Culture:* These are Christians who have separated themselves from the world in an attempt to retain purity by defining themselves over and against the culture. Think of monastics, the Amish, and some Pentecostal churches. In these groups there is a demand to preserve the individual's as well as the church's virtue in the face of a demonic, contaminating culture. The goal is to stay consistent with one's self-understanding as a Christian set apart from culture and to maintain the strictly defined rules of the group.
- *Christ of Culture*: In this type, culture is normative and Jesus is subsumed into it. This type has a positive view of culture and uses the message of Jesus to provide support for its highest ideals. Christians are called not just to be fully engaged in the world, but to see their faith in Christ and their citizenship as seamlessly interwoven. This type is exemplified by the Religious Right in American Fundamentalism and U.S. politics and by the proponents of the Prosperity Gospel.
- *Christ above Culture:* In this type, culture and Christ are not the same, but culture is still viewed positively and related to Christ in a way that draws the culture toward higher goodness through God's revelation. Thomas Aquinas' worldview typified this perspective wherein the church is seen as the vital link between the culture and God's revelation of grace. Thus, through the church, culture can be held accountable and even transformed. Great confidence is placed on human reason as well as the church to help followers move higher and higher in their upward climb to God. Two examples of this type would be the Roman Catholic Church with its emphasis on hierarchy and parochial education and Rick Warren's *The Purpose Driven Life,* which holds that

by following the teachings of the church, individuals can find God's purpose and meaning for their lives.
- *Christ and Culture in Paradox:* This is the Lutheran type wherein Christians can be "in but not of the world." In other words, Martin Luther's "two kingdoms" theory allows for a realistic approach in working within the culture, but also recognizes the abject sinfulness within humans and culture that ultimately renders it hopeless as a source of goodness. The other key component of this type is the concept of the hiddenness of Christ within the culture. Christ is indeed present within this world, but not in the places of "glory" where the world thinks to look. This belief encourages Christians to go to those apparently godforsaken places (homeless shelters, malaria bedsides, government offices) and do the work Christ calls us to do. Yet this worldview can lead some to a kind of quietism that refuses to engage the world because it is not part of the realm of God. (I will discuss this more below.)
- *Christ as Transformer of Culture:* This fifth and final type is much more positive about the ability of humans to rebuild a sinful society on the model of God's kingdom which Christ described in his teachings. Such optimism causes believers to see how God is transforming the culture right now, and to be inspired to join in this great work. It is a more realized eschatology wherein we can see the people, institutions, and work that is revealing what God is up to in the world to bring about salvation. Zwingli and Calvin would be proponents of this worldview that sees the church as norming the culture. The Social Gospel Movement and Martin Luther King Jr.'s belief that "the arc of the moral universe is long, but it bends toward justice," are examples of this fifth type.

This typology is not without its problems. Niebuhr acknowledged that these types can be reductionistic, so he encouraged readers not to be dismissive of people based on whatever type may fit them. Also, there are certainly particularities within each tradition that point to a more nuanced understanding of the types. Additionally, feminists, Black theologians, and other critics of Niebuhr's work point out that these types may overlook the ways in which gender, race, and colonialism impinge on these categories, including the question of whether there are, in fact, other categories as well.

Nevertheless, I list these five types in order to note that preaching in the Purple Zone works best within these three: *Christ above Culture, Christ and Culture in Paradox,* and *Christ as Transformer of Culture.* This is because a Purple Zone homiletic neither eschews engagement with culture and society (as *Christ against Culture* does) nor does it offer uncritical benedictions on culture and society (as *Christ of Culture* does). Rather, it stands at the intersection of faith and politics, willing to engage both. There is, however, one type that brings with it a particular tension when engaging culture—*Christ and Culture in Paradox*. The doctrine of the "two kingdoms" within this type warrants attention as we establish the foundations of Purple Zone preaching.

"Separation of Church and State" versus the "Two Kingdoms" Doctrine

In the survey "Preaching about Controversial Issues," 30 percent of respondents indicated that the principle of the "separation of church and state" was a valid reason to avoid preaching about controversial social issues in the pulpit. This phrase is based on Thomas Jefferson's metaphor of a wall of separation between religion and government in his interpretation of the First Amendment that "Congress shall make no law respecting an establishment of religion, or prohibiting the free exercise thereof." To be clear, while there is ongoing debate about the relationship between government and religion, the First Amendment was intended to prevent the establishment of a state church. It did not state that churches could not address issues that involve government. Thus, it would be inaccurate for someone to accuse a preacher of violating the separation of church and state by preaching a sermon that addresses contemporary issues of public concern—as long as the sermon was not taking part in *partisan* politics and advocating for a particular party or candidate.

However, when people cite "separation of church and state" as a reason not to engage public issues, it may actually have to do with their own discomfort in the preacher's willingness to traverse the boundaries between what Lutheran theology identifies as the "two kingdoms"—the earthly realm and the heavenly realm. Article XXVIII of the Augsburg Confession (the founding documents of the Lutheran Church written in 1530) put forth the notion that the earthly kingdom is the realm of politics and best left to the government. The heavenly kingdom, in contrast, is the spiritual realm of God and, thus, the purview of the church.

Some believe that the two kingdoms should not intermingle. They insist that clergy must limit their focus to caring for people's souls and preparing them for salvation. If people suffer injustice in this life, ministers are only to offer care and comfort, not raise questions about why injustice is occurring or what the church should do about it. Some justify this stance by referring to Paul's instruction in Romans 13:1–7, which begins, "Let every person be subject to the governing authorities; for there is no authority except from God, and those authorities that exist have been instituted by God." Or they may cite Jesus' words: "Render therefore unto Caesar the things that are Caesar's, and unto God the things that are God's" (Matthew 22:21). These passages are used to justify a clear delineation between the church and human governance.

The rigid dualism within the "two kingdoms" doctrine became especially pronounced in the 1800s, as seen in Lutheran theologian Christian Luthardt's (1823–1902) insistence that "[t]he gospel has absolutely nothing to do with outward existence but only with eternal life . . . . Christianity wants to change man's [sic] heart, not his external situation." Similarly, Rudolf Sohn (1841–1917), a Lutheran jurist, asserted that the concerns of public life "should remain untouched by the proclamation of the gospel, completely untouched."[2] This strict view on the demarcation between the "two kingdoms" often manifests itself in, or is confused with, the secular notion of the separation of church and state.

Unfortunately, both the "two kingdoms" doctrine and the principle of the separation of church and state have been used to rationalize the church giving uncritical support for the state, or at least quietly acquiescing to whatever happens in the realm of government. The problem with both positions is that they can be used to diminish or remove accountability of the state. Throughout history, the church's refusal to engage in the earthly realm of politics, let alone critique those in power, has had devastating consequences. When the church—and preaching—refuses to admonish, proscribe, and criticize corruption, negligence, or abuse of power by the state, it reneges on one of its major functions as an instrument of God in the world. That function is to provide prophetic critique on behalf of the marginalized and oppressed.

The rise of Nazism in Germany gives a stark example of what can happen when the church takes the "two kingdoms" doctrine too far. This doctrine provided theological cover for the rise of the Third Reich in Germany in the 1900s. Lutheran quietism led many pastors to withhold their critical voice and refuse to speak out about the Nazi regime. As a result, the church shares culpability in the torture and deaths of millions of Jews and other "undesirables" at the hands of Hitler, his administration, and those who followed his orders.

To avoid a repeat of this dereliction of duty, we can help our congregations deconstruct the rigid application of the "two kingdoms" doctrine by showing that there are both biblical and theological counterbalances to this position.

- First, the second table of the Ten Commandments has everything to do with human relationships, and thus authorizes people of faith to engage in discussions about how those relationships are attended to. God's Law is the primary force driving human beings to seek justice in their interactions with each other. (For an example of a sermon on the Ten Commandments and its relationship to prophetic preaching, visit https://thepurplezone.net/).

- Second, the recognition of ethical norms is intrinsic to human knowledge. In biblical parlance, God's Law is "written upon the heart" (Romans 2:15; Hebrews 10:16), so that even atheists and agnostics have a sense of right and wrong, even if they do not recognize or worship God.
- Third, Christians believe that God is still active in the world, and that God can work through political processes, just as God did throughout the Bible (see the stories of Joseph in Genesis, Esther, Daniel, John the Baptist, and Jesus, for example). Thus, there is no need to enforce an artificial gap between the realm of God and the realm of human earthly existence.
- Fourth, Jesus' instruction to "love your neighbor as yourself" (Matthew 22:39) has ramifications beyond individual interactions. As we learned in chapter 1, neighbor-love is the standard for the "Beloved Community" (also known as the Kingdom of God), providing the ethical norms for the just distribution of that which sustains life, health, learning, joy, the planet's ecosystems, and human relationships. In other words, the core of justice is care for the neighbor.

With all of this in mind, we need to consider the other two categories that underlie accusations of preachers being "too political" when addressing justice issues from the pulpit—emotions and relationships. Because these categories are often connected and intertwined, we'll look at them together.

Emotions, Relationships, and Power Differentials

In the survey of preachers about controversial issues, of those who indicated that they do not engage in preaching about social justice, more than half (55%) agreed with the statement, "Church should be a place where people come together, not be driven apart." Another statement, "The negative impacts on ministry are too risky," garnered agreement from nearly a third (28%) of respondents. Taken together, these statements indicate that pastors are deeply concerned about the emotional and relational fallout from preaching a controversial sermon.

One aspect of these emotional and relational dynamics has to do with power: who has it; who wants it; who abuses it; who fights over it; who fears losing it; who never had it; what's at stake in exercising it; how it's distributed; and who has agency to use it. Obviously, people's relationship with power—and how that plays out in a congregation—is complicated. But when someone accuses the preacher of being "too political," sometimes the intent is to exercise their own power to shut down discourse. What they often mean to say is: "Stop talking about this. Whatever issue you've raised, whatever stance you've taken, whatever prophetic claim you have made, you have triggered something that I/we do not wish to engage." The feelings of anger, discomfort, defensiveness, embarrassment, or vulnerability that a prophetic sermon might trigger are such that the "fight or flight" mechanism kicks in. Thus, getting the preacher to stop talking about it is the easiest way to avoid or squelch those feelings.

In fact, if you are a preacher and someone accuses you of being "too political" in your sermons, you might consider asking the person if this is, in fact, what they want you to do—to stop talking about whatever the issue is. And if they answer yes, you can then ask: Why? The person may or may not be able to articulate their real reason for not wanting you to preach about a particular issue. Or the reason they give for not wanting you to preach prophetically about an issue may be somewhat disingenuous. (For example, for female pastors, there is the complicating factor of being a *woman* speaking from a position of authority about issues that may make a person uncomfortable or angry. This reality is not one to which the person would necessarily admit, but it can be an additional dynamic to be aware of.[3])

Nevertheless, asking the "why" question can help uncover what the real issue is. If it turns out that the person is not opposed to the topic being addressed in the pulpit per se, you can ask what truly upset them. It may be that their concern is the rupturing of relationships in the congregation, for example. By using our skills of empathic listening and pastoral care, this conversation—if engaged in in good faith by both parties—can lead to deeper understanding and a willingness to learn and grow for pastor and parishioner alike. (In chapter 11, we'll discuss in detail how to handle negative pushback in a prudent and pastoral way.)

The Importance of Cultivating Trust

In an article for Duke Divinity School's Faith and Leadership Program, executive director David Odom noted that cultivating trust is essential for today's leaders in the church. His advice is especially applicable when preaching about emotionally charged topics and maintaining strong pastoral relationships: "To cultivate trust, leaders must contribute to a sense of safety, commit themselves to listening, empower others to act, learn from their mistakes, and promise only what they can deliver." Listening to others is particularly important today because

> many people in the United States don't remember a time when they were heard. Some feel that the American economy and society have left them

far behind. Others have been silenced for generations, their stories missing from history books and media coverage. As a result, many increasingly believe that they can be understood only by people like themselves. People not like themselves are dangerous. For protection, some people hide, while others lash out.[4]

When we are preaching in the Purple Zone, cultivating a sense of trust works best when it is carried out in the context of what Ellen Ott Marshall identifies as the "three commitments": *agape*-love (unconditional love-in-action that adheres to the principles of nonviolence), moral ambiguity (a willingness to wrestle with doubts and questions), and theological humility (making faith commitments as part of political conversations without imposing them on others). These commitments have the potential to "transform ideologically separated people into human beings with views that sometimes diverge and sometimes overlap, thus making dialogue, compromise, and reconciliation more possible."[5] These commitments are also essential for maintaining both strong relationships and compassionate care in the Purple Zone.

The process of deliberative dialogue in conjunction with accompanying sermons is one way to cultivate this trust. I am suggesting this model as one option for effectively addressing controversial topics and opening a way for the Holy Spirit to work within a politically diverse congregation, and even within congregations that are politically homogenous. I also believe that this process is helpful in the secular community, giving people tools to engage controversial issues on a deeper level and enabling them to respectfully listen to others and address problems in productive ways. For churches, the sermon-dialogue-sermon process may even offer a way for healing to take place where there has been damage and pain.

MORE THAN "POLITICS": FINDING A BETTER WORD

Recall from chapter 1 that many pastors in the survey stressed their belief that the pulpit is for preaching the gospel, not engaging in "politics." What they likely mean is that preaching is not intended to engage in *partisan* politics. In other words, the pulpit should not be a tool for any political *party* to use toward its own ends or for a preacher to push their own partisan agenda. However, we must reject the false notion that the gospel has nothing to say about contemporary issues or current events. Important to the task of Purple Zone preaching is to help folks develop a fuller understanding of what "politics" means.

The root of "politics" is the Greek word *polis*, which refers to "community" and "citizens." Thus, I teach my students that sometimes it's helpful to use alternatives to the word "politics," since it's such a loaded word. The terms we use to describe or talk about these topics can help avoid knee-jerk reactions that cause listeners to either tune out or react in anger. In sermons, Bible studies, and conversations, I have found the following terms and phrases to be helpful substitutes for the word "politics":

- Issues of public concern
- Community matters
- The common good
- Civic concerns
- Communal issues
- Societal matters
- Discerning public issues
- How we live together in community

Another way into the Purple Zone in a sermon is to come at "political" issues by asking a basic question: "What kind of community/church shall we be?" In other words, what is our identity as the people of God in the midst of this issue?

Let's look at two examples of how these phrases and questions can be integrated into a sermon. Here is an excerpt from a sermon I wrote about the need for the church to address climate disruption.

> How will we be as a society, as a church, as a human family in the midst of these environmental crises? The process by which we answer that question is called politics, because it has to do with the "polis"—the people, the community. It is a process that requires an honest and authentic wrestling with who we understand ourselves to be as people of God living in a broken, complicated world that we share with each other and the other-than-human inhabitants of this Earth.
>
> The church has a Word to speak in these situations. It is a Word that springs from the resurrection of Jesus declaring that a better future is possible, even when all signs indicate there is no hope. It is a Word that calls us into that future, inviting us into a discourse with each other to discern the best, most equitable way to make that future a reality.

Notice how politics is reframed as a process by which to understand who we are and how we will treat each other. The sermon also makes the case that the Bible has something important to say in the midst of this process of discernment about what to do regarding climate disruption.

As another example, here is an excerpt from a sermon by one of my students, Lucas McSurley, using the story of Moses and the burning bush

(Exodus 3:1–17) to explain in a more general way why the church can and should address political issues:

> As more and more important issues swirl all around us, I long to see that burning bush. A burning bush holding the voice of God could help us think through all the political issues of our day. Now, some of you hear the word political, and suddenly you're at the edge of your seat. Some may want to check out and disengage. But politics and faith are linked because our faith does not exist outside human relationships. Both our faith and our political policies are about how to best live together in community.
>
> One of the most interesting things about Moses' call story is that God is sending Moses to address Pharaoh in order to set the Israelites free. Have you ever thought about why God needs to address Pharaoh? Why doesn't God snap God's fingers and set the Israelites free, regardless of Pharaoh? The reason is because God most often works through human relationships. Notice how God introduces Godself—it happens relationally. God introduces Godself in relation to others: "I am the God of Abraham, the God of Isaac, the God of Jacob."
>
> Similarly, others know about God by being in relationship with us as Christians, and we also know God by being in relationship with one another. So no matter how much we may disagree, we continue to come together for worship, to gather around the altar. This is what it means to be the church. By remaining in relationship, especially through challenging times, we are revealing to each other how God relates to us.
>
> The image of a burning bush not only represents God but also represents us as the church. Notice that even though the bush was burning, the fire did not consume it. There was no destruction involved, even though the flame was heated and bright. Being the church engaged with public issues means to be in conversation, even heated conversation, but not be consumed. What if we showed the world how to disagree and still come together in the unity of Christ with respect and dignity in the midst of the tension? What if that light and heat from our discussions could convey the very presence of God into the world?[6]

As you can see, preaching in the Purple Zone acknowledges complexities in determining the kind of people we will be, thus indicating that public discourse is necessary. In Lucas' sermon, he reframed the question about what it means to be political by explaining how we can learn how to talk to each other in ways that do not destructively consume us. The image of the burning bush lights the way to move beyond partisan politics and harmful bifurcations (red/blue, Democrat/Republican, conservative/liberal).

Of course, sometimes the discourse does get too hot, and the flames can get out of control. As my former synod bishop, Robert Driesen, once reminded my clergy colleagues and me, we must recognize that even in the midst of these important conversations, our discourse will be flawed because we ourselves are only human and make many mistakes. Thus, we remind ourselves and our congregations that God is the one who is bringing about the future that has been revealed through the death and resurrection of Jesus. Sometimes that will happen through us; sometimes in spite of us. But we continue to have confidence in God's power and willingness to bring about that future. "We do not despair, but enter into the freedom God makes possible. It is because of this freedom that God invites us into conversation with all kinds of people. I join the conversation trusting that Jesus is Lord and not me."[7]

PREACHING POLITICS: WHAT DID JESUS DO?

Speaking of Jesus, it's important to point out that he also engaged in politics, in that he repeatedly addressed how our common life together—our politics—played out in issues of power and domination. His parables, sermons, acts of healing, exorcisms, and engagement with the public often confronted the ways that a particular group's politics—the ways it organized its life together—resulted in unjust relationships of exploitation. He spoke truth to power with words and actions of justice, liberation, and hope for the oppressed. From his birth, to his teachings, to his healings and miracles, to his arrest, execution, and resurrection, the life of Jesus took place within—and had ramifications for—the political systems around him.

As Audrey Borschel explains: "The gospels report that Jesus preached against some of the traditional interpretations of Torah, especially as they affected the social policies of the religious institution. Was his teaching political when he spoke truth to power, despite the fact that none of the gospel writers connected Jesus with a particular branch of Judaism or with a political movement?"[8] Yes, but not because he sought political power. In fact, she says, "In John 6:15–16, not only did he deny aspirations to be a king, but he escaped from those who wanted to effect his coronation. However, he spoke of a 'Kingdom of God' as a power structure in which God calls everyone to radical spiritual conversion through their practice of justice and love for all."[9]

At the same time, he was also *nonpartisan* because he engaged—and critiqued—conversation partners on all sides of issues. From Pharisees to Roman politicians, from women accused of adultery to men abusing their power, from people of different religions to his own disciples—Jesus engaged them all forthrightly and with authentic care and concern. The topics he discussed with them were the political hot-button topics of his day—taxes, poverty, hunger, the treatment of women, the status of outsiders, the exercise of power, and capital punishment (of which he would become a victim). These matters were important to Jesus; they were also important to the people who wrote the Bible because they saw fit to include them in the canon. These were issues that affected the well-being of individuals and the entire social order. If Jesus preached and dialogued openly about these issues, and if the biblical writers deemed it important to record all of this in scripture, it follows that Christians—especially clergy—are authorized to preach about and discuss important public issues in the church today.

What Purple Zone preaching emphasizes, perhaps in distinction to other modes of prophetic preaching that may be familiar, is the nature of Jesus' address. At every turn in the Gospels, Jesus' encounter with people is *dialogical*. From Matthew to John, we see Jesus in conversation with diverse groups of individuals with varying degrees and levels of power within the political systems of the day. Beginning with his early encounter as a twelve-year-old boy with the teachers in the temple, Jesus consistently engaged in dialogue. At dinner parties, along roadsides, on fishing boats, and in the halls of religious and governmental power brokers, Jesus was always willing to engage in conversation about the things that mattered. While there weren't the red-and-blue political parties that we have today, we could say that Jesus was certainly deep in the Purple Zone. Time and again he could be found discussing important public issues with women and men from across the political spectrum, spanning a diverse range of socioeconomic, religious, ethnic, and cultural markers.

Yet, even with his intention to engage hearts and minds, transform them and bring them into alignment with God's will, and usher them into the "Beloved Community," Jesus faced deadly opposition to his mission. Perhaps, then, the reticence of some preachers to preach prophetically is due to the knowledge that such sermons can lead to some form of "crucifixion," or at least a level of sacrifice that most are not willing to undertake. Fortunately, clergy are not called to die upon a cross for the sake of their prophetic proclamations. Jesus already did that. So while there may be times a preacher feels called to take a stand on an issue and "preach with their bags packed," as my mentor Karyn Wiseman says, Purple Zone preaching seeks to empower and equip both the pastor and the congregation to avoid the worst-case scenarios. The sermon-dialogue-sermon process begins with, is sustained by, and ideally results in Christ's *agape*-love. As Tisdale reminds us: "If the message we bring is genuinely born out of love—a love regularly practiced for even the most recalcitrant of sinners—hearts may well be opened to the prophetic message of the gospel in ways we cannot even imagine or anticipate."[10]

EMBRACING THE PREACHER-AS-TEACHER

One of the ways to enact the *agape*-love of Christ is to rethink the identity of the preacher when it comes to addressing taboo topics. Homiletician Richard Voelz notes that Jesus' identity as *teacher* is what drew followers to him, empowered his preaching, and gave him the authority to proclaim the Realm of God. Voelz suggests reviving the image of *preacher-as-teacher* in the pulpit in order to reestablish the necessary function of preaching for "ongoing instruction, catechesis, formation, and edification of the faithful (or would-be faithful) who are no longer as informed as they were in days gone by."[11] The preacher-as-teacher has the potential to re-enliven the prophetic task with both authority and deep love for God's people.

The preacher-as-teacher identity is not intended to connote a highbrow, boring lecturer pontificating about dusty doctrine and elite academic treatises. Rather, a preacher informed by critical pedagogy is a "public and transformational intellectual, someone who contributes to the formation of public life beyond the walls of the church."[12] Voelz suggests that by being reflective practitioners, empowering others to engage in critical thinking, and teaching toward transformation, preachers can effectively equip their hearers for the political and cultural struggles in which they find themselves.

This is precisely the kind of preaching envisioned for the Purple Zone as well. As Voelz notes, "Worshipping communities can neither retreat simply to inconclusive spiritual reflection nor engage in knee-jerk actions to issues as they come up." This fight-or-flight response simply will not do for Christians, because the fact is that the church "participates in the wider spheres of public life," whether leaders and parishioners choose to acknowledge this or not.[13]

Especially since the church is called on to help its members integrate their faith into the web of social, economic, ecological, racial-ethnic, cultural, and political relationships, the preacher-as-teacher is a helpful way to think about one's preaching identity. Voelz's approach not only enables parishioners to navigate "contested spheres" in a biblically and theologically informed way it also helps preachers sidestep what is, in fact, a false dichotomy between prophetic and pastoral preaching. The preacher-as-teacher "makes regular interventions into the lives of listeners to help them think in ways that empower them for transformative living," which is simultaneously a prophetic and pastoral act.[14] He explains:

> Teachers who place themselves within the sphere of critical pedagogy focus on places where suffering and oppression occur, looking to enact emancipatory practice, democratic change, and exercising civic courage . . . The preacher-teacher speaks with an aim to enable the gathered com-

munity to approach life with critical thought, then act with emancipatory impulses and courageous love.[15]

Further, Voelz suggests that when the preacher-teacher sees the preaching moment as one of liberating transformation, this brings about healing for individuals, as well as divided and broken communities. This type of preaching is also "ambitious enough to work toward the healing of socioeconomic and political systems. This is certainly a different sense of preaching as teaching: sparking the kind of critical thought that seeks to liberate and bring healing to the world we inhabit together."[16] Such critical thought enables preachers and their listeners to examine together "the church's role in taboos and contentious issues, summoning knowledge from a variety of resources, suggesting that reflection on this knowledge not only can, but must result in emancipatory practices and transformation."[17]

The sermon-dialogue-sermon method I am proposing is one way for a clergyperson to enact their role as preacher-teacher. Because the preacher invites the listeners into a dialogue through the preaching event, engages in a deliberative dialogue with their people about a specific issue, and incorporates that dialogue into a follow-up sermon, the congregation is no longer just a passive recipient of the preacher's homilies. Instead, both preacher and parishioners engage the "contested spaces" in the public square together, bringing their experiences, standpoints, values, and generative ideas into play. The homiletical approach Voelz envisions, then, is a co-creative and co-relational event that can strengthen the Body of Christ as it engages in the kinds of transformation which the gospel of Jesus Christ brings about.

In the chapters ahead, we'll continue to explore what it looks like for preachers to emulate Jesus' own dialogical, prophetic preaching and teaching ministry. In the meantime, we can begin the work of readying our congregations for engaging in the questions and conversations about how we will live as God's people and the church of Jesus Christ in the midst of the red-blue divide. Here are some tips for ways you can prepare your congregation for a sermon about contemporary issues and for entering the Purple Zone.

HOW TO PREPARE YOUR CONGREGATION FOR PURPLE ZONE PREACHING

1. **Teach your congregation the biblical examples of how people of faith engaged topics of public concern.** Help them to see that disagreement and conflict are not only part of God's story with us, but that the Bible itself contains many voices, perspectives, and

agendas which sometimes contradict each other. If God is okay with God's Word having these internal conversations, the church can learn to work with these complicated conversations as well. (In chapter 4, we'll look specifically at how to read and interpret scripture through a "dialogical lens.")

2. **Tell your congregation about the church's history of engaging controversial issues.** Focus especially on your denomination's past experiences of engagement in the public realm and the precedent it sets. This will help them understand both the ancient and recent historical context within which your own preaching will take place.

3. **Have a preparatory conversation with your congregation's leadership group (board, council, elders, etc.) before preaching the sermon.** Ask them what concerns they have and what suggestions they can offer for best approaching the subject. Alert key leadership that you'll be addressing a sensitive topic so that they are prepared and not caught off guard.

4. **Talk with clergy colleagues about your sermon.** Test-drive it with them and ask them to make suggestions for how to finesse the more controversial parts of the sermon. Seeking advice from trusted colleagues can both keep us honest and give us courage.

5. **Consider talking to folks in the congregation ahead of time who you suspect may be triggered by the sermon you will preach.** This is being "wise as serpents and gentle as doves" (Matthew 10:16). For example, on the Sunday of the baptism of Jesus, I decided to preach a sermon about protecting the waters of baptism from the threats of fracking. But one of my parishioners worked for the fracking industry. So I called him as I was preparing the sermon to let him know it was not my intention to target him personally, even as I preached a prophetic word. He responded: "Pastor, you have your job to do, and I have mine. Would you like to hear about my job?" He then described his work and how it supported his family, even as he noted the dangerous parts of his job. When I preached the sermon, he was present, and I made sure to speak about the complexity of perspectives as we are called to protect the waters of Creation.

6. **Invite different voices into your sermon preparation—and even into the sermon itself.** We'll discuss the process for doing this in chapter 8, where we will incorporate ideas from John McClure's *The Roundtable Pulpit*. For the time being, consider this example. When I saw that the lectionary included Jesus' teaching on marriage and divorce (Matthew 5:21–37), I decided to talk with three different

couples—one who had been married for fifty years, one who were newlyweds, and one who had married after previous divorces. I invited them to join in the sermon with me, and each of them shared their perspective on the text. Those hearing the sermon that day got a more well-rounded sermon than I would have preached if I had remained alone in my interpretation of the text.

7. **Be fair and avoid creating straw men or taking cheap shots against those who you believe to be on the "wrong" side of an issue.** Acknowledge the complexities of individual human sin, as well as systemic evil. Use the sermon to lift up the "big questions" that underlie the headlines or controversies. Then situate those questions within biblical and theological frameworks. (You'll see examples of how to do this in the chapters ahead.)
8. **Admit your own struggles with the issue.** Allow yourself to admit your own complicity, and ways in which your heart and mind needed to be changed in order to see things a different way. Share your humanity even while you maintain enough distance for prophetic critique.
9. **If you are a parishioner, ask to engage these questions with your pastor.** Does she or he feel comfortable engaging these issues in the congregation? Why or why not? What would need to happen in the congregation to enable more prophetic preaching to take place?
10. **Also, if you are a parishioner, talk with your fellow congregants about issues of public concern.** Ask what issues they consider acceptable to address, and which ones are off-limits. Ask their thoughts about the separation of church and state versus the doctrine of the "two kingdoms." Talk together about how your church could model healthy discourse around issues of public concern.

Even with all of this preparatory work, and even with the best of intentions, the pastor's sermon may still evoke strong pushback from some listeners. In the final chapter, we'll look at how clergy and congregations can process negative fallout from prophetic sermons. In the meantime, as we move toward establishing foundations for Purple Zone preaching, O. Wesley Allen reminds preachers what it means to be called as prophets:

> We cannot claim to serve a God of justice and be silent about [justice issues] in the pulpit. On the other hand, we're also called to be pastors to all of the members of the flock—to care for all the souls in our congregation, not just those with whom we agree. We cannot claim to serve the God of mercy and fail to offer grace to those who disagree with us.[18]

Indeed, finding and proclaiming the grace of God is key to preaching in the Purple Zone. Instead of merely fretting about upsetting our listeners, we can see times of conflict and divisiveness as opportunities to seek God's Peaceable Kingdom in our midst, even if it's not obvious or visible. As Allen observes:

> This is a moment in which God is offering the church a chance to engage in God's eschatological vision for the world. It is a chance for the church to cast aside its complacency and pick up the work of transforming the world instead of being conformed to it. It is a chance for preachers to reclaim the ethical voice that is the inheritance of the pulpit. It is a chance for us to make the church great again.[19]

With this goal of transformation through reclaiming the ethical voice in the pulpit, let's turn to establishing the homiletical foundations for Purple Zone preaching and learn what it means to preach a sermon in the "conversational" mode.

• 3 •

Homiletical Foundations for Purple Zone Preaching

𝒦arl Barth was the first to go on record encouraging Christians to "take your Bible and take your newspaper, and read both. But interpret newspapers from your Bible."[1] When we take our newspapers, news magazines, or newsfeeds from Twitter, Facebook, CNN, or FOX in one hand, we see the contours and angles that make up the ever-shifting architecture of the public square, both metaphorically and literally. Taxes, education, housing, immigration, pollution, and economics are just the beginning of the list of issues that have an impact on the quality of our lives individually, as well as our communities, our nation, and our "global village."

But what about when we have our Bible in the other hand? What does the Bible have to say about land use disputes or environmental devastation? What does God have to say about neoliberal capitalism or criminal justice? How would Jesus respond to questions about access to health care or gun violence? These are questions for both clergy and parishioners alike. The pastor alone cannot address these issues; rather, the whole community needs to wonder together about them. When they do, we naturally ask what the preacher will proclaim regarding these questions. As the one entrusted with the care of a group of Christians in a particular time and place, what will she or he say about topics such as equal rights or immigration? Will topics such as these make it into the sermon at all?

Both parishioners in the pews as well as a host of other constituencies beyond the walls of the church ask these questions. However, many assume, hope, or even demand that preachers not answer these questions in a public way, or in a way that has any bearing on how people or institutions conduct themselves in the world. In fact, it is often the case that our local communities, social institutions, businesses, CEOs, elected officials, and government agencies *dare* preachers to give an answer. Frankly, those in power often count on the church and preachers *not* to say anything substantive about these issues so that they may continue in their activities unimpeded.

For all of these reasons and more, the preacher's proclamation is meant not just for the Christian community, but also for the world in which the church exists, as we discussed in chapter 2. When preaching in the Purple Zone, such engagement with the world necessitates discussion, collaboration, and accountability by following Jesus' model of community-engaged preaching. Thus, we need strategies for gospel-centered prophetic and ethical preaching that steps into the public square in a way that is respectful, dialogical, cooperative, and, in the spirit of the preacher-as-teacher, aimed at edifying and building up the congregation and community.

Before we can think about strategy, however, we need to establish the foundations of a socially engaged homiletic—what is commonly known as "prophetic preaching." Then we need to understand what it means to see preaching as a conversation rather than an authoritative monologue. Let's start with exploring what we mean by "prophetic preaching."

WHAT IS "PROPHETIC PREACHING"?

Several homileticians have thought deeply about what prophetic preaching is, what it is not, and what distinguishes it from other types of preaching. We begin with preaching scholar Kenyatta R. Gilbert who identified what he calls the "trivocal impulse" of African American preaching. While Gilbert's description arises from the context of the historical Black church, his observations provide a helpful framework for understanding preaching in other cultural and ethnic settings as well. He identifies three aspects or modes of preaching that provide a way to understand the different intentions behind sermons: *the prophet, the priest,* and *the sage.* These impulses are not exclusive categories into which every sermon can be classified. Rather, they are modes of preaching that co-inform each other and sometimes overlap in a catalytic and holistic way. Ideally, these modes function in a "mutually influential relationship and are synthesized and appropriated in one's preaching life."[2]

Briefly, the *priestly* voice is characterized as the more "pastoral" impulse. Sermons in this vein offer comfort, hope, and a more spiritual focus on personal issues, while also providing institutional maintenance. The *sage* mode approaches sermons from a didactic perspective. They convey wisdom by way of teaching, explanation of doctrine, and, at times, exhortation. The third mode is that of the *prophet*. This voice focuses on ethics, engages in social critique, calls for justice, and boldly unmasks the systemic sin that holds individuals, communities, and the larger society in thrall. Taken together, Gilbert describes the principle marks of trivocal preaching in this way:

1. The *prophetic voice* expresses unrelenting hope about God's activity to transform church and society in a present-future sense based on the principle of justice;
2. The *priestly voice* encourages, through a variety of Christian practices, the Christian formation of listeners in order to enhance themselves morally and ethically; and
3. The *sagely voice* confers the preacher and congregation's wisdom; daringly, it speaks within the context of radical social and ecclesial change for the purpose of keeping vital the congregation's vision and mission.[3]

For Gilbert, the prophetic mode is "a mediating voice of God's activity to transform church and society in a present-future sense based on the principle of justice. The prophetic voice speaks of divine intentionality—what God demands and expects of God's own human creation." What are the main features of this type of prophetic discourse? It should oppose idolatry, refrain from absolutizing the present, and "drive toward a new unsettling, unsettled future." Further, "[i]t is a word that speaks to the predicament of human suffering from the perspective of God's justice. This speech, at all times, assumes a critical posture over and against established power. Last, the prophetic Word is a word of relentless hope."[4]

Dawn Ottoni-Wilhelm offers another definition of prophetic preaching as "divinely inspired speech enlivened by the Holy Spirit in the gathered community of faith. Prophetic preaching proclaims God's Word from within the Christian tradition against all that threatens God's reconciling intention for humanity and for all that creates and sustains a vital and necessary ministry of compassion to neighbors near and far."[5] While her definition does not mention the word *justice* per se, note how she mentions the care of neighbor which we emphasized in chapter 1. Ottoni-Wilhelm emphasizes that, "Because it is not exclusively either moral exhortation or prediction regarding future event, prophetic preaching envisions past, present, and future concerns within the context of the reign of God realized in Jesus Christ and empowered by the Holy Spirit."[6] Thus she frames prophetic preaching both within the context of time and from a Trinitarian perspective.

Leonora Tubbs Tisdale's description of prophetic preaching is more succinct. She says that prophetic preaching is "cutting edge and future oriented (yet not future predicting) and addresses public and social concerns."[7] She also provides a list of the "Seven Hallmarks of Prophetic Preaching," explaining that this type of preaching is:

- Rooted in biblical witness.
- Countercultural and challenges the status quo.
- Concerned with evils and shortcomings of social order; focused on corporate and public issues rather than individual or personal concerns.
- Names what is not of God (criticizing); names new reality God will bring to pass (energizing).
- Offers hope and promise of liberation.
- Incites courage and empowers hearers to work for change.
- Requires of preachers a heart that breaks with the things that break God's heart. This involves having:
  - Passion for justice.
  - Imagination, conviction, courage.
  - Humility and honesty.
  - Strong reliance on the presence and power of Holy Spirit.[8]

As David Schnasa Jacobsen has pointed out, however, the way prophetic preaching is often conceived is "something akin to the Lone Ranger." In other words, this type of prophetic preacher "drops in" as the hero, single-handedly saves the congregation from sin, and rides off into the sunset. The problem is that this Lone Ranger type of prophetic preacher

> adopts a stance of disconnection with the hearers and tries to convince them of a need to adopt a universalizable liberal principle. The issue here for me is not the validity of the ethical claim, but the image and stance of the prophet. The prophet is the righteous individual trying to reform the primitive system. Prophets are moral geniuses and religious innovators. They speak a word of individual insight in the hope of redeeming a corrupt social grouping.[9]

Purple Zone preaching is not envisioned as this singular prophetic-hero endeavor. While it is undergirded by Tisdale's principles, it seeks to embrace what Jacobson describes as a "public form of shared ecclesial engagement for the sake of the world God so loves."[10] Further, preaching in the Purple Zone includes a key element that is sometimes missing from prophetic preaching: *dialogue*. We'll learn how the process of deliberative dialogue has a specific role in Purple Zone preaching in chapter 5. In the meantime, let's take a closer look at the ways in which different scholars of preaching have encouraged the church to address moral and ethical deliberation about social issues by engaging the myriad of voices within the church and in the public square.

PREACHING'S CONVERSATION PARTNERS

Purple Zone preaching addresses the intersection of religion, culture, socioeconomics, and all manner of issues that have to do with the common good. Thus, it requires a homiletic for the public square informed by public theology. This public theology includes using biblical and theological resources for ethical and moral discernment, listening to and learning from victims of injustice, and organizing to confront systems of oppression while calling for positive social change. As the National Council of Churches once wrote:

> To interpret the Word of God in a sermon means making the Word of God *bear upon* a specific problem, a particular situation, a concrete issue, a definite life situation. The Word of God is nothing unless it strikes people in their lives, their communities, institutions, cultures, and their destinies. And it strikes them in judgment, mercy, and promise, aiming at *change* (repentance) to bring about more love, more justice, more truth, more freedom, more peace, and more praises of God in human life and affairs.
>
> If, therefore, the Word of God is properly interpreted in a sermon, a preacher may have to draw out specific implications and conclusions that indicate the significance of God's Word for now, for today, in our contemporary life situation. And the implication or conclusion should be critical of current trends, prevailing situations, etc.[11]

Similarly, Clark Williamson and Ronald Allen remind us that

> we are always called upon [to preach] to people who live in a new historical situation, one significantly different from that in which [the people of the Bible] were born. Preachers must speak plausibly to questions that are not only urgent but new, if they are to help people understand what it means to live a Christian life in the present . . . If we are to help people understand the world in which they live in the light of the Christian faith, we must also help them understand the Christian faith in the light of questions arising from the world in which they live.[12]

In other words, preaching has a word to say to the "powers and principalities" and the society that exists beyond the church walls. It is a word that puts the systems of domination (and those they hold in thrall) on notice that the crucifixions they perpetrate will not be the final word, nor will their oppressive reign endure without resistance. For Christians, however, any "issue preaching" must bring us to the person of Jesus Christ and what his ministry, preaching, teaching, healing, miracles, crucifixion, and resurrection mean for the communities and the very real bodies of human beings, animals, plants, and even Earth itself. Further, "the Word of God spoken is itself the Word of God in preaching or

God's own speech to us. Thus preaching has a dual aspect: divine activity and human activity, God's Word and human speech."[13] This dual function must be reflected in our prophetic preaching. We need to understand the human activity of the preacher who takes the suffering of humanity and Earth into consideration when proclaiming God's Word. At the same time, we need to articulate *God's* action of calling people both to awareness and repentance, and, most importantly, proclaiming and concretizing hope in the midst of despair.

Richard Lischer points out that our proclamation must also engage other dialogue partners such as "psychotherapy, anthropology, philosophy, ideology, politics, the arts, science, medicine, cybernetics, and ethics. This dialogue not only informs preaching; it makes it possible—and intelligible."[14] In the same way, Purple Zone preaching is responsible to the scriptures while being responsive to contemporary issues of public concern. Further, the preacher's attention to contemporary issues is not merely an imposition of external agendas or ideological concerns on the church's proclamation. Rather it arises out of, and is a natural extension of, the gospel's concern with "the least of these" and the Good News about the coming of God's "Peaceable Community."

This approach to preaching in the Purple Zone is strongly influenced by what John McClure identifies as a *liberation theology* approach to homiletics. This approach develops "a profound awareness of Christ incarnate in the pain and suffering of the poor, the marginalized, the oppressed, the shamed, the shunned, the outcast, the abused, or the disenfranchised."[15] McClure encourages preachers to attend to the margins by asking questions of both the biblical text and our particular preaching context:

- Who doesn't speak?
- Who's missing?
- Who goes nameless?
- What contradictions open the text toward "other-wise" interpretation?[16]

McClure also points to Martin Luther's understanding of sin and grace as the two poles within which prophetic preaching can find contemporary footing in addressing "social and structural oppression [as] the major expression of sin."[17] This sin is answered by the preacher's proclamation of grace as follows:

> God's will and power are identified not with what socially *is* but with what *will be*. Hope is an absolutely fundamental theological category. Anticipation of a new future grounded in faith in God conditions and motivates life. The Christian life is one of hope, consciousness-raising, learning from and suffering with the oppressed, . . . hope for and involvement in the work of social transformation, and joy in the present, rooted in faith's hope for and vision of the future.[18]

It is, of course, the promise of the resurrection that gives the commission and power to preach prophetically.[19] And Kenyatta Gilbert reminds us that the prophetic voice within trivocal preaching is not exclusive to or even distinct from the sagely and pastoral voices: "More than passionate and persuasive speech, at its core, preaching of this kind is Spirit-guided, three-dimensional, anointed discourse that speaks of divine intentionality, communal care, and the active practice of hope."[20]

Along the same vein, Tisdale emphasizes that it is the *pastoral need* of a particular people that gives rise to the need for a prophetic voice to speak alongside them or on their behalf. Meanwhile, the sagely or didactic voice can help educate our listeners about the importance of a contemporary issue as it relates to theological, doctrinal, sacramental, ecclesial, and biblical themes. Says Gilbert, "The common thread of all prophetic preaching is the recognition of injustice, and that the preacher will name injustice for what it is, and what justice should be. Thus, the prophetic witness is never imported; it is mediated, sent, and worked out in community, not in isolation."[21]

What I want to encourage in preachers is a confidence to exercise the prophetic voice on a regular basis—not just within the church's pulpit, but within the public arena as well, as they discern the call to do so. Further, this prophetic voice is exercised in *conversation* with the plurality of voices and viewpoints within and beyond one's congregation. In other words, I am proposing an expansion of Barth's dipolar engagement between contemporary issues and the Bible to include the people whose lives are affected by this intersection. Thus, we might amend Barth's words to say: "Take your Bible and take your newspaper, and read both *in dialogue with your community.* Interpret newspapers from your Bible *and share the task of discernment with the whole people of God.*"

This brings us to an important development in the world of homiletics—*conversational preaching*. Introduced in the 1990s, this approach to preaching was both an outgrowth of the "New Homiletic" and a corrective of it. In this section, I will briefly describe how conversational preaching emerged in the field of homiletics, then draw out implications for conversational preaching as we enter the Purple Zone.

FROM AUTHORITARIAN MONOLOGUE TO INDUCTIVE JOURNEY TO CONVERSATIONAL PREACHING

The New Homiletic

In 1971, a little book by Fred Craddock took the preaching world by storm. *As One Without Authority* was written as a reaction against authoritarian, deductive preaching that had characterized most sermons for decades. Craddock critiqued traditional authoritarian preaching as having "a downward movement, a condescension of thought, in the pattern."[22] He observed that this kind of preaching ignores the listener and assumes that the *kerygma* (a Greek word meaning "proclamation") is enough to bring listeners to faith without any concern for how the process of this proclamation actually happens. At the same time, Craddock noted the diminishment in authority ascribed to clergy by parishioners. Thus, he called for a new way of preaching that utilizes inductive logic as a more effective means by which to proclaim the gospel. In this way, he emphasized the primacy of the form of the sermon as much as the content. This approach to preaching became known as the New Homiletic.

Craddock proposed that the act of preaching is located in the dialectical movement between speaker and listener, inasmuch as the preacher listens to the scripture, commentators, and the Spirit in her preparation, then speaks what she has "overheard" to the congregation, who in turn listens to the sermon. This form reconceived the relationship between preacher and listener as one whereby the preacher leads the listener on a journey, bringing the listener into the process of discovery of biblical insights that occurred to her during her preparation.

While the inductive method revolutionized preaching in expansive and creative ways, Craddock made an assumption that needs questioning. He asserted that if the listeners make the trip, then it is *their* conclusion at which they arrive at the end of the sermon. But this ignores the fact that it is still the *preacher's* trip on which they are being brought along—not that there is necessarily anything wrong with that. But there is a subtly patronizing undercurrent here. Craddock's "journey" method is built on the premise that the listener will eagerly come along on the trip through the preacher's effective use of narrative, concrete examples, and evocative language that reenact the experience of discovering the gospel within the listeners themselves. This may sometimes be the case, but in Purple Zone preaching, we're looking for an alternative way to engage hearers that sees them more as co-creators of the journey rather than as passive recipients.

Lucy Atkinson Rose, in her book *Sharing the Word: Preaching in the Roundtable Church*, pointed out that the New Homiletic is still based on a model whereby the preacher is in a position of privilege as one who has the knowledge while the congregation is in the subordinate position and must be brought along to receive that knowledge.[23] All of this happens without any possibility of contestation. The preacher's experience of the Word is normative and may not always acknowledge those in the pew who have a radically different experience of the scripture. Thus, the New Homiletic continues the problematic assumption of authoritarian preaching in that it raises up the experience of one person in authority as paradigmatic and universal. Whether it happens deductively or inductively, there is still an assumption that the preacher's wisdom and insights are privileged over that of the hearers.

This is exactly the concern raised by some of the survey respondents to the questionnaire about sermons that address controversial justice issues that I discussed in chapter 1. Because many see the sermon as a one-way monologue, it precludes the opportunity for people to ask questions and engage in dialogue. For example, one respondent said, "I will bring up hot topics like this in a small Sunday School class, but sermons do not allow for dialogue." Another said, "[These issues] require more nuance and conversation than a sermon can offer in a divided congregational setting." Others pointed out that certain controversial justice issues take more time to discuss and digest than one brief sermon. As one preacher noted: "Setting this up for a sermon would not give enough time to truly unpack it. I think it needs a longer education timeline."

So is it possible to think about preaching as more of a "conversation" than a top-down diatribe? As a matter of fact, yes! Over the past twenty years scholars of preaching have developed a homiletical approach called "conversational preaching" that sees the preacher and the sermon as being part of a community of dialogue. Scholars such as John McClure, Ronald J. Allen, O. Wesley Allen, and Lucy Rose see conversational preaching as a means by which to engage many partners in a wide range of discussions, including dialogues regarding the church's tradition, the Bible, the local congregation and community, the larger society, and individuals who might not otherwise be recognized by the church.[24] This last was the particular focus for Rose.

Conversational Preaching

Lucy Rose offered a way to conceive of preaching that moves beyond the single talking-head espousing their views for the congregation to accept with passive ascent. Engaging John McClure's method of "collaborative preaching" (which will be discussed at length in chapter 8), Rose envisioned conversational preaching to be communal, nonhierarchical, personal, inclusive, and scriptural. Rose's proposal sought to remove the separation between preacher and congregation so that the relationship might be more of a give-and-take. "Conversational preaching," she said, "seeks to gather together these voices—local and global, present and past—paying particular attention to those that have been drowned out by the din around the round and rectangular tables of our world, paying particular attention to the whispers and pauses where people's voices are missing."[25]

This emphasis on including many different voices is especially important for Purple Zone preaching. The traditional model of prophetic proclamation whereby the minister harangues the congregation in a finger-wagging, camel's-hair-in-the-wilderness style is based on a model found in Hebrew scripture but, as David Schnasa Jacobsen notes, is anachronistic, impractical, and problematic today. While there is a certain tragic romanticism that we attach to prophets like Jeremiah, Amos, Hosea, John, and even Jesus, it's important to remember that none of the biblical prophets had a congregation like pastors do today. They set themselves (or God set them) outside of the established religious hierarchy and worshipping communities which enabled their critical distantiation. While there may be times when that kind of propheticism is called for, many find this style of preaching off-putting.

As it stands, the beleaguered, angry-prophet style of preaching fails to meet the needs of the congregation to be heard, affirmed, and invited into theological conversations about the social and political issues that they struggle with in their day-to-day lives and in the world around them. There are other ways to be prophetic within one's congregation that allow God's message of justice to be heard and metabolized. A pastorally sensitive approach to prophetic preaching enables the preacher to listen to and reflect on the needs of the congregation (even when those "needs" need to be challenged!). Such community-engaged preaching invites "a public, prophetic articulation of the gospel that not so much thunders an ethical-monotheistic 'thus says the Lord' to the monarch and his minions," says Jacobsen, "but humbly and prophetically 'names God into the world' in a way that makes connections with others—whether Christian, non-Christian religious, or even 'free thinkers'—for the sake of the world God so loves."[26]

Rose stressed that "within this community of shared faith and commitment, conversational preaching seeks to acknowledge a diversity of experiences, interpretations, and wagers, especially those on the margins without power, status or voice."[27] She made use of the image of *oikos* (Greek for "household") as a way to describe how the church may be re-formed in the spirit of conversational preaching:

> Within the household of God, domination and submission give way to partnership and cooperation; clericalism, or the hierarchical relationship between clergy and laity, disappears; everyone participates in setting the church's agenda and carrying out the church's ministry; and, in particular, those who are most marginal, whose voices have been excluded and silenced, are valued and invited back into the life-restoring conversations.[28]

This kind of inclusiveness is exactly what Purple Zone preaching is about. It entails developing relationships with one's parishioners and people within the community, listening to their voices, and inviting them into a dialogue about the important issues that affect our lives. It also means articulating uncomfortable truths in ways that are respectful while also reflecting one's willingness to be vulnerable, open, and trusting of the Spirit of Christ to guide the process of discernment around these topics of social concern.

As Ronald Allen and O. Wesley Allen explain, a conversational approach to preaching means that sermons are shaped "to contribute to postmodern individuals' and communities' approaches to making meaning in a pluralistic setting by offering a tentative interpretation of, experience of, and response to God's character, purposes, and good news."[29] Emphasis on the word *tentative* is key because the preacher's proclamation must be provisional and invitational, even as it is informed by his or her training, study, experiences, and engagement with other conversation partners. It also welcomes further conversation as the community continues to discern the theological, scriptural, traditional, and experiential implications of engaging these issues of public concern. As Ron Allen explains:

> A conversational approach listens to the voices in an interpretive situation (usually the Bible, church history/tradition, the experiences of the communities involved, scientific and other data) and helps the community consider interpretive options that are consistent with the community's deepest convictions (or challenge those convictions) and possible implications. The preacher helps the community toward an adequate interpretation of God's purposes in the context in which the sermon is preached.[30]

In the chapters that follow, there will be several sermons and sermon excerpts that will enable us to see these hallmarks of conversational preaching on full display. Before we examine these examples, I will share a five-fold approach to prophetic preaching that I have developed, along with a "dialogical lens" for reading and interpreting the Bible.

• *4* •

Five Paths of Prophetic Preaching in the Purple Zone

When I wrote *Creation-Crisis Preaching* to help pastors address environmental issues in their sermons, I drew on the metaphor of a tree to conceptualize different ways to approach topics such as climate disruption; safeguarding water, land, and air; and protecting vulnerable people and communities.[1] This conceptual framework was based on the phases of a deciduous tree's yearly cycle: flowering (raising awareness about environmental issues), leafing (calling for specific action), and fruiting (transforming people and society for long-term sustainable change). But as I was working on that book and talking with ministers about how they approach environmental issues in their sermons, I realized how difficult it is for many clergy to even mention a controversial subject such as climate disruption in a sermon, let alone preach a prophetic word about it. Following that book, then, I have decided to expand the threefold framework into what I call the Five Paths of Prophetic Preaching (figure 4.1). This diagram illustrates how these different strategies co-inform

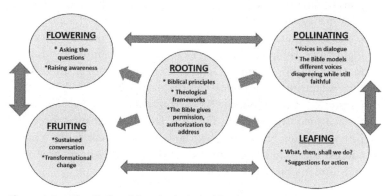

Figure 4.1.   Five Paths of Prophetic Preaching

each other. As we look at each of these paths in turn, notice that there is no linear progression from one approach to the next. Each of the paths connects to and through the others. They co-inform each other and provide numerous entry points to address issues of public concern. At the center of it all is the root system of biblical and theological principles that both anchors the tree and feeds it the nutrients it needs.

ROOTING

Rootedness in biblical principles and theological frameworks undergirds Purple Zone preaching. As we discussed in chapters 1 and 2, of the most important points to emphasize for listeners is that the Bible authorizes the church, and thus preachers, to address issues of public concern. Admittedly, some disagree with this on principle. As one person said in the survey, "Sermons should not be about [contemporary] topics but based on the Bible and its teachings."

While it is true that sermons based on the Bible and its teachings can transcend current events with themes and values that are timeless, such a statement is based on a false premise—that scripture and preaching are *only* meant for spiritual uplift and personal moral edification. Such a belief limits the power of God's Word. As we have established, Jesus, the prophets, and the Bible itself absolutely have something to say about contemporary issues because scripture addresses a myriad of topics. Thus, our preaching is authorized to speak to these topics from a biblical perspective. Consider just a few examples:

- Concerned about health care? Stories about healing—including questions about who should have access to care—are in the Bible. Think of Elijah restoring the life of the widow's son (1 Kings 17:17–24) and Jesus healing the paralyzed man let down through a roof (Mark 2:1–12, Luke 5:17–39).
- Climate change or other environmental issues keeping you up at night? The Bible has many verses and stories about how humans are to regard God's creation. Genesis 2:15, for example, shows God putting Adam into the garden to "till and to keep it." And in the final chapter of Revelation, the Tree of Life has leaves "for the healing of the nations" (Revelation 22:2).[2] If Jesus himself referenced weather patterns in his teachings (Matthew 16:2), certainly the church can address the issue of climate disruption and how it impacts our Earth and human communities.

- Thinking about why you or others are experiencing financial troubles and having a hard time making ends meet? Passages critiquing the injustice of a predatory economic system are found throughout scripture. Habakkuk 2:6–8, for instance, points to economic injustice and exploitation resulting in one's own destruction. And the Gospel of Luke has Mary singing a powerful song of the great reversal of predatory wealth in chapter 1:51–53.[3]

In other words, nearly every "political" issue you can name can be brought into conversation with a passage from scripture. Of course, the Bible does not address all our contemporary problems using our modern-day parlance. Further, preachers must avoid proof-texting or cherry-picking Bible passages to support their own partisan opinions, since this is an abuse of the text and the listeners. But as we learned in chapter 1, the Bible does provide us with the ethical framework of *justice* that can support our discussions about these issues.

FLOWERING

In the *flowering* approach to prophetic preaching, we raise awareness about justice issues and bring questions to bear from the perspective of theology, scripture, faith, and values. Consider, for example, the area of science and technology, which at first may appear to be outside of the Bible's purview due to the thousands-year gap between the ancient world and our own. But in fact, there are underlying questions about the applications of science and technology that have to do with justice, be it genetic engineering, the use of drones, advances in medical care, agricultural developments, military weaponry, the use of social media, self-driving cars, and even access to the internet itself. We can ask: What is fair and equitable when it comes to these technological developments? How can we responsibly exercise our human intellect while also keeping our ethics at the forefront?

On this flowering path, the Bible can offer guidance for these questions. For instance, Psalm 8 recognizes human beings as "a little lower than the angels," thus implying the potential for abundant good in harnessing human intelligence. At the same time, words of caution, correction, and accountability mark God's interaction with God's people, because there is also the risk of immeasurable harm from unchecked hubris and the idolatry of empire. The stories of the Tower of Babel in Genesis 11, Pharaoh in the book of Exodus, Nebuchadnezzar in the book of Daniel, and the critique of the

Roman Empire in Revelation all point to what can happen when humans accomplish much but fail to check their egos and keep the welfare of "the least of these" at the forefront. Notice, then, how flowering connects right back to rootedness in scripture. Rootedness means that we bring the Bible and theological frameworks to address all areas of life and that our preaching should do the same. Flowering brings the attention of the congregation to these areas of life from a biblical and theological perspective. Awareness can also spark an exchange between and among people of faith about the issue, what we might call "pollinating."

POLLINATING

For Christians, all of these contemporary issues must be brought into conversation with our understanding of a God who continues to be active in Creation and human history. This brings us to the *pollinating* aspect of prophetic preaching which emphasizes the fact that the Bible models for us what it looks like to have different voices in dialogue about justice issues. As we noted in chapter 2, Jesus himself engaged with a wide variety of conversation partners about subjects that mattered to his community and for people of faith. In fact, the entire Bible is replete with examples of dialogue among individuals from different constituencies who discuss how to handle complex public issues. Here are just a few examples:

- Moses appointing elders to help judge the affairs of the people (after heeding Jethro's sage advice) in Exodus chapter 18.
- Phinehas and the Israelites deliberating about altars and idolatry—and avoiding a war—in Joshua chapter 22.
- The Israelites rebuilding the temple, restoring community, and reestablishing public worship after returning from exile in the books of Ezra and Nehemiah.
- The early Christian community deliberating, debating, and discerning how they will "be church" together in the Acts of the Apostles, including who they will welcome, how they will feed those in need, and how they will distribute wealth.[4]

How does the pollinating approach work in preaching? Consider the issue of immigration. Both the Old and New Testament have stories about how to deal with foreigners. For example, God commanded the Israelites to show love to foreigners in Deuteronomy 10:19. At the same time, there is also the injunction against marrying people from other tribes in Deuteronomy 7:2–5. However, in the story of Ruth, Boaz shows mercy to—and ultimately marries—an outsider (chapter 2). Meanwhile, the writer of Hebrews in the New Testament encouraged the followers of Jesus to "show hospitality to strangers, for by this some have entertained angels unawares" (Hebrews 13:2). In a sermon about immigration, the preacher can help listeners recognize that if the Bible has divergent views, it's no wonder our communities and churches struggle with how best to deal with immigrants and refugees today.

That's exactly why rooting our preaching in the Bible is useful for these pollinating conversations. Because within the canon, there are various perspectives that span thousands of years and show us what it looks like for faithful people to disagree while discerning how to be the people of God. This aspect of pollinating will come up again in the discussion about using the *dialogical lens* for interpreting scripture in the Purple Zone. In the meantime, another path intersecting with rooting, flowering, and pollinating is leafing, wherein the sermon helps convert the light of the gospel into the action of the people.

LEAFING

When John the Baptist preached his prophetic sermon in the third chapter of Luke, he began by rooting his sermon in the words of Isaiah 4–6, then raised awareness about the need for repentance, thus following the flowering path (vv. 7–9). This sparked a conversation among his listeners (pollination). They asked the question: "What then, shall we do?" (v. 3:10). This brings us to the *leafing* phase of prophetic preaching. Sometimes called the "so what" or the "ask," this aspect of preaching offers concrete suggestions for how listeners can live out their response to the sermon's message. In the case of John the Baptist, his "ask" in Luke 3:11–14 was direct, specific, and contextual. *Share what you have with others. Be honest in your business dealings. Don't abuse your power. Be content and avoid coveting because it leads to breaking commandments.*

While preachers must be careful not to dictate the actions of their congregations or set out only one definitive way to put faith into action, giving suggestions and lifting up opportunities to take action gives the listeners a way to respond if a sermon so moves them. Like the process of photosynthesis converting sunlight and water into food for the tree, leafing allows the energy generated by rooting, flowering, and pollinating to be converted into deeds informed by our values. In fact, raising awareness about an issue without providing for any recourse to action can both frustrate the listeners and even result in the opposite effect of what the sermon intended, namely apathy borne out of feelings of being overwhelmed by the size and complexity of the problem. One way to counteract that feeling of being overwhelmed is to suggest concrete ways to respond and offer opportunities to take steps to address the problem. This allows the rhetoric to shift from simply opening minds and hearts to moving hands and feet in tangible ways. We'll see examples of how preachers can do this in the chapters ahead.

FRUITING

This brings us to the fifth approach to prophetic preaching—*fruiting*. This path allows for sustained conversation over time that eventually begins to transform listeners' lives, and perhaps even the community itself. The fruit of a tree not only nourishes those who eat it but it contains the seeds that can be planted in other places. Over the long term, these seeds can take root and grow, transforming the landscape. In the same way, preachers need to see their prophetic sermons as not only nourishing their immediate listeners but as containing the seeds for transformation in the long term. In this way, preaching is part of a larger movement of changing the landscape, establishing God's realm "on earth as it is in heaven." Preaching in the Purple Zone is more than just a one-time prophetic event. It draws deeply from the soil of biblical and theological reflection, engages the congregation in dialogue that enables them to learn a new way to be in productive conversation about the common good, harnesses the energy for enacting positive steps forward, and cultivates the slow-but-sure change in hearts and minds and communities. Again, we'll see examples of this approach as we move through the rest of the book's chapters.

With these five paths in mind, how might we design a sermon that prophetically addresses a public issue? Recall that there is no one starting point or necessary progression; rather, each route is linked to the others. This means that a preacher could use more than one path in a prophetic sermon. For instance, a sermon may start with raising awareness about an issue (flowering), speak to the biblical principles that inform our understanding of the topic (rooting), and then invite people to a formal dialogue about the issue (pollinating). Or a sermon may begin by noting all the different perspectives about a long-standing issue in the community (pollinating), list the ways in which people have suggested taking action (leafing), and then lift up a theological perspective to emphasize how God is working in and through the community's discernment and efforts to address the problem (rooting). As we'll see in chapter 8, a sermon *following* a deliberative dialogue would lift up the group's discussion about the issue (pollinating) as an example of how God is working in and through the congregation to create moments of deep listening and new connections (fruiting).

Now that we've explored these Five Paths of Prophetic Preaching, we need to spend some time thinking about the ways in which *conversations* happen in the stories of the Bible, as well as how the books of the Bible are themselves in dialogue. In other words, we need a *dialogical lens* for reading scripture that enables us to see how God works in and through our complicated, messy, conflicted, and yet faithful conversations in order to bring about discernment, justice, healing, and reconciliation. In this next section I'll show you how to employ this dialogical lens and then demonstrate how it can be applied to a scriptural text.

READING AND INTERPRETING SCRIPTURE THROUGH A DIALOGICAL LENS[5]

When I teach students the Purple Zone method of preaching, the first assignment I give them is to craft a simple "rooting" sermon that makes the case for why it is not only acceptable but necessary for ministers to preach about contemporary justice issues and for churches to discuss them. As David Lose says:

> The challenge and opportunity before us is to invite our people to actual engagement of the biblical story in an age where all kinds of grand stories and metanarratives clamor for their attention and allegiance. Our goal, that is, is less to develop biblical literacy than it is to nurture biblical imagination, where intimate knowledge of and regular interaction with the biblical stories invites patterns of thinking, speaking, and doing that would otherwise be unavailable to us.[6]

This "rooting" sermon primes the biblical imagination for addressing a specific controversial justice issue at a later time, as well as the deliberative dialogue sessions the preacher will eventually facilitate. This sermon helps congregations understand that dialogue about important—even controversial—issues is grounded in the witness of scripture. But you have to have your eyes peeled and your radar up for detecting and assessing the ways in which dialogue happens in scripture. In order to do that, I suggest using a dialogical lens for exegeting scripture.

Utilizing the dialogical lens requires us to draw from different exegetical methods. The historical-critical method is useful for determining the author of the work, its original audience, other intertextual sources, and the social, historical, or cultural influences with which the author may be implicitly or explicitly in conversation. Literary analysis will be helpful as we determine the characters and their roles in the story and the rhetorical techniques being used in the text. But the dialogical lens will also require some interpretive imagination, since the text sometimes only hints at the motivations and emotions of the characters and authors. At the same time, we need to consider the reader-response method because of the way in which the text will be heard and interpreted by readers in our contemporary contexts. Finally, the dialogical lens benefits from feminist interpretation, liberation theology, and John McClure's "other-wise" homiletic,[7] each of which enables us to ascertain the voices in the conversation that are not heard or acknowledged, but who nevertheless have a stake in the outcome. With these critical methods in mind, here are six steps for using the dialogical lens.

SIX STEPS FOR USING THE DIALOGICAL LENS

1. **Point out the dialogical aspects of the passage.** In broad terms, describe how this passage of the Bible is an instance of conversation, dialogue, or some other kind of interchange. Who is the (presumed) author, and who was the intended audience? What were the social, cultural, and political forces either in the background or directly present in the passage? In what other books or authors in the Bible is the text or author implicitly engaging in conversation? If the story is a narrative, who are the characters? Who speaks? Who is in the background? Who is in the scene but silent?
2. **Determine what's at stake.** What is the presenting issue? What are the fears or concerns of the author, the audience, or the characters? What are they afraid of losing? What or who is threatening to them? What are the overt or underlying tensions or conflicts?
3. **Identify the values.** This gets at the deeper ideals and principles that underlie a character's actions or writer's intentions. What is important to them? What do they cherish and hold dear? What is their "best self" that could emerge? Find the overlap—and the gaps. What desires, fears, and values do the characters or figures share? In other words, where are points of commonality among or between them? At the same time, where are there vast differences? What are the things the dialogue partners are unlikely to agree upon?
4. **Explain how God, Jesus, and/or the Holy Spirit is active.** What is God doing in the midst of this interchange? Is God's action

explicit, implicit, or apparently absent? How is the larger community wrestling with or expressing their faith in God?
5. **Recognize what the dialogue is teaching us.** What is this exchange, dialogue, or conversation teaching us about what it means to "be church" in the midst of contentious public issues? What can we learn about being faithful people who engage the conflicts and sin of the world, while maintaining the commitment to grace, hope, and love? What can we determine about who God is, what God does, and what God intends for us based on this interchange and dialogue in the passage?
6. **Suggest possible next steps.** What are next steps we might take based on what this biblical passage models for us? Are we sensing God's invitation to engage public concerns? Are we being invited into dialogue with each other, with this passage, and with God about specific justice issues? Are we learning what *not* to do based on what we see in this text? Are there common values we share that can be the basis for our response to a societal matter? What kind of church shall we be, knowing what the Bible models for us, and knowing what challenges our community is facing?

These steps and the questions therein will come into play when we craft sermons about specific issues we want to address in our sermons, as well as in the deliberative dialogue forums we will facilitate in our congregations. What this initial "rooting" sermon does, however, is to make the case that we are permitted, authorized, encouraged, and even urged to preach about public issues because scripture has already opened the conversation for us—we need only to step into it.

What would this kind of "rooting" sermon look like? What are different ways these steps can be used for employing a dialogical lens for exegeting scripture and crafting Purple Zone sermons? How do these steps connect with the Five Paths of Prophetic Preaching? In this next section, we'll look at an example of a biblical passage one of my students preached on using the dialogical lens, along with an excerpt from his sermon to see how this lens can be put into practice.

APPLYING THE DIALOGICAL LENS

To see how we might apply the dialogical lens, consider the story about Jesus' baptism in Mark 1:9–15. Keeping in mind that not all steps will be applicable or necessary, our sermon preparation might look something like this:

1. **Point out the dialogical aspects of the passage.** The author of Mark writes for an audience of first-century Christians living in the midst of persecution by the Roman Empire. In this narrative, the major characters are Jesus, John, God, the Holy Spirit, and Satan. The minor and/or background characters include the crowd gathered and watching the baptism, the Roman imperial system, Herod, the wild beasts and angels in the wilderness, and the people of Galilee.

    We can see that there are several conversations or exchanges going on simultaneously and at different levels between Jesus and John, between John and Herod, between Jesus and Satan (and the angels), and between Mark and the community for whom he writes. All of them are in some way involved with the Roman Empire.

2. **Determine what is at stake.** John and Jesus are intent on inaugurating Jesus' ministry. In the wilderness, Satan wants to tempt Jesus and keep him from his ministry. In the background is the Roman imperial system and Herod who both want to maintain their power. They are worried about Jesus and John disrupting and challenging them. They are threatened by any individuals who could amass enough people to lead an uprising. The crowds and the people of Galilee (as well as Mark's readers) are suffering under the oppression of both the religious and imperial authorities. They long for relief and freedom, both from their individual sins as well as from the systemic sins of the religious and political/militaristic systems in place.

3. **Identify the values.** Both Jesus and John value repentance and bringing about the Kingdom of God. However, Herod and the Roman Empire value power, domination, militaristic and political violence, wealth, hierarchy, and the ability to exercise their own agency and will without any accountability to human or divine authority. These values are completely incompatible with those espoused by Jesus and John.

4. **Explain how God, Jesus, and/or the Holy Spirit is active.** The voice of God and the presence of the Holy Spirit declare that Jesus is beloved and well-pleasing. Yet it is the Spirit that drives Jesus into the wilderness. The presence of the angels in the wilderness after Jesus survives the temptation by Satan indicates that God ministers directly to Jesus.

5. **Recognize what the dialogue is teaching us.** It took great courage for John to publicly proclaim a "baptism of repentance for the forgiveness of sins," and for Jesus to align himself with John, a controversial figure who challenged Herod's immorality and abuse of power. Jesus, too, showed courage when facing Satan in the wilderness. Yet at

every point along the way, God was there—in the voice from heaven, in the dove over the waters, in the wilderness, and through the ministry of the angels. Thus, we can determine that courage is required for dialogue, and that this courage is grounded in the presence of God who calls us beloved, compels us to enter "the wilderness," and ministers to us as we engage in contentious exchanges.

6. **Suggest possible next steps.** Perhaps we, too, are being invited into a dialogue about the politics of power, wealth, and temptation. What might it look like to live out our baptismal vocation by engaging those who oppose the will of God and the ministry of Jesus? Maybe it's time for our church to step into this conversation and listen to the voices that have a stake in this—from the rulers down to the common people. We must also identify and name God's presence in the midst of our baptism, our wilderness places, and our confrontations with those opposed to God.

Once we've worked through the six steps of the dialogical lens, the possibilities for utilizing the Five Paths of Prophetic Preaching reveal several options for crafting a sermon. In his sermon on Mark 1:9–15, one of my students, Ian McMichael, began by establishing the principles of baptism and what it means to become part of "God's community" (rooting). He then raised the possibility of the ritual of baptism calling us to engage the world—just as Jesus was called into the wilderness, and then into the community. Ian then contextualized the passage by raising the issue of immigration as a subject the congregation would be discussing (flowering and pollinating). He concluded by proclaiming that our baptism into Christ gives us the mandate to talk about the "hard stuff" (fruiting).

Here are some excerpts from Ian's sermon:

[Rooting]
Because we are loved and claimed by Christ through baptism, we are also called out into the world. We are called to walk and serve. We are called to sit down at the table and hear others. Our baptismal promise calls us to do that.

We see in other places in the Bible that the call to be in community with one another, grounded in the baptismal promise of Christ, is sometimes hard. During baptism either the sponsors or the one being baptized is asked to promise to "proclaim Christ through word and deed, care for others and the world God made, and work for justice and peace." That is a huge responsibility, and it isn't easy. And yet because we are washed in our common baptism as the community of Christ, we can depend on God to accompany us and lead the way.

[Flowering and Pollinating]
But how are we to work for the justice and peace of God? And what do we do if we disagree with others in the community as to what that actually means?

Just because we have been "sealed by the Holy Spirit and marked with the cross of Christ forever" does not mean that life will be easy. Or that everyone will agree. Baptism doesn't mean that the Holy Spirit acts like some mind-altering agent that makes everyone think the same way.

In the midst of a political climate that would like to pit one against another or the United States against the world, talking about these disagreements is more important than ever. If we cannot discuss current issues in church, then where can we? As a church we must enter into the wilderness of those who are opposed to God's purposes for us and this world.

In the sermons I'll be preaching in the weeks ahead, I'll be addressing one of those "wilderness" topics: immigration. I do believe that the Bible speaks to this issue. I also know that many of you might think a little differently than me. But our baptismal call is to talk about it, to learn from each other, and hear what the Word says from the mouth of someone who thinks differently than ourselves.

[Fruiting]
If we truly steep ourselves in the community of the baptized, nothing, not even tough conversations, can tear us apart. Bonded by our common baptism, we are not necessarily called to agree with each other, but we are called to listen to each other. We are washed by the Holy Spirit, fully aware that baptism doesn't immediately make things easy. But it simply and beautifully steeps us in God's grace so that, like Jesus, we are ready for the hard stuff. Let's talk about the hard stuff.[8]

Notice how Ian's sermon communicates that people of good faith can disagree about how to live out that faith. When preaching this text from a Purple Zone perspective, it's notable that Jesus went into the wilderness after his baptism—he did not stay in a place of comfort. He went to the difficult place and engaged with the adversary (Satan). But—and here's the key—he did not go alone. The text tells us that the angels were with him. In the same way, we can go into the wilderness of challenging places and engage with those who may be opposed to us. We can do this knowing that the angels of God surround us. And because we know that Christ has already gone ahead of us.

WALKING THROUGH THE PURPLE DOORS

Now that we have established the foundations for Purple Zone preaching, we're ready to apply these concepts. In the next chapter I'll introduce you to the sermon-dialogue-sermon method. We'll discuss how to choose a topic to address in your preaching and ways to craft a sermon that is a "Prophetic Invitation to Dialogue." This sermon will frame the issue to be addressed in the deliberative dialogue, which we'll cover in chapter 7. The goal of these chapters is to begin to transform the culture of the church from divisiveness and avoidance of difficult issues, to engagement in healthy and faithful conversation about those topics that concern the common good. As one of my students said in his sermon calling for the church to engage in public issues:

> We don't have to pretend like we don't have different ideas or political beliefs. We only need to believe that we, as the church, have something important to offer. And in a country so often divided between blue and red, I think it's appropriate that we all come through purple doors to get in here . . . and then again when we go back out.[9]

Indeed! It's time to open those "purple doors" and walk through!

• 5 •

Preparing for the Sermon-Dialogue-Sermon Process

Now that we have established the foundations for Purple Zone preaching, we're ready to apply these concepts. In this chapter, I'll outline the steps needed for preparing for the sermon-dialogue-sermon process. As we enter into the Purple Zone, we need tools, courage, and compassion to be the church in this divisive time. We are called to listen with hospitality, engage with integrity and prayer, and tackle tough topics with intellectual rigor. When looking for biblical models of this kind of listening with hospitality and engaging with integrity and prayer, one figure stands out: Lydia of Thyatira, the seller of purple cloth.

LYDIA OF THYATIRA, PATRON SAINT OF THE PURPLE ZONE

The story of Paul's encounter with Lydia and her household in Acts 16:11–15, 40, is a study in what it looks like to enter the Purple Zone. Lydia was from Thyatira, a city in north central Turkey. She travelled 591 kilometers (367 miles) northwest by land and sea to Philippi in Greece to establish her home and business of buying and selling purple cloth. This means that she had already ventured beyond her familiar place of origin; she demonstrated a willingness to leave her comfort zone and expand the circle of people and ideas she encountered. She met Paul and the other apostles when they found her with other women gathered for prayer "outside the gate by the river." The text says that she was "a worshipper of God," so we know that she was a faithful person and that she was already oriented in a way that was open to God's invitation.

The text tells us that Paul and his companions "sat down and spoke with the women who gathered there" (v. 13). This is important—they did not stand over the women. They sat down as equals to talk and listen. Lydia, in turn, listened to them. More than that, she *heard* them. "The Lord opened her heart to listen eagerly to what was said by Paul" (v. 14). In response, not only was she baptized but she had her entire household baptized as well. What's more, she extended hospitality to Paul and the apostles by inviting them into her home. We might imagine the whole lot of them sitting at a table, sharing a meal, with purple fabric draped around the room. It was a gathering of diverse people of various cultures from different parts of the Mediterranean world, united in their shared faith, knowing the challenges they faced.

Perhaps they even "talked politics." The controversial issues of their day might have included the fact that humans were being bought and sold on the market like so much purple cloth. Human trafficking was a reality of their time, much as it is in ours, though with a higher level of cultural acceptance in the ancient world. In fact, just after this brief scene of hospitality, Paul and Silas find themselves at a nexus of human trafficking when they release a young slave girl from her demon possession. This, of course, lands them in jail for disrupting the commercial enterprise of the girl's masters. After a dramatic series of events in which Paul and Silas confront yet another injustice—the prison system of their day—they return to Lydia's house to encourage and be encouraged.

In one short chapter, we see the Purple Zone in action—people of faith from different walks of life (and, perhaps, different political stances) brought together by the Spirit of God, united in baptism, and willing to engage the justice issues of their time. As Julie Cory, a pastor in Ohio, shared with me in a sermon she preached about Lydia, "When we risk turning around to swim upstream against the current of cultural norms, it is always risky. It means stepping out of our Red-Blue comfort zones and doing the subversive, culture-changing, radical life-changing work that we are called to by the gospel."[1] This is exactly the challenge the church is called to engage, and the story of Lydia shows us what this kind of risky hospitality looks like. Her "house church"—probably one of the first of its kind in that era—was the place where the faithful gathered to worship, encouraged one another, and even challenged each other about how best to live out the Christian faith in the midst of a hostile political and social culture.

Lydia knew the risk she was taking. Christians were being targeted and persecuted for their beliefs, and even killed for their resistance to the Roman Empire. But her courage, hospitality, and willingness to engage in dialogue in good faith—all within her regular practice of prayer and worship—shows us what it looks like to be the church in the midst of a divided and divisive culture. Lydia's house church was literally a "purple zone" that gives us a model for entering dialogue about difficult issues with discernment and compassion. We then emerge with new insights, build healthier relationships within the church, and carry this capacity for civic and public discourse into our communities and our country.

In these next three chapters, we'll learn one possible way to enter that discourse within the church—the sermon-dialogue-sermon method. My hope is that this method will aid preachers and parishioners in being courageous about the gospel, listening to the guidance of the Spirit, and trusting in the God who empowers us to speak the truth in love. This method offers a process that frames a controversial justice issue with biblical and theological integrity, invites people to engage in healthy and productive discourse, and then incorporates insights and observations from the dialogue into a follow-up sermon that witnesses to God's presence and action within our mutual discernment. By using the sermon-dialogue-sermon method, clergy and congregations may discover a way to build new and healthier relationships not just within the church but in the larger community. In the spirit of Lydia's hospitality, a Purple Zone church can be a place of holy risk-taking, sacred discernment, and surprising grace.

This chapter introduces the sermon-dialogue-sermon method, gives suggestions for how to plan your timeline for the process, and offer tips for how to choose a topic to address. In the next chapter, I'll explain how to preach a sermon introducing a controversial justice issue, what I call the Prophetic Invitation to Dialogue. You'll see several sermon excerpts to illustrate how this "prophetic invitation" approach can be applied for various scripture passages and within different contexts.

Keep in mind that the sermon-dialogue-sermon method is not a quick-fix or hit-and-run approach to prophetic preaching. It will require time for planning and preparation. But the time put in on the front end has the potential to yield positive outcomes that go far beyond a single sermon. As one of my students, Joanna Samuelson, observed, the time invested in the process "sends a message about the commitments and even the culture of a church. It communicates that *relationships are highly valued here even as we work through difficult issues together, and so this investment of time is worth it.*"

DETERMINING THE TIMELINE FOR THE SERMON-DIALOGUE-SERMON PROCESS

The sermon-dialogue-sermon process will take some planning, because it is not something that can be pulled off spur of the moment. Generally, you need at least two or three weeks from start to finish. First, you will determine your timeline and choose your topic. Then you'll preach your "rooting" sermon while getting the word out about the upcoming dialogue on the topic you've chosen. Just before the deliberative dialogue, you'll preach Sermon #1, the Prophetic Invitation to Dialogue, which will introduce the topic and invite people to attend the deliberative dialogue session. (We'll discuss exactly what this sermon entails in the next chapter.)

Then you'll facilitate the deliberative dialogue. This can be done immediately after the service, sometime during the week, or the following Sunday, but no later than one week after you've preached so that it's fresh in people's minds. Ideally, the session should be scheduled for approximately ninety minutes. The follow-up sermon (Communal Prophetic Proclamation) should be preached within one to two weeks of the deliberative dialogue and will incorporate what you heard and saw in the session. This sermon will be informed by the dialogue you heard as well as your ongoing biblical, theological, and pastoral reflection and discernment. The goal is to both deepen congregational engagement on this particular issue as well as help parishioners experience the results of *healthy* public dialogue informed and shaped by Christ-centered values.

Recall from the previous chapter that in order to prepare for the sermon-dialogue-sermon, you'll want to preach a "rooting" sermon first, or teach a forum that helps the congregation understand that the Bible not only has countless examples of dialogue within its pages but is itself a model of dialogue because it contains diverse voices that are in conversation with each other across the centuries about many challenging issues. You can also schedule a session just to introduce and explain what deliberative dialogue is and how it works. (Introductory videos are available at the National Issues Forums Institute website, https://www.nifi.org.) Also, the month before the sermon-dialogue-sermon process is to happen, put an article in your newsletter announcing the deliberative dialogue planned for the coming month, and put blurbs in the Sunday bulletin to remind people to attend. (See "Sample Newsletter Article" in appendix A.)

What might a timeline for the sermon-dialogue-sermon process look like? Table 5.1 shows some possibilities—all of which are only suggestions and can be adapted to your particular church calendar and congregational schedule.

CHOOSING THE TOPIC FOR THE SERMON-DIALOGUE-SERMON PROCESS

Once you have determined the timeline for the sermon-dialogue-sermon process, you'll need to choose the issue you want to engage in the delib-

Table 5.1. Suggested Timeline for Sermon-Dialogue-Sermon Process

Option A (over the course of two Sundays)
Sun., Oct. 9   Adult forum: Why It's Okay to Discuss Politics in Church
                  Sermon #1—Prophetic Invitation to Dialogue
Tues., Oct. 11   Deliberative Dialogue
Sun. Oct. 16   Sermon #2—Communal Prophetic Proclamation

Option B (over the course of three Sundays)
Sun., Sept. 18   Sermon: "The Bible, Politics, and Being the Church" (rooting sermon)
                  Adult forum: Introduction to Deliberative Dialogue
Sun., Sept. 25   Sermon #1—Prophetic Invitation to Dialogue
                  Adult forum: Deliberative Dialogue
Sun., Oct. 2   Sermon #2—Communal Prophetic Proclamation

Option C (over the course of four or five Sundays)
Wed., Oct. 20   Bible study on community discernment, part 1 (rooting)
Sun., Oct. 24   Sermon: "The Bible, Politics, and Being the Church" (rooting sermon)
Wed., Oct. 27   Bible study, part 2 (rooting, cont.)
Sun., Oct. 31   Sermon #1—Prophetic Invitation to Dialogue
Wed., Nov. 3   Deliberative Dialogue
Sun., Nov. 7 OR   Sermon #2—Communal Prophetic Proclamation
Sun., Nov. 14

---

erative dialogue. You may be wondering what actually happens in a deliberative dialogue? Briefly, "a deliberative dialogue forum does not advocate specific solutions or points of view but provides citizens the opportunity to consider a broad range of choices, weigh the pros and cons of those choices, and meet with each other in a public dialogue to identify the concerns they hold in common."[2] We'll learn more about the deliberative dialogue itself in chapter 7. For now, we begin the sermon-dialogue-sermon process by choosing a topic.

Start by exploring the issue guides available on the National Issues Forums Institute (NIFI) website to choose the topic you want to address. How does the NIFI decide the topics for which they write issue guides? Generally, the issue is one that affects people on many levels—individuals, families, communities, institutions, governments, businesses, and social policies. The issue is what we might call "wicked"—not as in evil, but as in complex. It's a colloquial term meaning "devilishly complicated," and is contrasted with "tame" problems, as illustrated in table 5.2.

Deliberation is necessary for "wicked" problems because when deciding on a course of action, there are compelling reasons on different sides that can clash.[3] The issue guides are developed to help participants begin to understand the complexity of these different issues, consider possible options for approaching the topic, and discern what steps might be taken to address it.

Table 5.2. Tame Problems vs. Wicked Problems

Tame	Wicked
Have a technical solution	Involve value conflicts and underlying paradoxes that cannot be formally resolved
Best handled by experts	Experts can help, but decisions involve tough choices and responsibilities that only the public should make
Can be clearly measured and evaluated	Include key aspects that allude to measurement and evaluation
General agreement on the nature of the problem	Different people would see the problem differently (and some may not even see it as a problem)
When a solution is found, most experts would likely agree and the problem may be solved	"Solutions" are never truly found, and the conversation will continue. Any actions will likely treat some aspects of the issue but may cause new problems elsewhere. The goal is to improve the situation and better balance competing interests, not to "solve" it for all time.

Source: Horst W. J. Rittel and Melvin M. Webber, "Dilemmas in a General Theory of Planning," *Policy Sciences* 4 (1973): 155–69.

As you peruse the NIFI issue guide web page (https://www.nifi.org/es/issue-guides/issue-guides), you'll see that there are guides for a wide range of topics. At the time of this writing, there are thirty-nine issue guides and advisories ranging from "Youth and Violence" to "Land Use Conflict" to "Economic Security." Even with this variety of topics, you may not find an issue guide for the topic you wish to discuss in your congregation. While you may wish to hold a dialogue about a different issue not covered by the NIFI in the future, for your first time trying the sermon-dialogue-sermon process in your church, I recommend picking an issue for which a guide is available.[4]

Choosing "Cool," "Warm," or "Hot" Topics

As you think about which issue to choose, you'll need to consider whether you should engage a "cool," "warm," or "hot" topic. A "cool" topic is one that would be less controversial in your context. In contrast, a "hot" topic is riskier because it has a greater potential of offending or raising the ire of congregants, causing conflict, or jeopardizing relationships within the church. This is not to say that any topic is intrinsically more hot or cool than another, as a topic's "temperature" depends upon the context of the church. It also depends upon the congregation's ability to tolerate the initial discomfort when first engaging a difficult issue. In other words, what is "hot" for one congregation may only be warm or cool for another.

For example, the issue guide "End of Life: What Should We Do for Those Who Are Dying?" might be considered a cooler topic because it's not as politicized to the same degree as, say, climate change or mass shootings.

However, for one of my students, this issue *was* a hot topic in her context because there had been several deaths in her congregation over the last year, some of which involved agonizing decisions about ending life-extending care for the patient. Because the feelings were still very raw for many people in her church, she decided to go with a cooler topic for her sermon-dialogue-sermon process. This illustrates the importance of ministers talking with their congregations about these issues in preparation for preaching and facilitating a deliberative dialogue about them. If clergy are in relationship with their parishioners and engaging them in conversation about their lives, they can better gauge the temperature of the potential topic.

Or you may, in fact, intentionally choose a topic that has been a long-simmering controversy but hasn't been dealt with in a healthy way. For example, perhaps your church is in a neighborhood where demographics are changing due to immigration. The sermon-dialogue-sermon method may be helpful for addressing the topic of immigration in your congregation because it can guide parishioners to talk about the challenges in a productive and healthy way. Or maybe your congregation is in a rural area that is dealing with the challenges of land development. A sermon-dialogue-sermon series exploring the theme of land use in the Bible and using the NIFI booklet, "Land Use Conflict: When City and Country Clash," could be helpful in facilitating a productive conversation on these issues in your context.

But if your congregation is more conflict-averse or has not developed healthy ways to talk about difficult topics, it may be best to start with a "cool" issue. Once a congregation experiences the sermon-dialogue-sermon process and learns how to have healthy dialogue, it's likely they'll be more willing to engage more controversial subjects in the future. How will you know whether to choose a cool, warm, or hot topic? This will depend on a variety of factors, including the congregation's past history with conflict and controversy, their ability to tolerate initial discomfort with potentially divisive topics, and even their "theology of conflict."

What Is a "Theology of Conflict"?

In its most simple terms, a theology of conflict is what we believe about the relationship between God and human conflict. Surprisingly little has been written on the topic. There is a great deal available on conflict *resolution*, peacemaking, and how to manage different levels of conflict in a congregation. However, comparatively little is available to help us understand how we think about God in relation to the things about which we disagree, dispute, and fight over. As homiletician Aimee Moiso notes, "few homiletic resources directly assess the dynamics of conflict in relationship to preaching—or how unexamined beliefs about conflict may be connected to our preaching pitfalls." The result is that

"Christian orientations to conflict are underdeveloped and in need of deeper reflection and understanding in order to be effective and faithful."[5]

Having some understanding of our own—and our congregation's—theology of conflict is important because it has both implicit and explicit ramifications for dialogue. For instance, if the assumption is that God does not approve of conflict, we may be reticent to engage any controversy at all. We may worry that we are disappointing God or going against God's will. Alternatively, if we believe that God works in and through human conflict in order to manifest God's will, we may be more willing to enter into dialogue about a difficult issue.[6]

To help us begin to unpack our theology of conflict, below are some questions to consider. You can answer these on your own, but I also recommend taking time with your church leadership and other groups within the congregation to discuss these questions. The answers will reveal a great deal about how individuals within the church, and how the system of the congregation as a whole, may respond to tensions that arise when you enter the Purple Zone in your preaching and deliberative dialogue.

QUESTIONS FOR DETERMINING A CONGREGATION'S "THEOLOGY OF CONFLICT"

- What does God think about human conflict? Does God think conflict is "bad," "sinful," and thus to be avoided? Or does God recognize that conflict is a natural part of human interactions and seek to guide us on the healthiest way to handle these tensions?
- What does the Bible reveal about God and human conflict? More importantly, how does our *interpretation* of scripture determine what we believe about God and conflict? Can we think of examples in scripture or human history when God used conflict in *constructive* ways to bring about transformation?
- What is God's role in human conflict? How does God function? Does God "pick sides" in an argument? Does God fight on behalf of a particular group or person? If so, what are the criteria God uses to determine on whose behalf God will fight?
- How does God regard *power differentials* when it comes to conflict? In other words, does God favor the one with strength and power? Or does God favor the one in the weaker position who is more vulnerable?
- If all parties are on a level playing field, how does God interact with us when it comes to conflict? Does God intervene or leave us to our own devices? What is God trying to say to us in the midst of the conflict?

- Is it possible to be in conflict and yet remain connected in the Body of Christ? Does conflict threaten our unity as a church? How does God maintain connection with us when we are conflicted?
- What does Jesus model for us about how to handle conflict? How does he respond to those who disagree with him? How do they respond to him?
- What is the role of the Holy Spirit in the midst of our conflict? Do we see the Holy Spirit working in and among us in the midst of the messiness? Do we believe that the presence of conflict indicates an absence of the Holy Spirit? Or is this where God's Spirit is fully present?
- What does our conflict reveal about the character of God? Of Jesus? Of the Holy Spirit? In other words, what does God do when humans are doing what humans naturally do—disagree, debate, and discern?
- How can our Trinitarian theology help us navigate tension in relationships? Are the three persons of the Trinity always in perfect harmony, or is there creative dissonance as well?

As you answer these questions to explore your congregation's theology of conflict, you may find that they give you insights to aid in your preaching as well. As Moiso notes, there is the potential for "our sermons to model the open, collaborative, and constructive responses to conflict that we want to see throughout the life of the church."[7]

Other Factors to Consider When Choosing a Topic for the Sermon-Dialogue-Sermon Process

Here are other important questions to help you determine what type of issue to engage in your sermon-dialogue-sermon process.

- **How long have you been in the congregation?** If you have only been in this particular church for a year or less, you haven't had much of an opportunity to establish relationships of trust. It would be advisable to get to know the people in your congregation, their history, and where the "landmines" might be before choosing a topic that might trigger unexpected pushback. You might consider choosing a cooler topic. And be aware that because you are new, you may not have a good handle on what a "cool" topic would be for this congregation. Therefore, consider talking with your church's board, council, elders, of staff-parish relations group.

- **What is the congregation's past history with conflict and controversy?** All congregations have conflict and controversy. This is normal because the church is a human organization and, as such, will have its share of disagreements. The presence of conflict, while universal, is also a matter of degree; some conflicts involve manageable, on-the-surface types of issues while others represent deep-in-the-core problems that have the potential to do more damage.

  It's also a matter of timing and how the conflict was processed. If the conflict was recent, or even current, and emotions are still raw, consider choosing a cooler issue for the sermon-dialogue-sermon process. If the controversy is in the past but there are residual negative feelings, perhaps a warm topic would be better. However, if the congregation has a healthy process for dealing with controversy and is more high-functioning when it comes to conflict, they may be ready and willing to tackle a hot topic.

- **What is on the hearts and minds of your congregation—or needs to be?** What voices are not "at the table" when it comes to justice issues?[8] What issue have you discerned needs to be address, but they (or you) are hesitant to bring up?

  For example, one of my students was in an all-white congregation that had had very little conversation about racism, so he chose the issue guide on "Racism and Diversity." Another student's church had a vibrant community feeding program but felt that the congregation needed to "take it to the next level" to think about advocacy on issues that lead to people seeking assistance in the first place. Thus, she chose the issue guide "Land of Plenty" to jumpstart the conversation (which we learn more about in chapter 10). In both cases, the preachers were attuned to the underlying dynamics and/or issues on the horizon for the congregation.

- **What is happening in the local community or national conversation that could be—or needs to be—addressed by the congregation?** For one of my students whose church was in the midst of a community experiencing a heavy influx of immigration, the "Coming to America" guide was ideal for facilitating a conversation about how to be the church in the midst of this growing population of newcomers. Another pastor I worked with decided to tackle the issue of gun violence because school shootings were making headlines almost weekly. She chose to use the issue advisory "How Can We Stop Mass Shootings in Our Communities?"

Once you've chosen a topic and determined a timeline, it's time to prepare for Sermon #1, the Prophetic Invitation to Dialogue. However, before we discuss the content of that sermon, let's take a moment to understand the form of preaching that is most useful for the sermon-dialogue-sermon process—the "topical sermon."

A WORD ABOUT "TOPICAL SERMONS" WITHIN THE CONVERSATIONAL APPROACH TO PREACHING

For some respondents in the "Preaching About Controversial Issues" survey, the willingness to address social issues in the pulpit was especially problematic for preachers who follow a lectionary or who are committed to strictly expository biblical preaching. For the former, the assigned lectionary texts for the day may not match up with the topic the preacher wants to address. For expository preachers, the concerns with a topical sermon range from being accused of eisegesis (warping a text's interpretation to fit a particular subject) to ending up with a sermon that sacrifices theological and scriptural integrity for the sake of addressing current events.

Ronald J. Allen's book, *Preaching the Topical Sermon*, addresses these concerns and makes the case that topical sermons need not be biblically thin nor abusive of the scriptural texts. Building on David Buttrick's notion of "preaching in the mode of praxis,"[9] Allen explains that while topical sermons may arise from a subject rather than a particular text, this does not mean that the Bible has no bearing on the topical sermon. Rather, "the center of the topical sermon is the interpretation of the topic in light of the gospel . . . A key question is, 'How does the gospel lead us to understand the topic?'"[10] For lectionary preachers who are concerned that a topical sermon will violate the integrity of their preaching, Allen emphasizes that the topical sermon does not "establish a route for the sermon to travel every Sunday. But it does mark a useful place on the homiletical map."[11] In other words, there may be times and occasions that call for a temporary pause in following the lectionary in order to address a topic that "can be better addressed from the standpoint of the gospel itself than from the standpoint of the exposition of a particular passage (or passages) from the Bible."[12]

However, a devoted lectionary preacher can also use the sermon-dialogue-sermon method with proper planning. If you are a lectionary preacher, the readings can guide you in determining a timeline. As you look ahead in the next month or two and see that there are texts that relate to a particular issue of public concern, you can plan your sermon-dialogue-sermon process accordingly.

Regardless of whether you follow the lectionary or choose your own texts, as I explained in chapter 4, what preaching in the Purple Zone emphasizes is interpreting the text through the dialogical lens. Using this lens helps congregants understand that just as the Bible contains a multitude of voices and standpoints on a wide range of concerns that were important to the original authors and audiences of its day, so, too, can Christians bring this same spirit of dialogue to the issues of our time. But just as important in Purple Zone preaching is that preachers themselves should strive to model the kind of dialogical spirit intended for the sermon. This is why the conversational approach to preaching is useful in the sermon-dialogue-sermon method.

Recall from chapter 3 that conversational preaching is an approach that seeks engagement with voices both within the congregation and outside the church.[13] Ronald Allen and O. Wesley Allen note that in a postmodern, post-apologetic world where Christians recognize the need to move beyond simply defending the faith or winning over converts, special care must be given to the ethics of conversational preaching. Since preachers "exert more power in a monologue than in back-and-forth interchanges," they must be "especially attentive to valuing reciprocity and asymmetry in and around the monological, conversational sermon."[14] In other words, the preacher must intentionally seek out voices of people who have different beliefs, experiences, backgrounds, and knowledge so as to avoid the stagnation and self-affirming echo chamber of those who share similar viewpoints and occupy the same stratum of socioeconomics, race, gender, and power.

Allen and Allen also explain why preachers must be especially careful with the trust, responsibility, and privilege with which they have been afforded:

> Since the sermon is a moment of privilege in which the community of faith quiets and allows the one voice of the preacher to speak, preachers must intentionally seek out times in the life of the congregation where they are in listening mode, allowing the perspectives of others to be commended to them and to critique their own . . . This reciprocal listening is a sign that the preacher values asymmetry in the congregation (and in the world in, and with, which the congregation interacts and makes meaning).[15]

As we will see in the ensuing chapters, deliberative dialogue is one form of civil discourse that can enable that kind of listening to happen. It is the Prophetic Invitation to Dialogue sermon that introduces the topic, frames it within a biblical and theological interpretation, and sets the stage for the dialogue. What, then, are the qualities, contours, and characteristics of this sermon? And what are the ethical commitments with which a preacher should approach this sermon? We'll answer these questions in the next chapter where we'll learn how to prepare and preach the Prophetic Invitation to Dialogue sermon.

· 6 ·

Preaching Sermon 1

Prophetic Invitation to Dialogue

PRESSING "PAUSE" ON THE STRIDENT PROPHETIC VOICE

Recall that in chapter 1, we learned about what *justice* means from a biblical perspective and why it is important for preachers to address controversial justice issues in their sermons. There is a caveat, however. Ronald J. Allen points out that on occasion

> ministers sometimes contribute to polarization by painting the world in stark and unambiguous terms of justice and injustice. Indeed, ministers sometimes contribute to polarization in the very classification of preaching as pastoral or prophetic—as if these are polar approaches—the first caring and nurturing while the second is confrontational and judgmental. Prophetic preachers can use adversarial rhetoric with intensity exceeding that of the most firebrand politician. In the name of the highest ends, some prophetic preachers engage in manipulative, even abusive rhetoric characteristic of other polarizers, such as caricature, name-calling, a them-and-us mentality, blaming, scapegoating, distortion, oversimplification, abandoning facts altogether, and playing to the fears of the audience.[1]

The Purple Zone preacher avoids this kind of polarizing speech. When it comes to preaching the Prophetic Invitation to Dialogue sermon that introduces the topic you and your congregation will address, the most important thing to remember is that in this sermon, *the preacher does not take a stand on the issue.* Instead, she acknowledges the complexity of the topic, considers many voices and perspectives, and frames it within a scriptural and theological context. In addition, the preacher specifically invites listeners to participate in a deliberative dialogue about the topic and explains how the Holy Spirit is part of this process of discernment within the Body of Christ.

I recognize that for clergy who favor a more strongly prophetic voice in their sermons, this approach may at first seem weak or watered down. But hear me out. This sermon is part of the larger process that will eventually lead to a bolder proclamation. The Prophetic Invitation to Dialogue sermon looks to invite people into the dialogue, not just make pronouncements that bring down the proverbial hammer or stir the pot (even if hammering or stirring is gospel-inspired!). As O. Wesley Allen describes it:

> Our sermons need to invite conversation about difficult topics instead of trying to put the punctuation on the end of those conversations. We need to open up congregational space for honest conversation in the place of divisive debate in which someone wins and someone loses. Conversation, as a postmodern form of communication, values diversity and reciprocity without saying, "Anything goes." A pastor who desires to hear what a congregant who disagrees with him has to say in order to appreciate the person and where she is coming from will be able to speak to and be heard by that person in ways a nonpastoral prophet never will.[2]

Purple Zone preaching attempts to hear and reflect the different voices and perspectives of listeners, inviting those voices and perspectives to be in conversation with one another in a formal way. One of the things I've learned is that in our severely divided political climate, *simply issuing the invitation to dialogue is itself a prophetic act*. It sends the message that church and community members' perspectives and life experiences are valued by the congregation and its pastoral leadership. In our time of virulent political tribalism that has so bifurcated this nation and many other countries, it *is* a prophetic act to preach toward an invitation to dialogue with prudence, restraint, and a posture of humility and respect. So pressing "pause" on our more traditional prophetic impulses in no way abdicates a prophetic preaching ministry.

AN INVITATION TO A "POTLUCK OF IDEAS"

Think of it like this: In this introductory sermon, you are the host who is inviting people to a "potluck of ideas."[3] You actually *want* people to come and participate in the dialogue, so why would you give the impression that either their "dish" is not welcome or that you are going to sneak in a menu of foods that are unpalatable? To avoid giving the wrong impression or inadvertently turning off people from wanting to attend, think about the person in your congregation who is the polar opposite of you politically. As you are working on your sermon, listen to it through their ears. What are the "trigger words" you need to avoid? What are the things you need to say that signal your openness and willingness to hear different perspectives?

In fact, one of the things you can do before you even preach this sermon and facilitate the deliberative dialogue is to reach out to those individuals who might give you pushback either quietly in their minds, secretly out of earshot, or right to your face. Let them know that the church will be embarking on this Purple Zone process, and that you would value their participation. Remember from chapter 2 that a key emotional and relational need for parishioners is to know that they've been heard and their views are taken into account, even when we disagree. Making the effort to extend a diplomatic hand before the process gets under way could go a long way toward the overall success of this journey into the Purple Zone.

As the host of this dialogue potluck, then, you will need to check your own biases and strong feelings about the topic when preaching the Prophetic Invitation to Dialogue sermon. A term you'll encounter in the coming pages is to be *passionately impartial*. This means that regardless of your thoughts and opinions on the issue, your goal is to remain neutral so that you can allow the process of community discernment to unfold.

This does not mean, however, that you must be *passionless* in this sermon. In fact, your passion for addressing this issue from the perspective of the gospel within this particular community is vital and can be expressed with genuine excitement and heartfelt concern. But rather than claiming to have the truth or the answers to the problem, we can approach the subject from a position of curiosity and openness to the wisdom and experiences of others. In this way, there is a greater likelihood that the preacher and congregation eventually arrive at the prophetic truth together. Even if there is no agreement about that truth, the experience of the process—if carried out in good faith—will still generate increased trust among the congregation, willingness to engage with other viewpoints, and an increased capacity to humanize those with whom we disagree. As homiletician Linda Clader explains:

> Our job is not to manipulate or direct our hearers into seeing things "our way," but to playfully nudge them or gently lead them or humbly offer them a means to see things "God's way." Perhaps the most important element we have to offer may be the gift of slowing down, of taking the time. In the end, the surprising answers to the challenges facing a community will come not because of our brilliantly polished sermons but at the initiative of the Spirit, and on the Spirit's schedule.[4]

This intentionality of slowing down and giving attention to a matter of public concern is both countercultural and modeled after the ministry of Jesus. The gospels show us that throughout his ministry he took time to listen to people, give them his full attention, and engage them in conversation—even if he disagreed with them and had to call out their hypocrisy. But with the exception of the foreign woman seeking healing for her daughter (Mark 7:24–30, Matthew 15:21–28), Jesus rarely dismisses a person who comes to him. And in that case, Jesus actually models what it looks like to be willing to change one's mind and learn from an exchange with another. So it is with our ministry in the Purple Zone as well. We take the time to listen to the concerns of a community or lift up an issue that needs attention, even if it is taboo. We pastorally introduce the issue through a sermon that is a Prophetic Invitation to Dialogue and prepare to facilitate a deliberative dialogue that helps the community discern who God is and who the church can be in the midst of the issue.

FOLLOWING THE FIVE PATHS OF PROPHETIC PREACHING IN THE PROPHETIC INVITATION TO DIALOGUE

As you are considering your approach to this Prophetic Invitation to Dialogue, let's return to the Five Paths of Prophetic Preaching that can help inform and shape this sermon. An important emphasis for this sermon will be "flowering"—drawing attention to the issue and raising awareness about the church's need to address it. Also necessary for this invitation to dialogue is "pollinating"—noting the various voices and perspectives about the issue *without passing prophetic judgment*. Linking into the way in which the Bible also models various voices and perspectives is what will "root" the sermon in the biblical principle of dialogue. The "leafing" aspect of the sermon will be to invite people to that dialogue.

Remember, this is not the sermon to suggest specific steps to take to address the issue—that will come after the deliberative dialogue with the follow-up sermon, the Communal Prophetic Proclamation. In this first sermon, your tone should be curious, wondering, and attentive to what and who God is calling us to hear and see. Thus the "fruiting" path is woven throughout the sermon and could be highlighted in the conclusion to help folks see the larger purpose of addressing this issue. The overall process is helping to plant seeds of God's transformational change for the congregation, and perhaps even for the larger community.

One other important aspect of the Prophetic Invitation to Dialogue is to admit your own complicity and struggles with the issue. While the sermon is not a place for confession or therapy, you may want to help listeners understand what's at stake for *you* in this and why you have discerned this is an issue that the church can and should address. By revealing your own vulnerability, you can avoid inadvertently setting yourself above and/or apart from the congregation in self-righteousness ("finger-wagging"). Instead, perhaps share what you are wrestling with regarding the issue, or how you recognize yourself as unwittingly contributing to the problem within the systemic sin surrounding the issue. In other words, share your humanity even while you maintain space for prophetic critique.

USING THE DIALOGICAL LENS FOR THE PROPHETIC INVITATION TO DIALOGUE SERMON

Recall from chapter 4 that the dialogical lens for interpreting scripture for a Purple Zone sermon involves six possible steps:

1. Point out the dialogical aspects of the passage.
2. Determine what's at stake.
3. Identify the values.
4. Explain how God, Jesus, and/or the Holy Spirit is active.
5. Recognize what the dialogue is teaching us.
6. Suggest possible next steps.

With the dialogical lens in mind, here is a possible sermon sequence to use in crafting the Prophetic Invitation to Dialogue. Keep in mind that this is just one possibility that could work for the introductory sermon:

- **Point out the dialogical aspects of the passage.** Begin by describing the contentious issue and then draw parallels to the points of contention the scriptural passage is addressing. Alternatively, begin by describing the contention in the text and then draw parallels to the public issue we are currently facing. (Readers familiar with Paul Scott Wilson's "Four Pages" form will recognize this as "trouble in the text/trouble in the world."[5]) Use your exegesis to highlight the ways in which dialogue is present within the text, in the background of the passage, or between the passage and the issue itself. Remember to notice those who are not "at the table" in an obvious way, but who nevertheless have a stake in the issue and the consequences of the conversation.
- **Determine what's at stake.** Again, draw parallels if possible between what is at stake for those in the text and what is at stake for those affected by the issue at hand. What are the fears, needs, concerns, threats, tensions, and conflicts?
- **Identify the values.** The biblical text should guide you to lift up the "big questions" that underlie the headlines or controversies sur-

rounding this issue. What are the deeper ideals and values that need to be identified? Where are there shared values, or where do values come into conflict?
- **Explain how God, Jesus, and/or the Holy Spirit is active.** Where or how do we see the Triune God at work? Even if the world of the Bible and the world of this contemporary issue are vastly different, lift up the teachings and actions of the prophets, Jesus, or the New Testament writers that might be helpful in addressing this issue.
- **Recognize what the dialogue is teaching us.** What can we learn about how to engage this issue from what we see in dialogue surrounding or within this passage? Are we seeing what *not* to do? Can we identify what it means to be faithful people who engage this issue even in the midst of systemic or personal sin? Can we discern the call of God to address this issue based on God's presence and activity within the biblical text?
- **Suggest possible next steps.** For this sermon, the next step is to invite people to the dialogue. Frame this invitation in a way that shows how our willingness to come together in dialogue about this issue is a sign of hope that the Spirit is working among us. Remind listeners that this is not about having a debate or coercing people to change their minds. It's about transforming the culture of the congregation from one of divisiveness (or avoidance) to one of healthy conversation that enables God's justice to take root and grow. You can say it like this: "I don't have the answers. But I'm very interested in the questions. And I'm interested in exploring those questions with *this* particular group of Christians in this congregation."

Let's take a look at an example of how these steps can be utilized in the Prophetic Invitation to Dialogue sermon. One of my students, Joanna Samuelson, chose the NIFI issue guide "Sustaining Ourselves" for her congregation's deliberative dialogue. She focused her Prophetic Invitation to Dialogue sermon on Matthew 22:15–22, the story about the religious leaders confronting Jesus about whether or not to pay the Roman tax. As you read her sermon, notice how she makes use of the dialogical lens for exegeting this passage, thus setting the stage for the invitation to the deliberative dialogue.

Sermon Excerpt: "Coined in the Image of God"

[Point out the dialogical aspects of the passage.]
In our Gospel reading for this morning, we have a politically tense, polarized and very divided society. Does that sound familiar to you? But instead

of the red state–blue state divide, we have the Pharisees versus the Herodians, two groups who were strongly opposed to one another. But they come together in order to confront Jesus and discredit him.

[Determine what's at stake; Identify the values.]
At the heart of this division here between the Pharisees and the Herodians is the issue of taxes. As you may recall, Palestine was a colony of the Roman Empire at that time, and the background to this story is that the Jews were required to pay taxes to the government that was occupying their own country. There are issues of power, wealth, inequality, and oppression all beneath the surface of their encounter with Jesus.

Not much has changed in two thousand years, has it? In our news cycle just this past week, there has been a lot about taxes and tax reform. Like the first century community of Jesus, we, too, are living in a highly divisive political time. And Jesus found himself right in the middle of a perplexing conundrum.

The Pharisees were hoping that Jesus would say that the tax should be paid so that the Jewish people would view him as a Roman sympathizer. The Herodians, on the other hand, were hoping that he would say no to the tax so that they could accuse him of treason and sedition.

[Explain how God, Jesus and/or the Holy Spirit is active.]
What is Jesus' response? Does he fall into their either-or trap? Of course not!

Instead, he replies: "Give therefore to the emperor the things that are the emperor's, and to God the things that are God's."

The way I see it, Jesus' response does two things. First, by refusing to answer their either-or question in the way they expect, he refuses to be pulled into their politically motivated scheme. Jesus will not be used as a pawn by either of these groups. And in fact, Jesus' response leaves it wide open—wide enough perhaps for some dialogue between the Pharisees and the Herodians!

Secondly, Jesus widens their question with his response by bringing God into the conversation: Give to God the things that are God's. In contrast to the image of Caesar on the coin, his response challenges them—and us—to consider that which bears God's image.

[Recognize what the dialogue is teaching us; Suggest possible next steps.]
This short, complex story about a small coin from two thousand years ago is still relevant for us today—especially in these politically divided times, especially in our public discourse about tax reform and government spending—the distribution of resources—and especially as we try to follow Jesus.

Our deliberative dialogue this afternoon is going to address these questions about how we as a community can fairly meet the needs of all citizens—including how taxes are part of this equation. We're going to have a conversation about sustainable living. We'll consider different points of view. And we'll remember that this story about that coin shows us that our belief in God significantly impacts all things secular, the everyday choices we make, including the way we vote, our infrastructure, the distribution of resources, and even the taxes we pay. We simply cannot separate the prophetic from the political!

In this story, Jesus invites us to consider what God might have to say about how we practice our faith not just in church on Sunday mornings but out in the public square every day of the week. This story about a simple coin is a humbling story. It's a story that grounds us in our truest identity. We are not simply our political affiliations. We are not our ideologies. We are children of God called to bring about God's vision of peace and justice and equality. Each one of us is created in the image of God. Each one of us is coined in the image of God! Thanks be to God.[6]

Did you notice how Joanna utilized the "fruiting" approach to prophetic preaching in the final paragraph? She moved the presenting conflict about taxes to a broader question of what this story—and our current debate about taxes—has to say about our identity. She reframed the issue in theological terms that help folks to see the larger purpose of addressing the topic of taxes and how to sustain ourselves and future generations. At the same time, she made a claim in the sermon that we are "children of God called to bring about God's peace and justice and equality." Here we can see that while the Prophetic Invitation to Dialogue sermon presses "pause" on the traditional prophetic impulse, it still makes important claims.

Now that we have our five paths of prophetic preaching in place using the dialogical lens, let's walk through some other examples of the Prophetic Invitation to Dialogue sermon. Along the way, I'll point out how these preachers utilized these tools in their sermons.

EXAMPLE 1: MENTAL ILLNESS

One of my students, Laura Ferree, chose the NIFI issue guide "Mental Illness in America" for her sermon-dialogue-sermon process. For her Prophetic Invitation to Dialogue sermon, she decided on Psalm 51 as her primary text, focusing especially on verses 1–2: "Have mercy on me, O God, according to your steadfast love, in your great compassion blot out my offenses. Wash me through and through from my wickedness, and cleanse me from my sin."

Sermon Excerpt: Prophetic Invitation to Dialogue about Mental Illness

> The sermon begins by describing the state of mind of the psalmist—the longing to be set free from sin. After this "rooting," she connects the passage with those who struggle with mental health issues. In this way she follows the "flowering" route by raising awareness of the issue.

Reading Psalm 51 and hearing the desperation to be washed clean, I thought about the people in our nation who struggle with mental illness. The Psalmist is crying out to God to be washed clean from the burden of shame, sin, and guilt so that they might be restored. Think of those who lie in their beds with depression. Or those who suffer from schizophrenia. Or those who have constant anxiety. The Psalmist's cries are their cries: "God wash us clean. Create in us a new heart. A new brain. A new nervous system. A new emotional center. Restore us to health. Let us live freely. Restore us to health."

> She continues on the "flowering" route by contextualizing the topic of mental health. She notes the ways in which their city, Seattle, one of the rainiest and most sunless cities in America, struggles with how to address mental health issues among the population of unhoused citizens. Then, she provides a few key facts about mental health.

Mental health issues permeate every facet of our society. No one is immune to the struggles of mental health. In fact, studies show that one in five Americans will have mental health problems in any given year. One in five! That is a lot of people! Here in Seattle, where it rains 213 days of the years, mental health issues especially affect our unhoused citizens. And yet we are largely silent on the issue as a church.

> She then makes the move to "pollination"—lifting up the need to talk about the issue of mental illness in the church.

In fact, the church is silent on many topics for fear of offending or alienating folks. But it is time we are honest with ourselves! It's time for the church to engage in difficult conversations, to come forward and acknowledge the mental health crisis, and our failure to address it. We need to hear the same words that the Psalmist uses in Psalm 51. These are words of desperation cried out to God, asking for full restoration of both physical and mental health.

Remember—the church is not a place where perfect people come. This is not a place where we neglect important topics or skirt around the necessary issues of our day. This is a place where we come together and admit our faults. We cry out in our own desperation. We admit our own struggles with mental health or acknowledge that we don't know how to care for our family members who struggle with mental illness. It is time for the church to end our silence on such important topics such as mental health, because it really is an issue of life and death.

> Notice how she frames this theologically, connecting with Jesus' willingness to dialogue, thus continuing on the "pollinating" route.

We have the strength to do this. We have a God who creates covenants with God's people and says, "I will be their God, and they shall be my people." Jesus shows us how to do the difficult stuff and sit with people who struggle with difficult issues. But we don't get to practice this very often. It still feels foreign to us to engage in difficult conversations.

> This leads to the "leafing" portion of her sermon—inviting listeners to take action by participating in the deliberative dialogue about mental health.

So I want to invite you to do just that. Immediately following worship, I will be hosting a deliberative dialogue session on mental illness where we can talk openly and frankly with one another about mental illness and our experiences.

> Finally, in the "fruiting" part of the sermon, she concludes by planting seeds for transformation.

In order to become more authentically the church, we are called to engage in the difficult conversations even if we don't agree with one another. I have to admit—that is really hard for me to say! I don't like divisiveness or discord. But that is not what this dialogue will be about. This will simply be a space to talk, as the Body of Christ, about our experiences around the issue of mental health and what we think the church can do moving forward. So please come and engage as the Body of Christ, remembering that we are one together. We are entering a covenant together just as God does with us.

> Notice the pastoral approach Laura takes in this sermon—forthrightly naming the taboo topic of mental illness, but doing so in a way that creates space for people with different experiences to find their entry point for the dialogue. Notice, too, the offer of a meal. In the spirit of the "potluck of ideas" I mentioned earlier, having actual food before the deliberative dialogue is an effective way to demonstrate the kind of hospitality intended for the discussion.
> Mingling over snacks or a meal gives participants a chance to informally talk before the session begins.

Remember that we are all beloved. So if you have cried out in desperation for your own mental illness to be healed, join us. If you have longed for God to heal your family member with mental illness, join us. If you are unsure about this topic and want to learn more, join us. And if nothing else gets you in the room, lunch will be provided! So please come as you are, as the body of Christ, remembering that we all long to be washed clean and have the peace and love of God.[7]

Before we close out this chapter, I want to show you an excerpt from a sermon about an even more contentious issue than mental illness—gun violence.

EXAMPLE 2: GUN VIOLENCE

Leslie Stephens pastors a congregation in Louisiana and chose to address the issue of gun violence and public safety in her congregation using the NIFI issue advisory "How Can We Stop Mass Shootings in Our Communities?" Using the scripture passage Matthew 5:43–48, her sermon focused on what it means to "love our enemies" in the midst of this very heated debate.

Sermon Excerpt: Prophetic Invitation to Dialogue about How to Prevent Mass Shootings

Leslie began her sermon by naming the questions and different angles people have for addressing the issue of gun violence, indicating that there are many perspectives on this complex issue. She then made the case for why the church needs to address this issue. Notice how she frames her argument in terms of the work of the Holy Spirit:

> As Christians, I think we have a unique responsibility to rise to the occasion and do all that we can to make a difference. We need to be the ones who lead the way in deliberative dialogue and civil conversation. We need to model what it is to come together as a community, even a community that has a diverse set of opinions. Even when it's difficult, even when we don't agree. We need to model what it is to continue to be in community and to still love and care for those with whom we disagree. The stakes are high but ignoring one another is getting us nowhere.
>
> I believe we can enter this conversation because the Holy Spirit lives and dwells in us. The Holy Spirit empowers us to do this, it gives us wisdom when we seek it. When we seek Christ's heart in our life and combine it with our own heart, it changes things in us. It helps us to see the people that others don't see. We stop dismissing people who are hurting and hear their cries for help. When we learn to have direct and intentional conversation with our neighbors, this is how change begins to happen. This is how things get better. This is how healing begins.

She then issued the invitation to the dialogue:

> And so next week, I want to invite you to a conversation. Next Wednesday we are going to have our first deliberative dialogue. We are going to come together, and we are going to ask how we might address the issue of mass shootings in our country. We are going to ask questions. We *are* going to disagree. I know all of you so well that I can guarantee this is going to happen. But that's ok. Because we are going to come together with our

common love and our faith. I know we can do this. I know that we can have these conversations. We are going to model for our community what it means to begin this process and to talk to one another and to listen to one another. To see one another as people and not as objects. This is our calling and so this is the invitation.[8]

To see the full text of Leslie's sermon, visit https://www.thepurplezone.net. You'll see how she wove in the call to dialogue with our baptismal calling and how she concluded by showing "what love looks like" when faced with the devastation of mass shootings.

AGAPE LOVE: PROPHETIC LOVE

Hopefully this chapter has helped you see that when sermons give people the permission to talk about difficult topics in a healthy way, we can help disabuse listeners of the notion that all conflict is bad or destructive. As one of my students, TJ Lynch, wrote in his reflection paper on the sermon-dialogue sermon process:

> I think it was almost freeing, in a sense, for folks to hear me say, "Yes, this whole faith thing can be tough at times, yet we are called to have these potentially difficult conversations." When people operate under the mindset that this journey of faith will be all rainbows and sunshine all the time, then as soon as things get difficult or tense we tend to think we're failing or doing something wrong. I think people are starting to realize that having these conversations and talking about difficult or controversial topics is not only permissible, but it's part of who we are called to be as followers of Christ.[9]

As I mentioned in chapter 2, the sermon-dialogue-sermon process works best when carried out in a spirit of trust rather than antagonistic propheticism. As soon as a person feels like they (or their viewpoint) are being attacked, they will shut down, making the process of God's transformation that much more difficult. As Philip Wogaman points out: "If the whole point of the prophetic word is God's love, how on earth can that message be heard if it is not expressed in a context of love? We cannot preach about love unlovingly; it is a self-contradiction."[10]

This Divine love will also carry us into the next part of the Purple Zone—the deliberative dialogue. In the following chapter, you'll learn exactly what deliberative dialogue is, how it works, and how to carry it out in your ministry context. Then in chapter 8, we'll see how the dialogue informs, shapes, and inspires the follow-up sermon, the Communal Prophetic Proclamation.

• 7 •

Deliberative Dialogue in the Purple Zone

> Surely this great nation is a wise and discerning people!
> —Deuteronomy 4:6

WHY WE NEED A DIFFERENT WAY TO "TALK POLITICS"

What frustrates you about politics? Perhaps it's the lack of trust in our leaders or the state of our system of government. Or it might be that any efforts to make changes have little effect and fail to make a difference. Not to mention the fact that any good ideas face seemingly overwhelming odds for getting them to the right people and scaling them up to a point where they begin to have positive effects. For others, it's the nagging feeling that we don't have power or agency in the political process. We doubt that even our community efforts have lasting effects when facing moneyed and powerful political interests. Sometimes we're not even sure where to begin because there are so many facets to the problems.

Because of these frustrations and more, the reality today is that many citizens have been reluctant to participate in civic life. Even the contentious 2016 presidential election only saw 58 percent of eligible voters at the polls.[1] At a time when our collective wisdom for problem-solving is so necessary, our discourse devolves into cynicism, polarization, and apathy. These underlying feelings and assumptions lead to some key questions:

- What would it take for ordinary citizens to rekindle their interest in civic engagement?
- How can we begin to help revitalize civic life in America?

- How can barriers be removed that inhibit citizens from discussing and acting on society's most difficult and most pressing issues?
- What role might the church and Christian citizens have in being the "yeast in the bread" for the rising of an empowered citizenry equipped for the work of building a more just and equitable society?

In my work with the Charles F. Kettering Foundation and the National Issues Forums Institute, I have found that *deliberative dialogue* is one process that can help citizens feel heard, engaged, empowered, and inspired to take action when faced with complex issues. My colleague, Dana Horrell, describes the need for deliberative dialogue this way:

> Deliberative work has become increasingly important given the sorry state of political discourse these days. Whether at the federal, state, or local levels, policy making has become an arena of deadlock and dysfunction. Ordinary citizens often feel marginalized when it comes to political decision making, as issues get framed in the media and by elected officials in a way that leads to divisiveness, so that elected officials and even voters make poor decisions because they are not allowed the time to discuss the options together. Deliberative forums are a tool that churches can use to help communities think better as they grapple with these issues.[2]

People who participate in these deliberative forums often come away with a better understanding not just of the issue that is explored but of their fellow participants in the discussion. This, in turn, can help to transform a church from a culture of divisiveness or avoidance (fight or flight) to one of healthy engagement with the issues that matter to them and their community. This chapter introduces the process of deliberative dialogue, explains step-by-step how to facilitate a deliberative dialogue, and provides practical tips for planning and hosting a deliberative dialogue in your congregation. Explanations of how to view different aspects of the dialogue through a homiletical lens are woven throughout the chapter. Since what happens in this dialogue will ultimately inform the follow-up sermon, the Communal Prophetic Proclamation, you'll want to keep your preaching antennae up as the dialogue unfolds.

THE KETTERING FOUNDATION AND NATIONAL ISSUES FORUMS INSTITUTE

The Kettering Foundation, based in Dayton, Ohio, was founded in 1927 by Charles F. Kettering, an inventor with over two hundred patents (most notably, the automobile self-starter). The nonprofit, nonpartisan research foundation trades insights from its research with a broad network of institutions, organizations, and individuals from over eighty countries. The foundation focuses on basic political research, striving to understand how citizens and political systems can work together. Since the early 1990s, the foundation has researched how democracy can be strengthened. The foundation's primary research question is: What does it take to make democracy work as it should?

That question is explored through the National Issues Forums Institute (NIFI), a nonprofit, nonpartisan organization that serves to promote public deliberation about difficult social issues. NIFI publishes issue guides and other materials used by local forum groups, including schools, civic organizations, and, yes, houses of worship. To be clear, the NIFI is a secular organization. But they partner with and encourage collaboration among forum facilitators, some of whom include clergy and lay leaders in houses of worship. Within its network of leaders from fields such as civics, education, and religion (to name a few), NIFI partners share information, best practices, research questions, and insights.

I first experienced the process of deliberative dialogue when co-leading a pastor's retreat in 2016 with Gregg Kaufman, a retired ELCA pastor and research associate within the Kettering Foundation. At the retreat where I first worked with Gregg, he trained the pastors in the process of deliberative dialogue developed by the Kettering Foundation and the NIFI. Then I worked with them on establishing scriptural and theological principles for engaging controversial issues in their sermons and providing strategies for preaching in the Purple Zone. Together, Gregg and I began to see how preaching, discipleship, and citizenship intersect and what potential there is for American democracy to be strengthened by the church's role as servant in the world.[3]

I now serve as a member of one of the Kettering Foundation's research exchanges focusing on how deliberative dialogue is used in faith-based settings. Through my work with them and in teaching seminary courses on the sermon-dialogue-sermon process, I have found the deliberative dialogue approach and the NIFI issue guides to be ideal tools for helping congregations engage difficult social issues. There are, of course, other organizations that specialize in civil discourse and dialogue.[4] But I believe the NIFI deliberative dialogue approach and nonpartisan issue guides are not only easily adapted to a congregational setting but also dovetail with core values of congregations. These values include uplifting the gifts and experiences of individuals to build and strengthen the community (1 Corinthians chapter 12). In addition, there is potential for deliberative dialogue to help congregations discern how they can best respond to the needs and concerns of their communities, and thereby answering Jesus' call to care for "the least of these" (Matthew 25:40).

THE CASE FOR DELIBERATIVE DIALOGUE IN THE CHURCH

Houses of worship are ideal laboratories for this kind of civic engagement to take place. As well, the deliberative process has the potential to complement the church's social teachings and policy work, especially at the congregational level. Churches were called "schools for democracy" during the founding of this nation. From the Social Gospel Movement, to the Abolitionist Movement, to the Civil Rights Movement, the church has been a significant institution for the development of American society. Today, denominations have established ministries to address all manner of justice issues from immigration and refugees, to homelessness, environmental issues, racism, and hunger, to name just a few. Advocacy efforts by churches and denominational offices have led to social and policy statements as well as direct action in the form of protest marches, letter-writing campaigns, and one-on-one meetings with lawmakers.

The church can make a vital contribution toward the restoration of public deliberation about important community issues by hosting, participating in, and training their leaders and congregants in the skills of deliberative dialogue. Indeed, such engagement with the public square is necessary for renewing the vitality of the church and providing moral and ethical resources for community conversation. There is great potential for the church to complement the efforts of secular organizations such as the Kettering Foundation, and simultaneously, for such organizations to provide helpful tools to teach us how to talk in healthy and productive ways about conflictual topics. The promise of such a mutually beneficial and reciprocal relationship invites us into new conversations to envision a better future.

At the same time, we must note that the church has not always been a congenial host of such dialogue. In fact, people of faith and even entire congregations have sometimes attempted to squelch public deliberation about controversial issues. There is plentiful evidence of this from perusing the responses and comments in my survey, "Preaching About Controversial Justice Issues," which I discussed in chapter 1. A significant number of clergy are opposed to engaging any contemporary justice issues in their preaching or teaching. Nevertheless, these instances do not negate the fact that our religion's own scriptures and history are founded on the very principles of relationship, engagement, listening, careful consideration, and intelligent, well-informed decision-making, as described in chapters 2 and 3. Despite the past mistakes, missteps, and misunderstandings revolving around the relationship between the church and the wider world, the gospel (and the church that proclaims that gospel to the world) has something positive to contribute to these issues, no matter how messy they may be. And when the church is willing to partner with and utilize tools from secular organizations committed to principles of dialogue, those contributions are even more significant. The Kettering Foundation and NIFI are just the sorts of partners to which the church can look for those resources.

Boosting the "White Blood Cells" in the Church

Part of what makes the deliberative dialogue process conducive to the church setting is because of the way it coincides with the idea of *responsibility ethics*. As theological ethicist Roger Willer explains, "Responsibility ethics recognizes human beings primarily as dialogical creatures. It sees human beings as answerers who live through response and interaction. The focus is on discerning what is a fitting response within the extremely complex situations of contemporary life that always include manifold competing demands and moral challenges."[5] Equipping parishioners to take up these moral challenges and discuss the complexities of what it means to live within the ambiguities of these controversial issues is one of the gifts a church can give to its members and, in turn, to society at large.

Participating in deliberative dialogue can contribute to higher levels of public engagement, foster a more broadened outlook, offer new ways to take part in groups, and provide an enhanced sense of empowerment for making a difference in one's community. These are all qualities that contribute to healthier churches as well. As one of my students, Joanna Samuelson, wrote in her reflection paper about the sermon-dialogue-sermon process:

> I believe that the regular practice of deliberative dialogue within the church setting has the potential to equip and empower the congregation to shape their faithful response to the needs of the world as inspired by the Word of God. That faithful response, of course, comes with commitment, consistency, and an investment in the deliberative process. I'd like to believe that, in this way, even the most divisive social or political issues could be discussed in the church setting. After all, if we believe the church to be a sacred and safe place, isn't it, then, the best place to sort through the most difficult issues?[6]

With her comment in mind, recall the analogy I made in the book's introduction about the church helping to create "white blood cells" in the Body of Christ. Leukocytes are produced in bone marrow. Deep within the skeletal structures of the human body is the spongy tissue that produces red blood cells, platelets, and white blood cells, or leukocytes. These leukocytes fight against invading bacteria, viruses, and fungi to help destroy infection. We might think of this Purple Zone work in our churches as taking place within the "marrow of the bone." These deliberative dialogues, sermons, and conversations guided by the Holy Spirit are producing the "antibodies" to neutralize the toxic "microbes" that weaken our internal structures, harm relationships, and compromise the health of our congregations.

What are these "microbes"? In biblical terms, Paul's letter to the Galatians describes them as idolatry, enmities, strife, jealousy, anger, quarrels, dissensions, factions, and envy (Galatians 5:19–21). In contrast, the "fruits of the Spirit"—the T-cells of the body, so to speak—are love, joy, peace, patience, kindness, generosity, faithfulness, gentleness, and self-control (Galatians 5:22–23). My hope is that you will find deliberative dialogue to be a powerful source of antibodies that can strengthen your church's capacity for health and wholeness when it comes to addressing the controversial justice issues of our day.

Let's look at what happens in a deliberative dialogue, and how you can facilitate a forum in your congregation.

WHAT IS DELIBERATIVE DIALOGUE AND HOW DOES IT WORK?

Deliberative dialogue is a form of communication where a gathering of participants interact in a small-group session to share experiences about a particular issue, consider different approaches to the topic, discern their common values in the midst of the discussion, and decide what steps can be taken to work on the issue. Deliberative dialogue is not a debate or a panel presentation. The discussion takes place within a structured forum wherein everyone is encouraged to speak in a respectful and open way, listen with the same respect and openness, and discern possible directions or action steps. Participants examine the pros and cons, consequences, and benefits of possible approaches to complex problems. The goal is not to reach unanimous agreement or to convince others about the rightness or wrongness of the positions presented. Rather, it's about finding shared values and, as a result, looking for a common direction, or at least next steps which the group might take together.

In chapter 5, I explained how to choose a topic to address by finding the NIFI issue guide that is appropriate for your particular congregation, and the need to assess whether you should pick either a cool, warm, or hot topic. After deciding on the topic and while preparing for the introductory sermon, you'll also need to plan for the deliberative dialogue that will follow. Hosting a deliberative dialogue is not something that can happen spontaneously. It takes time and advanced preparation to make folks aware that the process will be happening and to ensure that a diverse group of people are invited and encouraged to attend.

Inviting People to Participate in the Deliberative Dialogue

Because you need at least five people for the deliberative dialogue to be successful, I recommend reaching out to at least seven individuals with personal invitations to participate. That way you'll "seed the field" and ensure that you have a sufficient number of folks for the discussion. Consider inviting individuals who represent a wide range of perspectives, ages, political orientations, and life experiences. It's also prudent to invite the folks who tend to give the strongest pushback when you have addressed "political" issues in past sermons. Asking them to participate because you value their input can help avoid disgruntled comments later on. Because when people know that they have an opportunity to have a say, that their voice will be respected, and that their point of view is given consideration, it gives them a personal stake and buy-in on the process.

Is participation in the forum limited to members of the congregation? No, in fact it is advisable to invite people from outside the church to participate in the deliberative dialogue. Especially if you know of people in the community who have a vested interest in the topic, have a particular perspective to add, or can help round out the diversity of the group, including them in the dialogue can bring valuable voices to the discussion.

> **TIP:** *Make an effort to include youths and young adults in the discussion. Their presence can provide valuable perspectives on the issue. They will have different questions, experiences, concerns, and ideas that can challenge older adults to think more expansively. Inviting them also communicates that their input is welcomed, valid, and necessary for the life of the congregation.*

Preparing for the Forum

In the weeks prior to the forum, you'll print out copies of the issue guide that you've chosen and have them available for the congregation. You'll put them in a high-traffic area, such as the narthex or fellowship gathering area. Not only does this give people a chance to peruse the materials ahead of time, it can also spark interest in attending the forum.

In terms of supplies needed for the session, the only things necessary are a large flip chart or notepad on an easel (hint: the giant sticky-note pads work very well for these sessions) and some markers. Arrange the chairs in the room in a semicircle so that everyone can see each other. This room arrangement communicates to participants at the outset that collaboration, engagement, and egalitarianism are built into the deliberative process. I also suggest having people wear name tags, especially if the facilitator does not know everyone's name or if not all the participants know each other.

The NIFI recommends two hours for a deliberative dialogue. However, the students and pastors I've worked with tend to allot 90 minutes for the forums, given the time constraints of most church and clergy schedules. Less than 90 minutes shortchanges the process and does not give participants the time they need to process the information, think through the options, and allow the discussion to unfold naturally. In other words, deliberation takes time.

> **TIP:** *If you're planning to use a preset time for a deliberative dialogue, such as the Sunday School hour or a Wednesday evening Bible study, and you only have an hour for the discussion, consider splitting the dialogue into two parts, or even three. See Appendix B: Options for Planning One, Two, or Three Sessions for the Deliberative Dialogue.*

Roles within Deliberative Dialogue: Recorder, Timekeeper, Facilitator

You will need people to fill three roles within the deliberative dialogue: the recorder, the timekeeper, and the facilitator. (While some facilitators try to cover all three jobs, it's better if they are assigned to different people so that the facilitator is freed up to moderate the discussion without trying to write down the comments of the group and keep track of time.) *The recorder* writes down what the group says so everyone can see how the process of dialogue is unfolding, remembers what was said throughout the process, and analyzes the discussion for major themes. Using a flip chart, he or she writes in large legible letters to accurately record the pros, cons, themes, values, and next steps for each stage of the dialogue. *The timekeeper* reminds the group when each section of the dialogue is coming to a close and that it's time to move on. She or he clearly announces when a minute or two remains in each section, and then "calls time" when that segment is over and the discussion needs to move on.

The facilitator sets the tone for the forum and leads participants through the deliberative process. The responsibilities of the facilitator are to thoroughly read the NIFI materials, moderate the discussion with neutrality, encourage an exchange of views among the participants, press participants to focus on trade-offs, suggest points of view that may be missing, and keep the conversation respectful and on-task. Effective facilitators model friendly and relaxed behavior when welcoming people and introducing the issue. They manage the room well, model democratic attitudes and skills, and keep the deliberation focused on the options instead of getting sidetracked or stuck in unproductive conversations.

The facilitator *does not* need to be an expert about the issue under consideration. In fact, it's usually best that the person not be an expert so as to be able to focus on the role of facilitating rather than educating or being seen as a policy specialist. Certainly, the facilitator must read the issue guide carefully and make notes that will help guide the conversation. But the main job of the facilitator is to keep people focused on the approaches and moderate the conversation so that all voices are heard and the ground rules are followed. In the section below, "Analyzing the Issue, Weighing the Options," we'll look at specific strategies and techniques for moderating the deliberation.

In the meantime, it's important to know that the facilitator must *remain neutral* throughout the dialogue. If you have strong feelings about the topic, this is not the time to voice them. The key is to practice "passionate impartiality" so as not to unduly influence the dialogue or appear to have a hidden agenda. This does not mean, of course, that the facilitator should act like a soulless drone. On the contrary, a good facilitator demonstrates genuine curiosity, asks thoughtful questions, and provides insights and information when needed.

> **TIP:** *If the topic chosen for the dialogue is one about which you have strong feelings or opinions and you think it would be difficult to remain neutral if someone espouses beliefs or opinions that would "push your buttons," it's probably best if someone other than you facilitates the dialogue. For example, when it comes to the issue of climate change, I learned that it's best for me not to facilitate. My research about this topic and passion for environmental issues is such that I have difficulty holding back from wanting to advocate for the Earth and vulnerable communities. It's advisable for me to invite someone else to facilitate.*

Some may wonder whether the clergyperson always has to be the facilitator. Not necessarily. In fact, there may be times when it's best for the pastor to simply be the convener of the session and then to be either a participant, recorder, or timekeeper. Especially if the topic is one about which the pastor is particularly opinionated, as I mentioned above, allowing someone else to facilitate can be prudent. As well, because the pastor is naturally seen as "the expert" when it comes to spiritual and ecclesial matters, parishioners may be reluctant to engage in challenging conversations with their faith leader or may defer to whatever the pastor says. In other words, parishioners may be reluctant to exercise their own voices in the process if the pastor is the facilitator or a fellow participant.

> **TIP:** *Consider inviting another clergyperson from a neighboring congregation to take the reins of facilitating. You can then reciprocate the favor if they decide to host a deliberative dialogue in their own congregation.*

Obviously, there are both benefits and downsides to the pastor facilitating the conversation. However, I do recommend that ministers try their hand at facilitating a deliberative dialogue at least once, especially when introducing the process to the congregation for the first time. Learning to be a good moderator is a valuable skill that can be useful not just in these issue-driven conversations but in other aspects of church leadership as well. However, after folks have experienced the process and can see what's involved, the pastor may want to train others to facilitate deliberative dialogues in the future. This not only empowers lay leaders, it expands the pool of individuals equipped to moderate discussions about other topics and issues in the life of the congregation.

Shortly, we'll learn what happens in each part of the dialogue. But first, let's look at the format of the issue guides because they provide the content, framework, and information needed for carrying out the dialogue.

What You'll Find in a NIFI Issue Guide

At the time of this writing, there are nearly forty issue guides available from the National Issues Forums Institute on a wide range of topics. Each issue guide contains everything you'll need to facilitate the dialogue, beginning with a description of what deliberative dialogue is, how it works, and how the guide was developed. With every issue guide, the topic is carefully researched by teams across the country in consultation with various communities, as well as experts in the field. What impresses me about the guides is that they are nonpartisan, well-written, accessible for the lay person, and contain the right balance of text, charts, and images without being too long or cumbersome.

The key feature of the issue guides is that they always present *three* different and well-defined policy options for participants to discuss. The choice of three is intentional. Having only two options would turn the discussion into an either-or debate, which would only serve to reinforce the bifurcations already present. More than three would be too many for folks to discuss in the suggested time frame. The three options are meant to give participants the opportunity to weigh the benefits, disadvantages, and trade-offs of each one. It's also important to note that these are not three *solutions* to the issue, but *approaches*. The goal is not to solve the problem but to arrive at a fuller understanding of each other's stories, experiences, and values in order to find common ground upon which to take next steps.

Ground Rules and Opening Prayer

Before getting into the topic itself, the group will need to agree to ground rules for the deliberative dialogue. As *Difficult Conversations* author Katie Day explains, "Embarking on such a process needs to take place in the context of covenant—one that reflects commitments to God and to the community as well as the individuals within it. Participants need to know that there is a higher purpose to these conversations and that they are in this struggle together."[7] There are several good examples of ground rules for dialogue available through an internet search, but every NIFI issue guide also sets out guidelines for the discussion.[8] These typically include the following:

- Focus on the options.
- All options should be considered fairly.
- No one or two individuals dominate.
- Maintain an open and respectful atmosphere.
- Everyone is encouraged to participate.
- Listen to each other.

I have found that having the group take turns reading aloud the guidelines for conversation is a good way to make sure everyone hears them and agrees to follow them. It provides a common reference point in case the conversation takes a turn in the wrong direction. Taking a moment to remind participants of the guidelines to which everyone agreed can help get the dialogue back on track.

With these ground rules in place, the facilitator offers a centering prayer to set the tone and invite God's presence into the process. Here's a sample prayer:

> God of Wisdom, you have engaged your people in holy conversations in scripture, throughout the church's history, and in our own congregation. Send your Holy Spirit among us that we may listen and speak with respect as we honor the deeply held values and convictions that come from our faith and experiences. Engage our minds with clarity and curiosity, drawing from among us the insights that help us see your will for our dialogue, our church, our community, and our world. In the name of Jesus, we pray. Amen.

Introducing the Topic and What's at Stake

Once the ground rules have been established and the prayer concludes, the facilitator introduces the topic in a general way. Whether or not participants had a chance to read through the issue guide before the start of the dialogue, you'll want to spend a few minutes highlighting the major points of the issue, as well as some of the key facts, charts, and statistics provided in the guide.

Then, the facilitator asks a key question: "What's at stake for you regarding this issue? In what ways has this issue affected you personally or someone close to you?" In other words, what's their "skin in the game"? Participants are invited to respond to the question by sharing—in one or two sentences—why the issue is important to them on a personal level. This is a key step in the dialogue because it gets beyond partisan talking points and media spin. It brings the conversation immediately to the "heart" level of engagement. This is not to say that information and facts are not important, but having people share their stories about why the topic matters to them introduces the component of *narrative* in providing context for the issue.

For example, David Allred pastors a church in a city in Tennessee that has seen the devastating effects of heroin addiction. In a deliberative dialogue he facilitated on the opioid crisis using the NIFI issue advisory "What Should We Do about the Opioid Epidemic?", participants shared a multitude of perspectives and stories. Family members of participants were in drug rehabilitation centers. Friends were victims of violence during drug deals. One participant shared the pain of their own battle with drug addiction. From the outset, people saw how the issue of opioids touched their friends, neighbors, and community members in direct and indirect ways.

> **TIP:** *If your group is larger than ten people, it's better to split into smaller groups of three to six for this part so that sharing can be done in a more intimate way and within the allotted time. If the group is larger than ten, the sharing can take so long that the remaining segments of the dialogue are shortchanged. I have found that it's best to give groups five minutes to share amongst themselves, and then turn back to the larger group and call out what their group talked about, which can then be written on the notepad. This allows for each person to be heard, as well as for the larger group to get a sense of the range of personal touchpoints for the issue, without eating up too much time at the beginning.*

From a preaching perspective, this time of personal sharing is critical because it will be useful in grounding the follow-up sermon in the real-life experiences of those in the congregation. This is not to say that the preacher should reveal confidential information in the sermon. But take note of the diversity of ages, occupations, walks of life, experiences, and political orientations of those involved in the dialogue. If someone does share a particularly poignant story, and they grant permission for it to be used as a sermon illustration, the result can make for a powerful preaching moment in the Communal Prophetic Proclamation sermon, which will be discussed in the following chapter.

Should the facilitator also share their perspective, opinions, experiences, and/or positions on the issue during this introduction? While some may contend that she or he should be forthcoming with this information so that participants know where they stand, my experience is that it's best not to share this viewpoint, at least not until the dialogue concludes. Remember that the facilitator's job requires neutrality. If people ask your opinion, remind them of your responsibility to guide the conversation without bias, no matter your personal opinions, and to treat all participants with respect. This is not to say that the facilitator can't share their connection to the issue. For example, if the facilitator had a family member in a drug rehabilitation center, he might want to share this in order to reveal his own "skin in the game." As long as the facilitator does not reveal his opinions about the issue in sharing this bit of personal information, this openness can help create a sense of trust and model vulnerability within the group.

Analyzing the Issue, Weighing the Options

Once everyone has had a chance to share why the issue matters for them, the next stage is deliberating about the three approaches to the topic. Allot equal time for each of the options. At the top of each large sheet of paper, write the title of the approach and put "Pros" and "Cons" in two columns underneath. Give equal time to consider the consequences for good and for ill of each option.

> **TIP:** *If your group is larger than ten people, use the small groups again for discussing each option. Some facilitators have the groups discuss the pros and cons of one issue for a few minutes, then have groups report out for the recorder to write down the thoughts and ideas for all to see. Then they do this for the other two issues, ebbing and flowing between small group and large group. Other facilitators prefer to have the groups go through the three options in succession and report out after they're all done. Either way is fine, depending on what works best for you and your group.*

This stage of the deliberation asks people to recognize that every action will have a downside and to realize that every decision has trade-offs. In the issue advisory about the opioid crisis, for example, there are three options: 1) Focus on treatment for all; 2) Focus on enforcement; 3) Focus on individual choice. Within those options, there are both "Actions" and "Drawbacks" listed. In option 1, one possible action is to greatly expand the number of drug treatment centers, especially long-term facilities. The drawback to that action, however, is that more treatment centers will be located in neighborhoods around communities where they could pose problems. Participants will discuss what they think are acceptable trade-offs, what other factors need to be considered, and what they agree are important underlying values within the options.

The role of the facilitator is vital at this stage of the dialogue. The facilitator listens for deeper concerns that motivate a participant's comments rather than taking them at face value. For example, in the opioid discussion, a participant may offer a very strong opinion that all the drug users should be locked up in prison. The facilitator can follow up with a question such as, "It sounds like you have very strong feelings about this. Can you say what in your experience has led you to this conviction?" Or, "I wonder if you can imagine what a family member of a drug user might think about this suggestion?"

In other words, an effective facilitator asks clarifying, thoughtful, and probing questions to surface underlying values and ferret out costs and consequences. In appendix C, "'Cheat Sheet' Questions to Encourage Deliberation," you'll find a list of helpful questions facilitators can use to encourage deeper reflection, work through key tensions, and identify common ground. From a preaching perspective, these questions are not only useful for the dialogue, they are also helpful for approaching the Communal Prophetic Proclamation sermon that will be preached after the dialogue. The questions allow the preacher to consider different perspectives and standpoints, flesh out the context, and think forward to consequences of different action steps.

> **TIP:** *Be aware that it's likely that participants will point out that there are other factors that have a bearing on the topic that are not mentioned in the issue guide or advisory. Additionally, some may balk that the three options do not include other approaches that they think should be considered. This is to be expected. Remember that the materials are only a means by which to enter into the dialogue; they are not the definitive authority or final say on the topic. The NIFI materials are a tool for opening the conversation. While the facilitator will need to keep the discussion within the boundaries of the three options, the group's process will also take on a life of its own.*

Reflecting on Recurring Themes, Shared Values, and Common Ground

After analyzing all three options, the next stage is reflecting on the conversation as a whole in which the group looks at the three sheets of paper with the pros and cons listed under each option. The facilitator asks: "What are some common themes that kept coming up throughout our discussion? And what commonly held values do you see emerging from the three options?" As people identify those themes and values, the recorder writes them on another sheet of paper. While the group may not agree on the means by which to achieve or enact those values, the goal is to at least name the points of common ground.

Returning to the opioid crisis dialogue, when my colleague David Allred facilitated the dialogue in his congregation, several themes and values emerged, including: identifying the "pain points" for people, focusing on mental health (especially with young people), safety, accountability, compassion, forgiveness, families, and relationships. Granted, there were differing opinions on how safety might be achieved, for example, but when a group is able to sift through the pros and cons and lift up these values, it can be a real moment of clarity. It shows them how much they do have in common in terms of what's important to them and what people hope and long for regarding this issue.

From a preaching perspective, these shared values are essential for the follow-up sermon. They can be lifted up as evidence that the Holy Spirit was working and moving within the process to help the group see what common ground unites them, even in the midst of diverse opinions and perspectives. These values can also be correlated to appropriate biblical principles, thus enabling the congregation to see the ways in which this issue dovetails with scriptural narratives, teachings, and overarching themes.

> **TIP:** *The group will quickly come to realize that these different values compete for our attention, resources, and time. This is a point in the dialogue when people sometimes get frustrated. So it's important to remind them about one of the goals of the process, which is to help groups become better able to move beyond the obstacles of "false polarization" and "analysis paralysis" in order to prioritize, innovate, and spark collaborative action.[9] We'll see examples of how this works in the next chapter.*

Suggesting and Discussing Next Steps

The final stage of the deliberative dialogue is to consider possible action steps. The facilitator asks, "Based on our shared values and knowing that we have a wide spectrum of experiences, political affiliations, and personal convictions, what are two or three things that might be next steps for us in continuing to address this issue?" This is a time for brainstorming, so as people make suggestions, do not critique, judge, or dismiss any ideas. The recorder simply writes the suggestions on the final sheet labeled "Next Steps."

This part of the process is very organic and contextual. The ideas people suggest will depend on what they've just talked about when discussing the three approaches and common values, what they see as prioritized needs in their church or community, and what sparks their interest and imagination. For instance, it may become apparent that certain voices and perspectives were missing from the dialogue. Someone may suggest, then, that the church host another session and invite more people—particularly those whose views were underrepresented. Or a group may decide that there was an aspect of the issue that they need to know more about. In that case, someone may have the idea for the church to plan for a speaker or a group of panelists to address the topic. Others may be ready to move into steps that involve advocacy or activism. For instance, one person may want to organize a letter-writing campaign to send to the local newspaper and elected officials. Or another may suggest scheduling a meeting with a local elected official to discuss the issue. In the chapters ahead, we'll look at several case studies to see the ways in which different congregations identified next steps that spoke to their situations and primary values.

> **TIP:** *I suggest that after a list of next steps has been compiled, the facilitator should ask the group to identify the three that seem to have the most energy or appear to be the most doable in the short term. While it's not necessary, the pastor may also ask if any individuals would like to follow through with any of the suggestions and make plans to put the steps into action.*

Remember that "solutions" are not the point of this process. The underlying paradoxes of competing interests and conflicting values are difficult to resolve. But by the end of the deliberative dialogue, the hope is that participants are better equipped to rank the values they hold dear and address the tensions among themselves in more productive ways than before the process began. In this format, instead of hearing disconnected voices espousing inflammatory rhetoric and simplistic framing that demonizes opposing viewpoints, they will have experienced a process that encourages mutual understanding and genuine interaction across perspectives. The resulting improvement in the quality of our public discourse is a solution in itself. Not only is this process positive for democracy but for the church as well, which is just as in need of meaningful interactions and a culture of engagement as other human institutions.

Concluding the Deliberative Dialogue

As the session draws to a close, it's a good idea to do a final check-in to ask how people are feeling about the process. What's their takeaway? What did they learn? What surprised them? What's one word they would use to describe how they feel now that the session is ending? This helps to provide closure and gives the facilitator immediate feedback on the process. The facilitator then hands out the evaluation forms (available in the leader guides) for people to fill out before they leave. (These forms are sent back to NIFI to contribute to their ongoing research.) The forum concludes with prayer, and the facilitator thanks everyone for attending.

At the end of the deliberative dialogue, then, there should be at least six sheets of paper up on the walls, as seen in figure 7.1. Before taking down the sheets of paper and recycling them, be sure to take photos of them to share with group members and others who were not able to attend the dialogue but may be interested in the results. These sheets contain the wisdom of the group, a record of the process, and will serve to jog your memory when it comes time to prepare the follow-up sermon, the Communal Prophetic Proclamation.

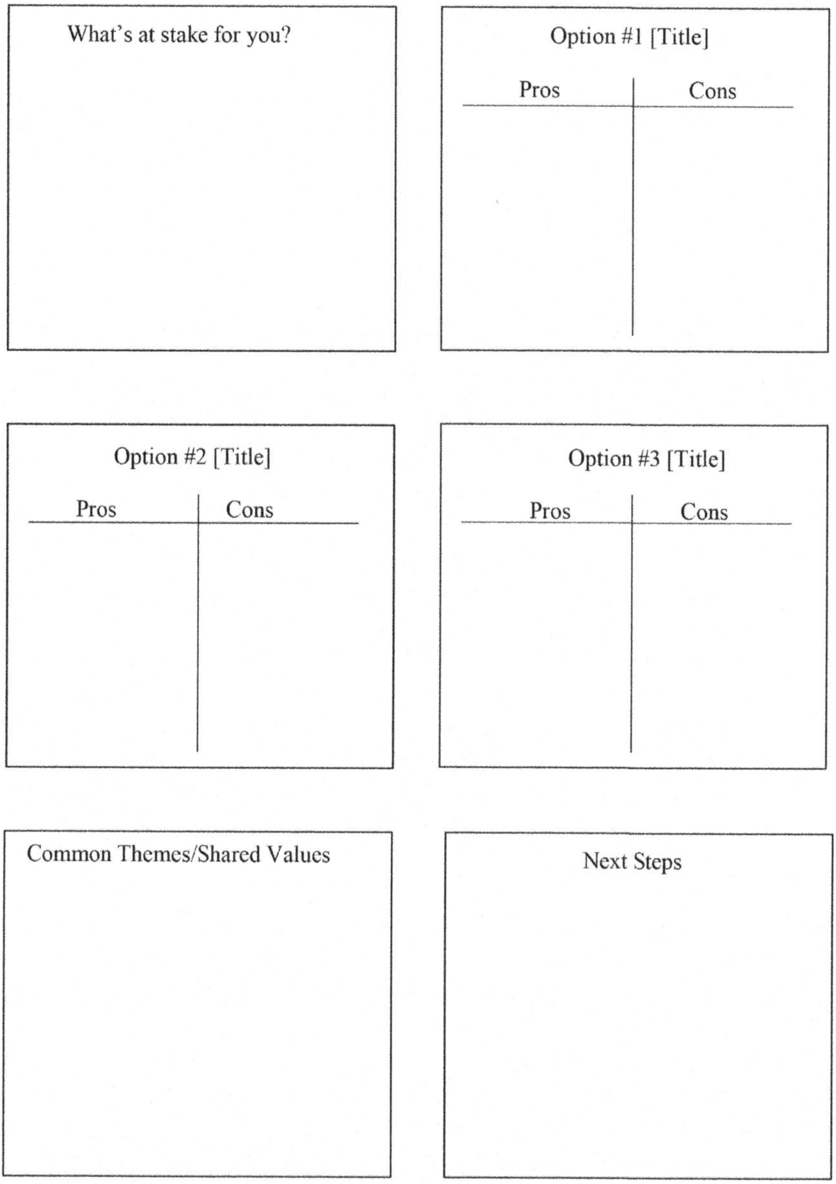

What's at stake for you?	Option #1 [Title] Pros | Cons
Option #2 [Title] Pros | Cons	Option #3 [Title] Pros | Cons
Common Themes/Shared Values	Next Steps

Figure 7.1. Recorder Sheets in a Deliberative Dialogue

TIPS AND STRATEGIES FOR EFFECTIVE FACILITATION

When facilitating a deliberative dialogue, thinking on your feet is a necessary skill that comes naturally to some but can be developed by nearly anyone. To aid in that skill-building, it's helpful to keep in mind different approaches that can be employed when moderating a discussion.

- The Referee—When the conversation is humming along, there's no need to interfere unless the ground rules need to be enforced or the timekeeper's announcement that it's time to move on needs to be repeated.
- The Interviewer—There may be times when specific questions asked of participants can push the conversation to go deeper or clarify certain ideas and positions. Especially if the conversation stalls or hits a bump, having a list of questions prepared ahead of time can be helpful. See appendix C for the "cheat sheet" that contains those probing questions.
- The Devil's Advocate—If the group is fairly homogenous or if there are obvious gaps in the representation of different perspectives, the facilitator may need to offer views that are not present in the forum. Sometimes problematizing and troubleshooting the consensus of the group can yield new insights.
- The Weaver—Especially when working toward the common values portion of the dialogue, the facilitator can help participants identify and build upon common ground. Finding the common threads that weave their way through the dialogue allows participants to gain a wider view and analyze their own process of discernment.

With any of these strategies, the facilitator will need to make choices on how to guide the conversation. When a participant shares a perspective or idea, one option is to acknowledge it and simply move on by asking for additional comments. Another option is to paraphrase what the person just said. Especially if what the person said was lengthy, paraphrasing can help the recorder find the right words for writing key phrases on the notepad. Asking follow-up questions is another option, especially when playing devil's advocate. One of those questions can be about how participants are reacting to some of the ideas they have heard others share. Ask if the idea resonates, brings up questions, or raises concerns in order to invite others to engage the idea, thus furthering the process of deliberation. Finally, returning to the issue guide to raise another question or point mentioned is another way to usher along the discussion.

Mediating Conflict within a Deliberative Dialogue

Passions can run high when people discuss difficult social issues. Despite the best of intentions, old patterns of engaging complex problems are deeply ingrained. Instead of wrestling productively with the tensions, participants may be tempted to fall into either-or thinking, use an "us-versus-them" mentality, frame opponents as "the bad guy/gal," or resort to narrow or shallow thinking about competing interests and values. When this happens, the facilitator has an opportunity to guide the discussion back to engaging the "higher brain" and away from the reptilian fight-or-flight part of the "lower brain." Here are some suggestions for mediating conflict within a deliberative dialogue:

- **Name and acknowledge the feelings.** "As we can see, this is a difficult issue, and emotions are running high. Let's take a moment to do an 'emotion check-in.' In a word, can each of us share what you're feeling at this point?" Acknowledge that the feelings are normal and necessary for helping us make moral and ethical decisions.
- **Validate how well the group has been doing in the deliberation so far.** Then give a friendly reminder about the ground rules.
- **Empathize by sharing how you, too, have felt strong emotions when you participated in a previous discussion about a difficult topic.** Then share a bit of wisdom that another facilitator passed on to you when it comes to making space for these places of tension, such as using "I wonder" questions or inviting people to share their stories of how they came to believe what they do.
- **Model higher-level thinking.** Use phrases like, "I'm curious" and "What would we think about" in order to access more reflective levels of thought.
- **Offer a brief prayer.** Recentering after a tense moment of conflict can help participants regroup and recall the foundation of faith that binds them together. For example: "Holy Spirit, you are truly in this place. We offer our feelings into your care so that we may continue in our dialogue, guided by your wisdom for your purposes. Amen."

Reining in the Talkative Individual

One of the most difficult skills to master is how to diplomatically intervene when a person is dominating the conversation or is simply taking too long to tell their story or make their point. One way to prevent this behavior is to emphasize in the ground rules that participants should keep their comments brief, so there is time for everyone to share their thoughts. Even with this being said, it can be challenging to rein in a verbose participant. Here are some techniques that usually work:

- Take a few steps toward the person, then turn slightly away toward the rest of the group. This kind of body language can signal to the person that the group is ready to hear another voice.
- When they take a breath, jump in with, "You know, what I really appreciate about what you're saying is this: [paraphrase what you've been hearing, or lift up a major theme]. I wonder if anyone else can relate to this?" This is a way to pivot to other participants.
- If subtle hints don't work, make the "time-out" sign with your hands. Explain that it's important to hear other perspectives and ask the group what voices they haven't heard from yet.
- Once in a while, a person is loquacious because they have a highly informed opinion or necessary information. While their intentions are good and their input is valuable, it can also divert the deliberation process and become a lecture. If you sense this is happening, you can say something like: "This is a really important perspective. I wonder if you might consider being part of a panel discussion on this topic at some point in the future? In fact, that could be one of our 'next steps' going forward. How about we hear some other perspectives as well?"
- If all else fails, say, "I just want to remind us all of the ground rules we agreed to regarding participation and allowing for equal sharing. I'd like to hear from someone who hasn't had a chance to share yet."

Drawing Out the Quieter Participants

The opposite challenge is when no one seems to want to talk or when one or two individuals are either reserved or silent. Before rushing into a new question or pushing people to talk, remember that it's okay for there to be pauses and silence. People need time to think and process what they want to say. When it's time to draw out quieter members of the group, consider these kinds of questions:

- What makes this issue real for you?
- Can you give us an example of what was just said?
- What values or personal principles come to mind when you think about this issue?
- What seems to be most important to those who have these opinions or ideas?

I do want to note that some people may just want to observe the conversation, or they may not have anything they want to share. That is perfectly fine. But the facilitator needs to make sure that the person is given room to share their voice if they so desire. Thus, when asking questions of those who have not yet talked, it can be framed in this way:

- Do you have anything you would like to add to that point?
- Was there a perspective about this issue you wanted to share?

Also, if the facilitator notices that someone has been trying to speak, but just can't break in, she can simply say, "I see Sam is trying to share something with us. What would you like to share, Sam?" In this way, the facilitator can draw out the quieter individuals without putting them on the spot in a way that is uncomfortable for them.

In any case, if a person mentions up front that they do not feel comfortable participating in the dialogue, you can suggest that they serve as the recorder or timekeeper for the session. That way they have a role to play and can listen without the expectation that they must speak.

BUILDING THE CAPACITY OF ACTIVE CITIZEN-BELIEVERS

By this point, it should be apparent that deliberative dialogue is a viable approach to building capacity for genuine, meaningful engagement on difficult issues that impact the lives of individuals, communities, and society at large. Moreover, houses of worship are ideal sites for civil discourse to take place, since there is (in theory) a broad cross-section of citizenry in terms of age, professions, gender identity, race, ethnicity, and political affiliations. In this way, churches can be ideal Purple Zone "laboratories" in which to carry out experiments in civil discourse.

For example, one of my students, Kenneth Greble, facilitated a dialogue on health care, a problem that was of particular concern to his aging congregation. By engaging the issue guide, "Health Care: How Can We Reduce Costs and Still Get the Care We Need?", the participants not only wrestled with the complexities of the health care system, they pooled their community's wisdom by sharing with each other how they had handled certain medical issues. As well, they offered each other tips on navigating the labyrinth of health insurance challenges. They started networking with each other and exchanged tips and helpful hints. In other words, deliberative dialogue has the potential to galvanize individual and collective action as well as improve community problem-solving.

At the interpersonal level, Ken saw how the dialogue encouraged people to open up about struggles they were having with their own health and finances—something not usually discussed over cookies at coffee hour. He observed a deepening of relationships and an increase of compassion in the members toward each other. This, in turn, led the congregation to begin talks about establishing a parish nurse program. This illustrates an increased capacity for community problem-solving.

Dana Horrell notes that cultivating active citizen-believers helps build stronger, healthier, and safer communities and congregations:

> Group discussion does not have to be twisted by anger or marred by disrespect. Deliberation is possible, even concerning controversial matters such as immigration, community policing or gun violence. By hosting forums, church leaders can offer a space where difficult issues get raised, and though perhaps not resolved, at least considered respectfully and well. Along the way, churches might help their neighbors learn how to be better citizens.[10]

When people know each other's stories, understand each other's values, and identify a common goal toward which to put their efforts, this increases civic capacity. Citizens become more involved when they know they are trusted—and can trust others—to share ideas and engage in civil discussion. In the process, the Holy Spirit works through us in the wider world, enabling us as Christians to offer our gifts to the civic realm. Because when we engage these issues, we do so grounded in the Triune God who has made us, redeemed us, and sanctified us for the sake of the world and to work for the common good.

• 8 •

Preaching Sermon 2

Communal Prophetic Proclamation

TAKING A SEAT AT THE *ROUNDTABLE PULPIT*

John McClure's 1995 book, *The Roundtable Pulpit: Where Leadership and Preaching Meet*, introduced a new approach to the weekly task of preaching that involved collaboration with one's parishioners in preparing for the sermon. A central question of the book is how principles and practices of truly participative dialogue can be incorporated into preaching, given that sermons are essentially monological.[1] His answer is to use a collaborative method as an alternative to the "sovereign" clergy-centered style or the inductive approach.[2] Recognizing the need for preachers and their congregations to develop a public theology that reconnects the private and public realms, McClure's roundtable pulpit method has the preacher meet with a group of parishioners each week to discuss the text for the upcoming sermon. The insights from the discussion are then rhetorically woven into the sermon.

The premise of McClure's book is that "the best way to empower congregations for ministry and mission is through the use of collaborative forms of leadership and preaching."[3] More than simply an innovative technique, McClure's approach was envisioned to "help the preacher come to an understanding of the nature of biblical proclamation that can become the centerpiece of an effective form of congregational leadership, and perhaps, a repaired form of Christian community."[4] In this way, the text, the preacher, and the congregants come "face to face with one another in a context in which otherness, rather than homogeneity, is valued and taken seriously."[5] Trusting both the collective wisdom of the congregation, as well as the guidance of the Holy Spirit, the clergyperson leads these conversations that hold up the experience, wisdom, spiritual reflections, and gifts of the people within the congregation. The sermon then proclaims the Word drawing on this dialogue to contextualize the issues and share how the gospel is present both in the scripture and within the community of faith. Thus, the church becomes "a learning community where Christians share power and permit themselves to be instructed by one another's differences."[6]

In the sermon-dialogue-sermon process of preaching in the Purple Zone, this principle of representing the diversity of voices undergirds the sermon following the deliberative dialogue—what I call the Communal Prophetic Proclamation. It is *communal* because it arises not from the preacher's study exclusively but from the midst of the community within which the Word is proclaimed. It draws on and emerges from the process of dialogue that takes place within the community. It is *prophetic* because it expresses "unrelenting hope about God's activity to transform church and society in a present-future sense based on the principle of justice," to borrow from Kenyatta Gilbert.[7] Put another way, it addresses public and social concerns with an eye toward the biblical precepts of justice and righteousness. It is *proclamation* because it is a sermon that announces the Good News about God's purposes of integrity, freedom, compassion, reconciliation, joy, abundance, healing, and hope for the world.

Through the life, ministry, death, and resurrection of Jesus Christ and empowered by the Holy Spirit, this preaching forthrightly names the trouble of this world *and* invites hearers to envision God's transformation. Taken together, the Communal Prophetic Proclamation sermon helps listeners come to terms not just with the justice issue under consideration but with each other as a community and the quality of relationship to which God is calling us. As McClure puts it, "it implies that members of the community of the Word decide on ways to stand *with* and *for* one another by claiming tentative *directions* of thought and action as God's Word."[8]

McClure's idea that "all members of the community have an interpretive and proclamatory vocation" finds doctrinal footing in what Martin Luther called "the priesthood of all believers."[9] This doctrine asserts that because Christ gives access to God to all believers (rather than mediated through a priest), every Christian can do ministry within their own sphere of influence in whatever station of life they find themselves. When applied to the preaching ministry, the priesthood of all believers supports the notion that the experiences, insights, and discernment of the people in the congregation should be heard and incorporated into the sermon. When this happens, the church lives out its communal life of faith through an ongoing dialectic of reflection and proclamation.

McClure describes the process of roundtable preaching in this way:

> Leaders create roundtable conversations designed to provide opportunities for laity to interpret the gospel and make their voices heard in ways that can

have impact on the congregation's identity and mission . . . The preacher does not present sovereign declarations or the purposes and goals of the church from the pulpit . . . Instead the preacher collaborates with members of the congregation, galvanizing in the pulpit the actual talk through which the community, in response to the biblical message, is experiencing and producing its own congregational life and mission.[10]

Ronald Allen and O. Wesley Allen Jr. pick up on another of McClure's suggestions about harnessing the *asymmetry* in conversation to enhance the moral vision of the congregation. Asymmetry means that there are differences among the conversation partners, that they are not a homogenous group echoing each other's ideas. Allen and Allen assert that asymmetry is necessary for the ethics of a conversational sermon because it introduces outside ideas, pushes the participants to consider the "other," and holds them accountable to those others. Preachers, then, must not only utilize reciprocal listening to indicate the value of this asymmetry, but also "value and represent some degree of asymmetry *in* their sermons. They must find ways to represent a diversity of serious voices found in and around the congregation in their sermons so that hearers can engage a range of perspectives in considering the tentative proposal being offered by the preacher."[11]

Especially during this divisive time in our nation—or any time conflict threatens the foundations of a community or society—the preacher has a unique position and opportunity to model a dialogical approach to a contentious issue while also examining it through the lens of the gospel. What makes the difference in moving beyond either fear-based hesitancy or anger-based prophetic rhetoric are the stories, experiences, and values from within the congregation to which the preacher listens deeply. In his book *Preaching in the Era of Trump*, O. Wesley Allen Jr. reminds us that "preachers in a postmodern context . . . must find ways to offer to their congregations *experiences* of those events, stories, values, and ideas from which they hope the hearers will make meaning."[12] This chapter provides strategies and techniques to do just that.

REVIEWING THE SERMON-DIALOGUE-SERMON PROCESS TO THIS POINT

Let's review what you've done to this point. You preached a "rooting" sermon (or led an adult forum or Bible study) about the need for addressing issues of public concern in the church based on biblical and theological precedent. You chose a topic to address in your congregation and preached the Prophetic Invitation to Dialogue sermon encouraging listeners to take part in the deliberative dialogue forum. In that sermon you took a neutral position on the issue while still raising awareness about, and making a case for, why it should be engaged in your congregation. Then you held a deliberative dialogue in which participants wrestled with this issue in respectful and thoughtful ways.

In the dialogue, you introduced the topic, established ground rules for the discussion, and invited people to share why this issue was important to them or how they relate to it on a personal level. Then, the group deliberated about three possible approaches to the issue by weighing the pros and cons, after which you guided them to identify common themes and shared values that undergirded their discussion—even if there was disagreement about how those values could be actualized. Finally, the group discussed possible next steps to address the issue in their particular context given their shared values.

Now it's time to reflect on what you noticed, the insights you gained, and what you learned as you either facilitated, participated in, or observed the deliberative dialogue, depending on the role you had. What follows are questions to help you recollect and sift through what happened in that forum. Your answers to these questions will feed directly into your preparation for the follow-up sermon, the Communal Prophetic Proclamation.

QUESTIONS FOR REFLECTING ON THE DELIBERATIVE DIALOGUE

General Information about the Session

1. How many people attended?
2. How many men/women/people of other genders were present?
3. What was the age range of the participants? How many youth, young adults, middle-aged adults, and retirees were present?
4. What was the socioeconomic range of the participants?
5. What was the racial/ethnic spectrum of the group?
6. What do you guess to be the political affiliations of the participants? What percentage were conservative, moderate, progressive, or a mixture?

Content of Deliberative Dialogue Forum

7. In the opening section, when people shared how this issue affected them personally, what stories stood out to you?

8. How would you characterize the discussion? Was it relatively calm or intense? Were there moments of tension? If so, what were the points of contention?
9. After the group deliberated about the three options, what common themes and shared values did they identify? What passages, stories, or images from scripture align with these themes and values?
10. What ideas were suggested in the "next steps" section? Which ones seemed to generate the most energy? In what way might these ideas be the workings of the Holy Spirit within the group and/or the congregation?
11. Were there any "a-ha" moments of sharing within the group that shifted perspectives?
12. How did you feel when the forum was finished? What feedback did you receive from participants after it was over?
13. What did you learn about this group and/or the congregation from this deliberative dialogue?
14. What did you learn about yourself in this process?

Answering these questions will give you the basis for constructing the follow-up sermon. This is not to say that every answer to these questions will be included in your sermon in some way. Rather, these are for your use as you develop the form and content of your sermon. As you'll see in the sermon samples further on, the information and insights gained from taking these notes after the deliberative dialogue will give you the details, themes, focus, and direction your sermon needs.

In the Communal Prophetic Proclamation, you will help the congregation understand how the deliberative dialogue dovetails with the mission of the church, the ministry of Jesus, and the vision of reconciliation, wholeness, and hope that God is putting before the congregation. Using the dialogical lens for exegeting scripture, this sermon will biblically and theologically frame the prophetic word regarding this justice issue and offer an interpretation for how this process of communal discernment impacts the ongoing life and ministry of the church. At the same time, this sermon will show listeners that there are ways to be prophetic and engage issues of public concern that can be generative rather than mired in antagonism.

Shortly, we'll look at how to choose the biblical text that will provide the foundation for this sermon. But first, let's look at the key elements and basic characteristics of the Communal Prophetic Proclamation sermon.

CHARACTERISTICS, TONE, LANGUAGE, AND COMPONENTS OF COMMUNAL PROPHETIC PROCLAMATION

Characteristics of the Communal Prophetic Proclamation Sermon

Recall that in "Sermon #1, the Prophetic Invitation to Dialogue," the key was to show restraint when exercising the prophetic voice. Rather than making bold prophetic pronouncements, the goal was to outline the contours and complexities of the topic, make the case for the church to address it, and invite parishioners to participate in the deliberative dialogue. Now it's time to shift into a more prophetic mode—but with one caveat. In "Sermon #2, the Communal Prophetic Proclamation," *the preacher DOES NOT impose their position on the issue but raises up the prophetic discernment of the group from the dialogue.* In other words, this sermon continues with the premise that the strength of the preacher's prophetic words increases when it moves beyond their singular voice to include the voices of the people whom the pastor serves with and alongside.

This *communal* aspect of the prophetic sermon after the dialogue is especially important because the preacher is entrusted with being the sole communicator and interpreter of what was a group event. As McClure points out: "While the sermon remains a non-interactive, single-party communication event, *it is embedded within, and re-presents an actual interactive, multiple-party communication event (the sermon roundtable).* The sermon avoids being coercive or manipulative inasmuch as it is faithful to the collaboration and feedback that actually took place."[13] Thus, the sermon following the deliberative dialogue entails a responsibility to be true to the spirit of the dialogue and to those who participated in it, even while being responsive to the prophetic claim of the gospel upon us, our listeners, and the community. In the roundtable pulpit, this means that the preacher will

> sometimes permit sermons to travel in directions that the congregation wants to go instead of toward the preacher's preferred destination. The preacher may argue against this direction in the pulpit, establish the possibility of traveling on alternative pathways, or put new and important baggage on board the sermonic vehicle. Ultimately, however, the direction a sermon takes is determined collaboratively.[14]

The tone and the use of language in the Communal Prophetic Proclamation sermon are what communicate this prophetic collaboration experienced in the deliberative dialogue.

Tone of the Communal Prophetic Proclamation Sermon

The Communal Prophetic Proclamation exhibits a tone of what Dale Andrews has called "prophetic care."[15] Knowing how vital trust is to the preaching relationship with one's hearers and seeing that those bonds of trust were likely strengthened by facilitating or participating in the deliberative dialogue, it's important to stay the course in the follow-up sermon. Even if the justice issue stirs righteous anger within us (as well it might), we must be careful not to express that anger in such a way that the congregation feels it being directed at them personally. It may be the case that the attitudes and actions of some in the congregation contribute to the issue being a problem in the first place. Nevertheless, Tisdale warns, "If prophetic preaching is born out of thinly disguised anger at a congregation, out of frustration with a congregation, or out of a desire to appear loving so that the message will be heard and accepted, people will know it. We cannot fake love in the pulpit."[16]

It is this *agape*-love that must infuse itself into every aspect of our prophetic preaching. And, hopefully, that *agape*-love was modeled for you by the participants in the deliberative dialogue. Hearing each other's stories and struggles, coming to a deeper understanding of how a person came to their stance on an issue, and even seeing small shifts so that empathy and compassion can begin to arise—all of this contributes to having a heart (and one's sermon) powered by love.

In addition, the Communal Prophetic Proclamation sermon bears the responsibility of potentially leading others toward a future deliberative dialogue. This sermon carries the weight of both concluding the process and opening the way to another sermon-dialogue-sermon series in the future. Consequently, "if the message we bring is genuinely born out of love—a love regularly practiced for even the most recalcitrant of sinners—hearts may well be opened to the prophetic message of the gospel in ways we cannot even begin to imagine or anticipate."[17] How we communicate that love is directly dependent on the language we use in the sermon.

Language in the Communal Prophetic Proclamation Sermon

When describing the premise for using collaborative language in a sermon, McClure draws on what David J. Hesselgrave calls the "'rhetoric of listening,' a form of communication in which preachers listen to and follow hearers toward purposive but always changeable goals. This means that *the collaborative sermon must both describe and imitate in the pulpit the collaborative process.*"[18] McClure devotes an entire chapter to explaining what the language of the collaborative sermon sounds like. Adapted for the Communal Prophetic Proclamation sermon, we can say that this collaborative language

> will either *describe* the dynamic as it took place at the [deliberative dialogue] or it will *imitate* directly one of these dynamics. Imitation means that you repeat in the pulpit the same dynamic that took place in the [deliberative dialogue], perhaps using some of the same language, without actually telling the hearer that what you are saying has taken the form of the conversation that took place at the [dialogue].[19]

As an example, recall from chapter 6 that Laura Ferree engaged the topic of mental health in her first sermon. In her follow-up sermon after the deliberative dialogue she used *description*: "To begin the dialogue, we shared what stake we had in the conversation and why the conversation was meaningful to us. Stories were shared about personal struggles with mental health, family and friends who struggle with mental health, and noticing how mental health plays a role in our city's homelessness crisis."

If she had chosen instead to *imitate* the dynamic, she could have said, "As we sat in a circle for the dialogue, we heard the many ways mental health issues impact our lives. 'I struggle with depression.' 'My family member has been trying to manage mental illness for years.' 'When I volunteer at the homeless shelter, I encounter many people with mental health issues.'"

Without revealing any information shared in confidence, both description and imitation allow the congregation to experience the dialogue that produced the sermon. Consequently, they are indirectly included in the dialogue and become part of the ripple effect of the discussion. As McClure describes it:

> A congregation is a web of conversations. In order to focus these conversations on the gospel and the mission of the church, participants in these conversations can be included in an ongoing, core-conversation (the sermon roundtable), where the Word of God for the congregation is discerned. Sermons describe and imitate these core-conversations so that all may hear the variety of ways in which the congregation is coming to terms with the gospel of Jesus Christ. Collaborative preachers bring into the pulpit the actual "talk" through which the community articulates its identity and mission.[20]

Components of the Communal Prophetic Proclamation Sermon

Now that we've established the characteristics, tone, and language of the Communal Prophetic Proclamation sermon, it's time to look at the mechanics. There are three basic components that should be included in this sermon:

- **Reintroduce the topic addressed in the Prophetic Invitation to Dialogue and briefly explain what happened in the deliberative dialogue.** Even if parishioners heard Sermon #1, at least a week or two will have passed since then, so a review will be helpful. Also, those who are hearing about this for the first time will need to be oriented as to why the topic was chosen and be given some basic background about it. In summarizing the dialogue, you can draw on your notes from questions 1–6 above. One thing to emphasize is the diversity of the group in whatever way you noticed it. Establish that what you are saying in this sermon arises out of a multiplicity of demographic and political standpoints in order to establish credibility and authenticity for the sermon.
- **Share insights that emerged from the deliberative dialogue session about the topic.** Especially lift up the shared values that reflect the biblical witness (see question 9 above). It's important to interpret these values using a biblical and/or theological lens. How were Jesus' teachings and ministry reflected in the dialogue? In what way did you see the Holy Spirit at work amongst the participants in the discussion?
- **Recount what the group suggested as possible next steps.** This will be an opportunity to point out how God is working through the church in the midst of this difficult issue during this fractious time.

Note that the order in which these components are woven together in the sermon is up to the preacher and depends on the sermonic form chosen. We'll see different examples of sermons further on. In the meantime, let's discuss how to choose a biblical text for the foundation of the Communal Prophetic Proclamation sermon.

CHOOSING THE SCRIPTURE FOR THE FOLLOW-UP SERMON

A key difference between McClure's roundtable and the deliberative dialogue is, of course, the subject matter. In the roundtable conversation, the focus is on a specific biblical text, which can lead participants to make connections to contemporary issues or apply the text to particular modern-day situations. The deliberative dialogue, in contrast, focuses on a specific *topic* which participants may or may not connect directly to biblical passages or religious themes in the midst of the discussion. The "common values" section is the natural place for this to occur. But the issue guides are not written with a religious audience in mind, so it will be up to the preacher to help participants—and the sermon hearers—to make explicit connections to the church, the Bible, and the life of faith.[21] In the Communal Prophetic Proclamation, then, the preacher interprets the deliberative dialogue experience through a biblical and theological lens. This way the congregation understands how this topic and the process of dialogue are in concert with the faith and life of the church. So, how might a preacher go about choosing the biblical text for this sermon?

In chapter 5, we discussed the challenges of adhering to the Revised Common Lectionary for the sermon-dialogue-sermon process. While the texts may serendipitously align with the topic about which the sermons and dialogue will be addressing, it's not advisable to shoehorn a text to fit the issue just to make it work. Therefore, you may opt to preach topical sermons throughout this process.[22] However, if you decide to stay with the traditional lectionary, you may find that there are general themes within one of the texts assigned for the day that lend themselves to an idea you are lifting up in this sermon. For instance, one student had chosen climate change as his issue for the sermon-dialogue-sermon process, and it so happened that the Sunday when he preached the follow-up sermon, Psalm 23 was assigned for the day. The contrasting imagery of green pastures with the valley of the shadow of death served as an apt illustration for talking about the stark differences between what God intends for our planet and what humans have wrought.

Also, for those using the Narrative Lectionary or semi-continuous readings over a series of weeks, there may be an opportunity for having the sermon-dialogue-sermon process overlay nicely. As an example, Karleen Jung, a pastor in Kentucky, planned to read through the book of Ruth with her congregation over four weeks. She chose the topic of immigration for her deliberative dialogue because Ruth and Naomi's story is about immigrants, foreigners, and the challenges of communities integrating outsiders. By the time she came to the fourth week, she had completed the deliberative dialogue and was able to use the final chapter of Ruth as the scriptural basis for her Communal Prophetic Proclamation. (We'll learn more about Karleen's process in the final chapter.)

A third option is to wait to choose the text for the basis of the sermon until *after* the deliberative dialogue. That way you can follow the guidance of the Spirit—and the insights from those gathered—to settle on a scripture passage that best speaks to the topic and the message you want to convey. Of course, not all preachers have the option to wait to choose their texts, especially if they have musicians and choirs who need sufficient planning time and a set schedule for picking appropriate music. In any case, whether you have the flexibility to pick your text after the dialogue or are obligated to choose from among preset readings, you can use the following six rubrics to help you think about how you might engage scripture for this sermon. Some of these you'll recognize as adaptations of the dialogical lens introduced in chapter 4:

- **Themes and images.** What themes and/or images from the deliberative dialogue resonated with you, and what scripture passages, images, or stories do they bring to mind?
    - For instance, one of my students addressed the issue of hunger and chose Acts 4:32–35, the story of the first Christians sharing in generosity. The sermon emphasized that just as the Acts community demonstrated being bound together in faith, the dialogue group saw how those tethers of love provide the means of distributing resources.
- **Prophetic texts.** When thinking about the prophetic aspect of the justice issue your group addressed, what text might help frame a sermonic approach to the issue that draws on the discussion in the deliberative dialogue?
    - For example, one of my students preached a sermon about economic security and used Amos 5:18–24 to name the fear expressed by people who shared their experiences with economic hardship: "Like fleeing from a lion, only to be met by a bear" (v. 19). However, the preacher also proclaimed the intention of God to have "justice roll down like waters, and righteousness like an ever-flowing stream" (v. 24). The preacher went on to give concrete suggestions that people of faith could carry out to unblock that river and let God's righteousness flow.
- **Dialogical texts.** What passage from scripture comes to mind that models the kind of interchange you observed and experienced in the deliberative dialogue? In what ways do you see an exchange between author and audience, social and political forces, the passage and other portions of scripture, or the characters in the passage itself? What can we learn about God's intentions for us and our potential as God's people equipped for this interchange?
    - For example, one student's topic was health care, and he chose the parable of the seeds falling on good soil in Matthew 13:1–9. He pointed to the conversation between Jesus and the disciples as an example of the dialogical nature of the text and then connected this to the way in which the deliberative dialogue had yielded ideas "a hundred-fold" for helping seniors in his congregation and community connect with each other around how to navigate the complexities of medical care and insurance.

- **Mirroring values.** Thinking about the *values* that your group named in the dialogue, what biblical passages or stories ring a bell for you?
  - For example, if your topic was racism and a primary value was that of *equality*, Galatians 3:28 might be ideal ("There is no longer Jew or Greek, there is no longer slave or free . . ."). Similarly, as one of the sermon samples below demonstrates, a deliberative dialogue on the topic of mental health revealed that *accompaniment* for those facing mental illness was a primary value. Thus, the image of the Good Shepherd in John 10:11–18 illustrated this value and connected it to the guiding and accompanying love of Christ.

- **God at work.** As you consider God's interactions with God's people in scripture, how did you see God working in the midst of the dialogue?
  - In one of the examples below where the congregation addressed gender-based violence, the preacher chose the story from Exodus of Miriam and the women dancing and celebrating their freedom. The preacher emphasized God's intention to liberate people from violence, just as God liberated the Israelites from their violent enslavement in Egypt.

- **Faith in action.** This corresponds with the "next steps" phase of the deliberative dialogue and emphasizes how we might respond to God's invitation to engage public concerns. You might think of a biblical text in which the author, the characters in the story, or the people involved in the passage respond to the transformative love of God with concrete actions.
  - For instance, one pastor chose to address gun violence in the deliberative dialogue. The text she chose for the follow-up sermon was Matthew 5:43–48 in which Jesus instructs his followers to "Love your enemies and pray for those who persecute you" (v. 43). The preacher recounted specific suggestions made by the group to enact that kind of love, including offering more community events for youth, organizing volunteers to mentor troubled youth, and planning a future deliberative dialogue on mental health issues.

Whichever of these criteria you use for integrating the scripture with the deliberative dialogue, you'll find that utilizing the Five Paths of Prophetic Preaching will be helpful for thinking through how you might strategize this sermon. In this next section, we'll revisit those approaches.

RETURNING TO THE FIVE PATHS OF PROPHETIC PREACHING

Recall that in chapter 4, I introduced the Five Paths of Prophetic Preaching: rooting (in scripture and theology), flowering (raising awareness), pollinating (encouraging dialogue), leafing (suggesting specific action), and fruiting (transforming the culture for sustainable change). The Communal Prophetic Proclamation sermon can utilize any and all of these routes depending on the topic, the nature of the deliberative dialogue, the scriptural text, and the function of the sermon. Let's take each of these in turn, recognizing that the routes chosen or emphasized will depend upon the topic of the sermon and what you want it to accomplish.

- **Rooting.** The biblical principles and theological frameworks that undergird the topic are essential for this sermon. Not only will you point out the way the scriptural passage is in dialogue about the issue but you will note how dialogue is present within the text itself. You'll also highlight the shared values that reflect the biblical witness.
  - When preaching about the opioid issue, for example, I could choose Mark 1:21–28, the story of Jesus casting out a man's demons. I would point out the different voices and characters in the story—the people in the temple, including the priests, scribes, and Pharisees (though they are not named as such), the disciples, Jesus, and the man with the unclean spirit. I would frame addiction as being one of those "unclean spirits." Then, drawing from the shared values that were named during the dialogue, I would point to Jesus' model for how a community can confront and cast out those demons.
- **Flowering.** Given that most people in the congregation will already have some awareness about the issue under consideration either from hearing the Prophetic Invitation to Dialogue sermon or by participating in the deliberative dialogue, you won't need to spend too much time on this path. There are key elements from the dialogue, however, that can help to reintroduce the topic, or to introduce it in a different way. The opening section where people shared their "skin in the game" may provide you with stories or an illustration to help put a face on the issue. Of course, if you want to use a person's name or give telling details, you'll need to first ask permission of the person who shared their story. The other way to use the flowering approach is to put the three options in the dialogue in the form of questions.

○ For example, a sermon on the opioid crisis might say something like this: *Just this morning, we opened our newspaper to see yet another headline about the opioid crisis. Our state is among the top ten with the highest opioid-related overdose deaths. The rate of deaths here is nearly double the national average. Knowing that God cares about our minds, bodies, and spirits, how do we respond to this crisis as people of faith?*

Last week a group of people gathered in the fellowship hall to discuss this very question. We heard stories of people whose lives have been forever changed because of addiction to opioids, and we wrestled with different ways we might approach this complex problem. Should we focus on treatment for all and devote more resources for turning around the epidemic? Should we focus on enforcement and keep our communities safe by preventing people from becoming addicted in the first place? Or should we focus on individual choice and allow people to use drugs safely as long as they are not harming society or committing crimes?

- **Pollinating.** The Communal Prophetic Proclamation sermon will focus a great deal on this aspect of prophetic preaching. Whereas the first sermon invited people to the dialogue, this sermon will describe what it was like to have different voices in the deliberative dialogue together. Using the rhetorical techniques of *description* or *imitation* described above, you'll help listeners get a taste of the discussion. The preacher makes clear that this is what it looks like for faithful people to disagree while discerning how to be God's community in the world.

  ○ To make the dialogue aspect even more obvious, you may even consider asking two or three people who attended the dialogue to share what they heard and saw during the forum. This could be scripted with the individuals and the preacher, reader's theater style. Or you could carry it out "Donahue-style" with the pastor going into the congregation and giving the microphone to the individuals. Whatever format you choose, this aspect of the sermon emphasizes the dialogical aspect of the group's discernment about the issue. The pollinating aspect will also come to the fore when putting the issue in dialogue with the biblical text chosen for the sermon.

- **Leafing.** When you recount what the group suggested as possible next steps, this will be an opportunity to identify these ideas as evidence of God working through the church in the midst of this difficult issue during this fragmented time. These next steps fall under the leafing category because they encourage the listeners to take part in or support the actions suggested in the deliberative dialogue.

- ○ For example, if one of the next steps suggested in the dialogue about the opioid crisis was to start a support group for family members and friends of those dealing with addiction, the preacher might announce that there will be a brief meeting after church for those who are interested in such a group. Or if the suggestion was made to consider partnering with a local organization already working with people battling addictions, the preacher may announce that the church will host a forum to hear a speaker from the organization. Whatever is suggested, the key is to highlight this as evidence that the Spirit of God is already moving and working among us and through us in the midst of this complicated and divisive issue. In this way, people will see that the church is actively engaged in this prophetic work of justice to bring about the Realm of God.

- **Fruiting.** Remember that the fruiting aspect of prophetic preaching allows for sustained conversation over time that eventually begins to transform the lives of individuals and the culture of the church.

  - ○ The conclusion of the sermon might pull back for a wider view of where we started with this issue (wanting to avoid it for fear of causing conflict) to where we are now (willing to have conversation, being able to take part in a process of discernment, and potentially willing to take next steps to engage the issue concretely). In this way, the preacher points to the work of God as arising organically from within the community itself while being rooted in scripture and guided by the knowledge and experience of those taking part in the dialogue. The preacher might also invite further conversation for those whose interest is piqued after having heard about the process. In any case, this sermon helps to cultivate the slow-but-sure change away from either avoidance or divisiveness to one of engagement and communal discernment.

Above all, this sermon needs to name God's presence in this particular time and place regarding this particular issue. It should offer a compelling vision of what is possible, knowing what God intends for the community in terms of justice, healed relationships, and wholeness. This sermon points to the dialogue as a means of activating prophetic imagination and inviting us into God's intended future. This is done through what Dale Andrews calls "bridge building," an image we'll turn to in the final chapter.[23] On this bridge, our trust and hope in God's future causes us to act in a way that brings that future into existence today.

Let's look at two examples of how the Communal Prophetic Proclamation incorporates the deliberative dialogue into the sermon.

EXAMPLES OF COMMUNAL PROPHETIC PROCLAMATION SERMONS

Example 1: Mental Illness

Returning to Laura Ferree's sermon-dialogue-sermon process, recall that in her Prophetic Invitation to Dialogue sermon on mental illness, she forthrightly named that the church needs to address the issue and created space for people with different experiences to identify with the sermon and, thus, participate in the dialogue. At the deliberative dialogue that followed, twelve people attended ranging in age from early thirties to mid-seventies. The group consisted of white men and women occupying the middle- to upper-class range of the socioeconomic spectrum and leaning politically moderate to liberal. They discussed the pros and cons of the three approaches in the NIFI issue guide: (1) put safety first, (2) ensure mental health services are available to all who need them, (3) let people plot their own course. The robust conversation yielded many insights about the issue as well as ideas for how their congregation might take steps to address mental health in their community.

The Sunday for Laura's follow-up sermon happened to be Good Shepherd Sunday, so she chose to focus on the lectionary texts assigned for the day: Psalm 23, 1 John 3:16–24, and John 10:11–18. The cover of the bulletin for the worship service contained two images. One was a picture of Jesus as a shepherd carrying a lamb on his shoulders, protecting it from a wolf. The other image depicted Jesus carrying a person who was clearly in pain. She began her sermon by inviting folks to reflect on those images, asking them, "Where do you see yourself? What emotions do these images stir up for you? Do you identify with the lamb draped over Jesus' shoulders, or do you identify with Jesus carrying the person who is in pain?" In the sermon she made a connection between Jesus as the Good Shepherd and the need for the church to serve that role when it comes to people dealing with mental illness. Here are excerpts from the sermon with notes describing the mechanics and how she used the Five Paths of Prophetic Preaching.

Sermon Excerpt

> Here she reintroduces the topic of mental illness. You may notice that this is a deductive sermon, wherein she states her thesis at the outset of the sermon: that the church has a role to play regarding the issue of mental health.

About a month ago a group gathered to discuss Mental Health in America. We shared personal stories together. We brainstormed ways to advocate for those who struggle with mental health. And we recognized that the church has a role to play in advocating and supporting those who struggle with mental health.

> In this paragraph and the next, she weaves together both the "flowering" and "rooting" paths by raising awareness about the issue and connecting it immediately to the biblical image of the Good Shepherd.

To begin the dialogue, we shared what stake we had in the conversation and how this issue impacted each of us. Stories were shared about personal struggles with mental health, family and friends who struggle with mental health, and how mental health plays a role in our city's homelessness crisis. As I look at these images of Jesus as the good shepherd, I think about these stories. Maybe this person draped over Jesus' shoulders is struggling with mental health. Maybe you identify with that person. Or maybe you feel like Jesus carrying a person as you try to support a family member or friend who struggles with mental health.

People spoke about feeling concern, pain, hopelessness, and fear around this issue. Similar emotions are evoked by the Gospel this morning as we hear about the wolf that snatches up the sheep because the hired hand runs away in fear. I think that mental illness can often feel like a wolf prowling, and those struggling with mental health may feel like those sheep—abandoned and vulnerable while the wolf prowls and attacks every aspect of their life. How helpless and terrifying that must feel. The isolation can be unbearable.

> Here she utilizes the "pollinating" path by recounting the dialogue about the three options in the issue guide and some of the discussion about the complexity of the issue.

So, during this dialogue we looked at three possible approaches to noticing and assisting those with mental health issues. I experienced this as a meaningful discussion where the Spirit was clearly present. We recognized that many of the problems related to mental health can be connected to wider systemic issues such as access to medical care, family dynamics, and, for young people, bullying at school. We determined that we need better resources in our schools, as those are the places where many signs of mental health difficulties are initially displayed. But teachers often don't have the support or resources to recognize or help those students. Finally, there is always a stigma attached to mental health issues. Sometimes family members are in denial about their children's mental health, or as adults we don't want to be labeled as someone who struggles with mental health.

> Over these next three paragraphs, she follows the "leafing" path by asking how the church can act on the issue and sharing ideas suggested by the group.

With these reflections in mind, we talked about what we can do as a church. As we discussed ideas, I was reminded of the images from Psalm 23—God accompanying us in every aspect of life, from the green pastures and still waters, to the valleys of death and the onslaught of enemies. It raises the question—how can the church be God's shepherding presence when it comes to those who are struggling with mental health?

> Notice how this paragraph is simultaneously affirmational of the process, the diversity of ideas, and the group's capacity for response.

I was impressed with the way the Spirit inspired us with different ideas and willingness to serve. We dreamed about supporting the school across the street by being lunch buddies or simply giving a space for students to feel noticed. We discussed organizing to send letters to city council, school boards, and the state to make them aware that mental health issues are a growing concern that cannot continue to go unnoticed. The energy in the room was amazing and this group wanted to harness that energy for action and change. Even more, there was enthusiasm for having more of these kinds of dialogues to discuss other issues and create action plans. I was truly inspired by this dialogue.

The reading from 1 John says, "Little children, let us love, not in word and speech, but in truth and action." I believe this is exactly what our dialogue group was doing. They were taking time out of their busy Sunday to discuss a growing crisis in our nation and they were willing to respond beyond word and speech and move into truth and action. We have heard a lot recently about how we need to move beyond thoughts and prayers into policy and change. Honestly, for a while this idea challenged me because I know that our thoughts and prayers are extremely important. But the more I reflected on it the more I realized that our thoughts and prayers—our words and speech—should guide our actions to bring about change. We aren't called to simply sit in our seats and notice from inside the church. We are called in 1 John to go beyond ourselves and take action! We are a church that follows the Good Shepherd, and I can already see how God's presence is leading and guiding us.

> Her conclusion is one of "fruiting" in that she casts the vision of the church as being part of the Good Shepherd's mission and what it means to enact God's love.

Whether you identify with Jesus or the person being carried in these images, know that we have a Good Shepherd who guides us. A Good Shepherd who notices the forgotten sheep. A Good Shepherd who carries us out of harm's way and away from the wolf. A Good Shepherd who teaches us how to be love in the world. We are growing into the love that the Good Shepherd has taught us. We are enacting God's love in the world, proclaiming that no wolf is strong enough to snatch us from the loving embrace of the Good Shepherd. As the church, we can do the work of the Good Shepherd by our words and love as we live out God's truth and action in the world.[24]

Example 2: Gender-Based Violence

One of the pastors I trained in the sermon-dialogue-sermon method, Colleen Bookter, serves a congregation in Louisiana and chose the topic of gender-based violence to address in her sermon-dialogue-sermon process. For her Prophetic Invitation to Dialogue, she chose to preach on Exodus 1:15–2:10, the story of the midwives sparing the Hebrew baby boys and Pharaoh's daughter saving baby Moses from a violent death. She connected this story to the reality of abuse and violent deaths that continue to happen in our own time. She then invited listeners to follow the model of the midwives and Pharaoh's daughter who talked with each other in order to solve a problem. By engaging in a deliberative dialogue about gender-based violence, they, too could discuss how the church might address this issue and take steps to prevent it.

Eight people attended the deliberative dialogue—men and women ranging from young adults to retirees, all white and mid- to upper-middle-class, including those with both conservative and progressive political orientations. Colleen was surprised at the willingness of participants to share personal experiences with abuse situations right from the beginning of the dialogue. Their rich conversation highlighted several shared values and resulted in concrete suggestions for how the church might take action on this issue, which are evident in her sermon below.

This follow-up sermon was based on the story of Miriam leading the women in song after crossing the Red Sea (Exodus 15:1–12, 18–21). She begins the sermon by briefly recounting Miriam's story and how she was part of the efforts to end violence against her people. She then weaves in the experience of the dialogue throughout the sermon. In this excerpt, I've noted how the Five Paths of Prophetic Preaching are employed.

Sermon Excerpt

Colleen leads by asking the question that begins to connect the scripture passage to the contemporary issue of gender-based violence, thus starting on the "flowering" path.	I wonder what Miriam's song means for us today? How is her voice calling out to us? In what way can the singing and dancing of these women give us a framework to think about the experience of liberation from violence for

women and other vulnerable people in our own time?

Last month when I preached, our text challenged us to think about gender-based violence. It was that text that started the dialogue about what the Christian response to sexual and domestic violence should be. A few days after that sermon, a group of people gathered to talk about this issue. In this group, we had a variety of people—men and women; conservative, moderate, and liberal; college students, working adults, and retirees. Some with personal experience with sexual or domestic violence, some just wanting to create a world without such problems.

> Notice how she points out the diverse range of experiences, ages, political views, and walks of life of the dialogue participants, invoking the "pollinating" path.

As each person shared their stories and thoughts about gender-based violence, I couldn't help but think about Miriam and the women who had watched their own people suffer violence for generations. This biblical saga reminds us that violence is a very old problem that goes back to biblical times.

> With just a few sentences, she deftly connects back to the biblical story, thus using the "rooting" path.

In our conversation, instead of focusing on our differences in political ideology, we focused on three key ideas of how we might tackle this issue. First, through education. Second, through direct action to survivors. And third, through advocacy, reaching out to legislators. For each of these responses, we talked about the pros and cons, the advantages and drawbacks to each approach. We didn't solve the problem at hand, but we did have a fruitful conversation where we thoughtfully looked at ways we can respond to gender-based violence.

> Here and in the next paragraph the "pollinating" path is clear as she describes the dialogue and points out the common values identified by the group.

As you can imagine, all of us around the table didn't agree on everything. Discussions around domestic violence and sexual abuse can be both difficult and controversial. But as a people of faith, we knew we were called to put our political divisions aside and focus on how we can respond as Christians. Once we did that, we identified many shared values. Our group valued human life, preventing abuse, addressing violence, and saving lives. We valued the desire to be a witness in support of those affected by this problem. We were committed to raising awareness and providing education around gender-based violence. And we valued the desire to respond to domestic and sexual violence in a unified manner.

Some of us were passionate about finding ways to prevent the more horrendous acts like rape and physical violence that threaten people's lives. Others were interested in starting with subtler actions—such as getting at the root of micro-aggressions that are part of the larger problem of violence.

> In this paragraph we see some "leafing"—lifting up suggestions for addressing the problem of gender-based violence.

Just as the Israelites began to wonder what life outside of slavery and oppression might be like, together around the table we all began to wonder what it might be like for women today to be free? To be unafraid? To dance! To sing! To celebrate who they are as children of God. And to do so without fear.

> In this next section, she not only roots the sermon again to the biblical story but also asks prophetic questions that will set up the prophetic response that follows.

What might it be like for us to raise children in a world where we aren't fearful of them becoming victims of domestic violence or sexual abuse?

What might it be like for people today to take out their tambourines and to sing praises to the Lord knowing that the world was a little safer?

Around that table, we all agreed that it is essential that the Church respond and speak because too often in the past, religious traditions have been used to defend abusive patriarchy. To bind victims to marriage commitments that are undermined by intimate violence. To exhort people to "offer up" suffering as a kind of sacrifice rather than change the conditions that cause it.

> Here she speaks a profoundly prophetic word—but notice how she frames it. The exhortation comes from "we," and is not just her own pronouncement.

We must speak because the value of human life compels us. We speak because if we keep silent, if we ignore the human cost and spiritual degradation of domestic violence, then we are failing the people we are called to serve.

We speak because when we do, we can help transform the world, healing the wounds we see before us, and bringing us closer to the kind of place God intended for us to live in.

> Building on the communal discernment, the conclusion of the sermon boldly proclaims a vision of the church speaking up and speaking out on the issue of gender-based violence. And she does it in a way that frames it within the biblical story while also emphasizing the possibility of transformation. Thus, "fruiting" is the final path of this sermon.

We speak because we follow a Christ who liberates, so that one day, all God's children can grab their tambourines and join Miriam and the women in singing their song of liberation.[25]

NAMING *WHO THE CHURCH IS* IN COMMUNAL PROPHETIC PROCLAMATION

As we can see from these two sermons, "collaborative preaching respects differences as well as similarities in relationships. It generates a more participative, communal process of prophetic discernment in a congregation."[26] Communal Prophetic Proclamation in the Purple Zone is one way for preachers to tap into the social context of their congregations and, together with their parishioners, develop a prophetic voice. As O. Wesley Allen reminds us:

> Instead of preachers calling the church to become *who we ought to be* (ethically speaking), we should name *who the church is* (theologically speaking). We should speak of mission, reminding hearers that mission is who we are (instead of who we ought to be). People will want to live up to that which defines them. Their heads will be raised (meeting the preacher's eyes) with a sense of pride and purpose, saying, "You know, that *is* who we are! Let's get moving."[27]

In the next two chapters, we'll look at several case studies of preachers naming who the church is and calling, leading, and inspiring their hearers to live into that mission. Let's get moving!

• 9 •

Case Studies from the Purple Zone, Part 1

Immigration

HOW TO HANDLE THE "ELEPHANT IN THE SANCTUARY"

When it comes to addressing controversial justice issues in the pulpit, O. Wesley Allen describes the challenge of how to deal with the "elephant in the nave (and the chancel?)." On the one hand, preachers are tempted to either avoid it "and hope it will continue residing in our midst without doing too much damage. We are tempted to preach spirituality, self-help messages, and a gospel of individual grace. We are tempted to soothe our consciences by saying the pulpit is not a bully pulpit, and proclamation and politics have nothing to do with one another."[1] On the other hand, we're tempted to forge ahead as if doing battle. "We are tempted to don the mantle of the angry prophet, speaking truth to power regardless of the consequences."[2]

Yet, as Allen insists (and hopefully this book has made clear thus far): "When we step into the pulpit, our job is not simply to proclaim the gospel but to get the gospel heard—to get it heard so that it might be believed and lived. Neither ignoring the elephant in the sanctuary nor verbally berating it will accomplish this."[3] As we've seen in the preceding chapters, the sermon-dialogue-sermon method is one model for discerning the gospel and its proclamation in, with, and among the members of the church. In other words, prophetic preaching both informs and is informed by the process of dialogue with the congregation and community. By helping our listeners understand and accept that addressing social issues is both biblically and theologically authorized, and by showing them a way of engaging these issues in the spirit of dialogical hospitality, we can come to deeper relationships based on listening and compassion. This, in turn, allows the life- and world-changing love of God in Jesus Christ to transform our hearts and congregations from the inside out rather than from the top down. Ideally, this process can serve as a healing "balm of Gilead" to soothe the sin-sick soul of a person, a congregation, a community, and even a nation.

"THREADING THE NEEDLE"

Such an endeavor is, of course, no easy task. Preaching in the Purple Zone requires planning, patience, and building the skills of facilitating dialogue. It also involves trying a different approach to prophetic sermons than what we may be used to or trained in seminary to do. An image that has stuck with me is one described by one of my students, Branden Hunt, who preached a sermon introducing the topic of immigration. After the sermon, he was approached by a parishioner who said, "You did well in threading the needle with that sermon."

The parishioner recognized that Branden was working within a tight space politically (the congregation was a mix of conservatives, moderates, and progressives), and managed to find a way through homiletically. Preaching from the lectionary, Branden used the story in Matthew 22:15–22 about the Pharisees and Sadducees trying to trap Jesus with a question about paying taxes. He explained that just as Jesus could not be trapped by what seemed to be only two sides of the coin (pay the tax or not—either way is a no-win situation), so the issue of immigration has more than two sides. There is more to the complexity of immigration than the zero-sum game of, say, building a wall versus letting in all immigrants indiscriminately. Branden then issued the invitation to his listeners to engage in deliberative dialogue about immigration following the service to explore that complexity from a faith perspective.

Immigration, it turns out, was the topic most often chosen by the students and pastors I have trained in the Purple Zone over the last year, from June 2017 through August 2018. A third of them picked immigration to address with their congregations, attesting to the priority of this issue for many clergy and churches, as well as for our nation as a whole. The popularity of this topic is also not surprising given the high ranking it received in the survey I conducted in which I asked pastors to indicate what issues they planned to address in the coming months. Immigration ranked third, after economic and racial issues.

With the exception of one student who developed her own materials, the preachers I trained all used the NIFI issue guide, "Coming to America: Who Should We Welcome, What Should We Do?" Within this guide, the three options for approaching the issue of immigration are:

Option 1: Welcome Immigrants, Be a Beacon of Freedom
This option says that immigration has helped make America what it is today—a dynamic and diverse culture, an engine of the global economy, and a beacon of freedom around the world.

Option 2: Enforce the Law, Be Fair to Those Who Follow the Rules
This option says we need a fair system, where the rules are clear and, above all, enforced. With an estimated 11 million people living in the country illegally, our current system is unjust and uncontrolled.

Option 3: Slow Down and Rebuild Our Common Bonds
This option recognizes that newcomers have strengthened American culture in the past. But the current levels of immigration are so high, and the country is now so diverse, that we must regain our sense of national purpose and identity.

One of the reasons students chose this topic is because of the faith-based moderator guide available for this particular issue. Gregg Kaufman (whom we met in chapter 7) developed the guide to enable faith communities to more easily use religious framing to discuss the topic of immigration in a way that connects to their values as informed by scripture and religious teachings. The moderator guide includes background information about the history of religious organizations' involvement with resettling refugees and helping immigrants become integrated into American society and congregations. The opening includes questions that directly relate to the experiences of the local faith community:

- How might we discern God's will for our Jewish, Muslim, and Christian faith communities regarding the needs of immigrants, refugees, and undocumented immigrants?
- What makes this issue "real" for you and your faith community?

Then for each of the options there is supplemental information about the way faith communities have engaged each approach based on their public statements and humanitarian work. There are also faith-based questions for each option, such as:

- What does your faith tradition say about welcoming the stranger? Are there sacred texts that might inform your deliberation?
- How might this option offer opportunities or tensions relative to religious organizations' immigration ministries?

144   *Preaching in the Purple Zone*

In this chapter, we're going to see how several pastors approached this one issue. You'll see the variety of ways in which they used scripture, the content of their deliberative dialogue forums, and the contexts of their local communities to inform both the form and content of their sermons.

CASE #1: STRUGGLING IN THE WILDERNESS

Background

Dan Gutman served as a student intern at a congregation in Ohio with over one thousand mostly middle-class members. He described the political orientation of the city in which the congregation was located as far-right conservative but noted that their congregation had more moderates than most churches in the area, along with a few progressives "who mostly lie low and keep quiet." The congregation was racially white, but the community had a rapidly growing population of immigrants from the Marshall Islands.[4] Thus, he chose immigration as his issue to address in the sermon-dialogue-sermon process.

Prophetic Invitation to Dialogue Sermon

Dan's Prophetic Invitation to Dialogue sermon focused on Numbers 21:4–9, the story of the Israelites grumbling against Moses while wandering in the wilderness, the result of which was poisonous snakes biting them as divine punishment. After setting the scene by recounting the story of their escape from Egypt and their desperation for food as they wandered in the wilderness, Dan pivoted to a modern-day example of immigrants crossing through the wilderness.

Sermon Excerpt

> In this paragraph and the next, Dan's "flowering" path fuses with the "pollinating" path in that the way he raises awareness about the issue of immigration is by highlighting the different angles and questions people bring to this topic.

Of course, we can't talk about the Israelites in the wilderness without thinking about people in our own time who are, literally, migrating through a wilderness. I'm talking about the issue of immigration. And the parallels are uncanny, aren't they? Here's a group of people leaving behind everything they know for a chance at a better life, a life of freedom, prosperity, and hope. The Psalm for today talks about God gathering in people from every direction. Elsewhere in the Bible we hear about God's commands to love and welcome the stranger, the foreigner, and the alien. Even with this biblical story as our background for this modern-day dilemma, however, when the church asks the question, "What should our response as Christians be to the issue of immigration?" the answer isn't so clear.

What about when that person has come here without following the proper protocol? What if they're here without documentation but were brought here as a child? What if they have the proper documentation but they're taking a job that could have gone to someone else? Or what if they're taking the jobs no one else wants, providing the cheap and necessary labor needed to keep food prices low for struggling families? What about if they intend to do harm? What about fears about immigrants based on harmful stereotypes? What if some immigrants are bringing drugs into our communities? What if some are trying to escape a country corrupted by drugs and drug lords and gang violence?

> In these next three paragraphs, Dan "roots" the question of immigration in the way in which people talk about the topic. Thus, he frames a prophetic critique of the current state of discourse within a biblical context.

The questions are overwhelming, aren't they? In fact, as a society struggling with the issues of immigration we now find ourselves in a wilderness of uncertainty. And just like those Israelites, we've gotten a bit impatient, grumbling in that wilderness. We start pointing fingers, complaining about the other side, distrusting each other, and dramatically proclaiming, "What are you trying to do, kill us?!" Of course, the reality is that there are lives at stake. Innocent people get hurt while we bicker back and forth.

For the Israelites, the consequence for them was death. Suddenly, poisonous snakes came upon their community and started biting people. Only when people began dying did they recognize their sin. The problem wasn't their objection to starving to death in the wilderness; it wasn't their concern for themselves and the ones they loved. It was the way they went about it. Instead of having an open and direct conversation with God and Moses and each other, they spoke behind each other's backs, grumbling, complaining, and speaking against one another and God. That was their sin.

Doesn't this sound an awful lot like how we handle the issue of immigration? That same poison of contention and backbiting has crept into our communities. Haven't we lived in the consequences of our sin long enough? Haven't we had enough of all of the grumbling and complaining, the blaming and infighting? Isn't it about time to invite God into the conversation?

> "Leafing" takes the form of an invitation to the deliberative dialogue. Notice how he uses a theological framework for this invitation.

Here's the good news. First, we're going to have the opportunity this afternoon to do just that together—invite God into our conversation by engaging in a deliberative dialogue about immigration. It's going to be an open, honest, and direct conversation exploring three possible approaches and our common values, so we can begin discerning what a faithful response might be from this community. I hope you'll be able to join us for that.

> Dan makes a strong prophetic exhortation in these next two paragraphs while also proclaiming the gospel.

But here's the better news. After all the grumbling and fighting, God didn't abandon the Israelites. God told Moses to lift up a poisonous serpent on a pole so that anyone who had been bitten could look at it and be saved. In other words—face this issue head on. Stop lurking around like snakes in the sand. Engage with one another in direct, healthy, constructive ways.

God doesn't abandon *us* either. Instead, the gospel lesson today tells us that God, in the incarnation of Jesus Christ, has been lifted up on a cross, and we who have been bitten by the poison of sin can look to him and be saved. No longer condemned by our past, but invited into the light, into a better way of being in community together. . . .

> In these concluding paragraphs, Dan brings in the Gospel reading of the day, which further supports the "pollinating" path, highlighting the dialogical aspect of the passage about Jesus and Nicodemus. He also reminds the congregation of God's redemption and Christ's love and light promised to them as they undertake the dialogue.

Did you notice—this whole passage in the gospel [John 3:11–21] happens in the midst of a conversation, a dialogue with Nicodemus? Nicodemus comes to Jesus secretly, under cover of night, slithering like a snake trying to be unseen. But Jesus challenges him to be forthright, to ask his questions directly and openly. He says, "For all who do evil hate the light and do not come to the light, so that their deeds may not be exposed. But those who do what is true come to the light, so that it may be clearly seen that their deeds have been done in God."

Jesus is inviting us into the light. Our dialogue about important and difficult issues is one we can have openly, in full confidence that the Holy Spirit will be our guide and will help us discern together how to be the church in the midst of this issue of immigration. We are not left alone in the poisonous darkness of our sin but are invited out in the open, redeemed by God, and into the love and light of Christ. That's the hope we carry with us as we do our best to work out these difficult topics together. We do this in faith, in hope, in Christ.[5]

Deliberative Dialogue on Immigration

Dan's deliberative dialogue forum drew thirty people—many more than he had anticipated. He decided to break them up into three smaller groups, counting off by threes. This was a good move on his part because it shuffled the participants and allowed for more diversity of thought and insights. He also chose to use the faith-based moderator guide developed by Gregg Kaufman which turned out to be helpful in terms of moving people out of their preconceived political ideals and into perspectives informed by their religious values. After deliberating about the three options, the groups rejoined to discuss the values they had in common. Things like *understanding, respect for the law, morality,* and *love* were named. But the theme that kept recurring was that of *personhood*. This led some in the group to take the initiative to follow through with the action items discussed in the "next steps" portion of the forum, including reaching out to their denominational office on immigration and refugees, and developing a list of local resources for assisting immigrants. To see how Dan developed all of this in his excellent Communal Prophetic Proclamation sermon, visit https://www.thepurplezone.net.

CASE #2: TELLING THEIR STORIES

Background

Jenny Perkins was a student pastor at her small church in a large Texas city when she chose the immigration issue for her sermon-dialogue-sermon process. The congregation was progressive and had a history of social justice activism. Due to their proximity to the border with Mexico, her congregation's community was right in the thick of the controversy over how best to handle the waves of refugees and immigrants crossing into the United States. While Jenny's church had already committed to being part of the sanctuary church movement, they were trying to decide what that meant for them. There are many levels of involvement possible for congregations ranging from organizing vigils and marches, to training immigration advocates, to sheltering an immigrant individual or family facing deportation.[6] Jenny's hope was that the congregation would consider the latter option and open their doors to receive and protect immigrants. The deliberative dialogue she facilitated, however, challenged her assumptions and made her rethink their options for addressing this issue.

Prophetic Invitation to Dialogue

Jenny did something unusual in her choice of biblical texts. For both of her sermons, she preached on Mark 10:46–52, the story of Jesus healing the blind beggar named Bartimaeus. This decision to preach from the same text twice was not her intention at the outset but rather arose after the dialogue and her reflection about it. In her Prophetic Invitation to Dialogue sermon titled, "Their Stories, Bartimaeus' Story, Our Story," she focused on what it means to listen to those we seek to serve. After the deliberative dialogue, she realized that the same text provided a key interpretative frame, but from a different angle.

For her first sermon, she projected on a screen the artwork of three different women being held at a nearby detention center while she read the desperate stories of each one. Through a volunteer art and writing project run by a local chaplain, the stories and images made by the women helped them to find their voices and share their heartbreaking experiences of violence and extreme poverty in their homelands. They tell of children threatened by gangs, harrowing journeys through mountains and deserts, and longing for peace and safety.

Jenny then pivoted to the story of Bartimaeus and his own desperate cries for healing which were met with orders from the crowd and disciples to be silent. But Jesus instead silences the crowd and asks the powerful—and empowering—question: "What do you want me to do for you?" The question gives the man agency over his own life and healing. Jenny connected this to her congregation's discernment process about what it means for them to be a "sanctuary church." She made the case that just as Jesus listened to Bartimaeus and gave him a chance to speak, so, too, did they need to speak and listen to each other, explaining that they would have an opportunity to do this in the deliberative dialogue. Ideally, this dialogue would lead them to listen to immigrants in their community, thus giving them agency in their own lives. And for the church, the dialogue could provide discernment on how to live into their identity as a sanctuary church.

Deliberative Dialogue on Immigration

Jenny's congregation already knew they wanted to be welcoming to immigrants and refugees. What they didn't fully understand for themselves was what being a "sanctuary church" meant for their church. So she developed a discussion guide with three options: 1) Educate the community on immigration issues; 2) Direct action for immigrants; and 3) Advocacy on behalf of immigrants and refugees. Jenny admitted in class that she hoped the dialogue would lead the congregation to begin planning how they might shelter an undocumented individual or family. However, the dialogue showed her that this is not where the church's discernment was heading.

About twenty-five people (mostly white) attended the forum ranging in age from their forties to their mid-seventies. As they weighed the pros and cons of the three options, several common values emerged, including *witnessing to our faith, helping those in need, building community,* and *using resources wisely*.

But the one that stood out was that of *safety*. Several members expressed anxiety about advocacy and activism because of concerns about their safety and that of the congregation. Some of the individuals in the congregation were themselves socially targeted because of gender-identity issues and did not feel comfortable with the idea of the church taking on an activist role and bringing public attention to itself in that way.

Jenny listened deeply to these concerns, along with the still fervent desire of the group to do what they could to help immigrants and refugees. The energy from the group coalesced around education—educating themselves and the community about immigration and refugee issues. Upon reflection, she realized that if they hadn't had this dialogue, she might have pushed the congregation in a direction they were not ready to go. While she was a bit disappointed that her vision for the congregation being a sanctuary church did not materialize in the way she had hoped, it so happened that another opportunity presented itself that aligned with the values of the group and the goal of education.

Communal Prophetic Proclamation

In her follow-up sermon, Jenny reminded the listeners of the story of Bartimaeus being heard by Jesus and gaining his sight. She then referenced the theory by liturgical scholar Gordon Lathrop that Bartimaeus appears again in the Gospel of Mark—as the young man who witnessed Jesus' resurrection.[7] As she recounted the experience of the deliberative dialogue, she framed it as a "Bartimaeus' experience," where each person's voice was heard, and they were able to see more clearly what a "resurrection ministry" might look like for their congregation as they considered their options for engaging in the sanctuary church movement.

At the end, she shared that after the deliberative dialogue, she received an email that the artwork she had shown in the first sermon was being turned into a travelling art exhibit. The organizers were looking for churches to display the artwork in their building for a month and host a community event to promote the art and stories of the immigrants being held in detention centers. So the council voted to approve a month-long exhibition of the work and to host a community event about the art. This action aligned with their goal of education and with their values of community, living out their faith, raising awareness about the plights of refugees and immigrants, and wisely managing their resources without risk to anyone's safety.

For Jenny, this was a "Bartimaeus moment." While she had to let go of the hope for the church to shelter an immigrant or refugee, her eyes were opened to the church's mission and ministry finding new life and purpose in hosting the immigration art exhibit. Recall from the previous chapter John McClure's statement that a preacher using a collaborative approach will "sometimes permit sermons to travel in directions that the congregation wants to go instead of toward the preacher's preferred destination."[8] This was precisely Jenny's approach to the sermon-dialogue-sermon process, and it yielded a sermon that spoke authentically to the congregation's discernment for witnessing and acting on their faith and values regarding the issue of immigration.

CASE #3: LIGHT THROUGH A MOSAIC OF STAINED GLASS

Background

Lucas McSurley described the Ohio church in which he served as a seminary intern as a "liberal bubble" surrounded by a strongly conservative community. He estimated the political spectrum of his congregation to be 70 percent liberal, 25 percent moderate, and 5 percent conservative. The church even "nested" a Hispanic immigrant congregation, a commitment that appeared to be in alignment with their progressive values. However, Lucas perceived the congregation as being unusually silent after the election of Donald Trump when arrests of undocumented immigrants rose and separations of families increased. While there were pockets of folks, including the senior pastor, who spoke out, the church as a whole did not come to the aid or defense of the targeted individuals. Since that time, the leadership of the congregation had worked to repair the trust that had been damaged with the immigrant community. Lucas saw potential for a deliberative dialogue on immigration to contribute to the mending process. When he shared with the church leadership about his idea for the deliberative dialogue, they together reached out to the Hispanic congregation to invite their members to attend the forum. The dialogue and resulting sermon were profoundly shaped by having their voices at the "roundtable pulpit."

Prophetic Invitation to Dialogue

For his first sermon, Lucas chose the story of the call of Samuel in 1 Samuel 3:1–21. He highlighted the dialogical nature of the text—God calling to Samuel; Samuel and Eli conversing about the strange voice in the night; Samuel listening first to Eli and then to God. While the message God had for Eli and his household was not a welcomed one, it was a necessary corrective.

Lucas then pointed out that just as this holy dialogue raised many questions for Samuel, Eli, and the whole community, so does God's invitation to address the issue of immigration raise many questions regarding the tension between unity and diversity, human dignity and personal safety, economic opportunity and exploitation. He invited the church to the dialogue to participate in God's intention of transformation:

> Take notice of God's action in this story. Nothing that Samuel did prompted God to speak to him. God initiated, and God spoke to Samuel—just as God comes to each one of us. God spoke to Samuel with the intention of transforming the entire system that was under Eli. God shows up, and then God transforms.[9]

Deliberative Dialogue on Immigration

Lucas intentionally reached out to the Hispanic congregation nesting in his church to invite them to this dialogue. That alone communicated care and concern and showed that he honored who they are and what they could contribute to the dialogue. Of the fourteen people who attended the session, four of them were from the Hispanic church, which added an important perspective to the discussion. For example, when it came to listing the common values, those who represented the Hispanic community said that their goal was *cooperation*. In contrast, the participants from the white church named the goal of *inclusion*, expressing a heartfelt desire to engage people from different races and backgrounds.

The "next steps" part of the dialogue yielded particularly fruitful results. The group suggested specific ideas for helping the Hispanic congregation feel more welcomed in the space, including signage throughout the church *in Spanish*. "Once this idea was on the table," Lucas said, "we were dumbfounded that this hadn't been done already!" The dialogue also birthed a joint Three Kings celebration the following January where the two communities shared a meal, played games, and continued building relationships. Reflecting on the dialogue, Lucas said, "This process opened the door for trust and it made a huge stride in rekindling the energy that these two communities had when the Hispanic community was first invited to share the space."

Communal Prophetic Proclamation

For his follow-up sermon, Lucas worked with Isaiah 9:1–7, particularly the verse, "The people who walked in darkness have seen a great light; those who lived in a land of deep darkness—on them light has shined" (v. 2). He began by describing a time he saw a beautiful stained-glass window in a cathedral and the way the morning sun filtered through the shards of glass, filling the church with color and light. He used this image to describe the deliberative dialogue experience with members of the two congregations.

> We gathered to have a dialogue about the complexities of immigration in this country, and to weigh the pros and cons of different approaches to this issue. What a gift it was to have members of the Hispanic congregation with us. We learned a lot about each other. We spoke about the need for education, to teach one another about our culture, history, and traditions. The more we spoke about our faith and families, the more we began to notice the beauty within each of us. Take a look at the stained glass right here in our own church this morning. Notice how each piece is different in size and shape, yet all the pieces come together to make one awe-striking image. We, too, are more beautiful when we come together.[10]

Lucas then framed the metaphor of the stained glass theologically, explaining that "God is the ultimate source of light, lighting not only our church, but the entire world around us. As Christians, we are called to be stained glass, to show how the light can shine into our community of faith." He also emphasized that no stained-glass window is made of just one color or with the same sizes and shapes of glass. Likewise, if certain people are excluded, the stained-glass window will be missing pieces and fail to be as beautiful as God intends it to be. "God shows up, and a masterpiece is created with all of our differences." He then shared the different ideas for cooperation in ministry between the two congregations, including the ideas for new signs, joining in the Three Kings festival, as well as jointly addressing the issue of homelessness in their county.

Toward the end of the sermon, he offered a bold prophetic claim—that hosting the Hispanic church was not an act of charity. "No, this community is at the very core of who we are. They are the center piece of God's stained-glass window."

CASE #4: BRIDGING AND SHEPHERDING IN A BILINGUAL CONTEXT

Background

Ian McMichael served as a student intern at a congregation in a southern state that consisted of a home church and a satellite mission that ministered to Spanish-speaking immigrants. Fluent in Spanish, Ian spent the majority of his time in the satellite congregation and chose to address the topic of immigration since a substantial number of the congregation were undocumented residents. But not all of those who attended the church were Spanish-speaking. Some were English-speaking whites as well, which created interesting dynamics among the parishioners. The congregation was also mixed in terms of its politics. Not only were there different people in the congregation holding differing political perspectives but, within their own political stances, some were conservative on certain issues and more progressive on others.

Prophetic Invitation to Dialogue

With these dynamics in mind, Ian designed his first sermon around the image of Jesus as "bridge-builder." His scriptural text was Hebrews 5:5–10 which refers to Christ as a "high priest." He pointed out that the Latin word for priest is *pontifex*, literally "bridge builder," and contrasted Jesus' ministry of building bridges to that of the divisive language and politics today that focus on building walls and keeping people separate from each other. In this sermon excerpt, you can see how Ian preaches first in English then in Spanish (thus building bridges between the two languages as well):

> Instead of building walls and dividing, Jesus builds real and tangible bridges to bring God's people together as the community of Christ. In the actions of Christ, we see that everyone has value. It doesn't matter if you don't speak English, or if you just came to this country, or what color your skin is. Everyone in this world has value. Everyone in this *church* has value.
>
> *En vez de hacer muros y dividir, Jesús creó maneras reales y tangibles para unir a la gente de Dios en la comunidad de Cristo. En las acciones de Cristo vemos que cada uno de nosotros tiene valor. No importa si nos hablas inglés, si acabas de llegar a este país o el color de tu piel. Todos en este mundo tienen valor. Todos en esta iglesia tienen valor.*[11]

He went on to say that Jesus, as a bridge builder, invites us into conversation with each other. This led to the invitation to the deliberative dialogue about the issue of immigration. He ended the sermon by saying: "Let's help each other, in the name of Christ, continue to build bridges between people. Amen. *En el nombre de Cristo, ayudémonos los unos a los otros a construir puentes entre todo el mundo. Amén.*"

Deliberative Dialogue on Immigration

The group that participated in Ian's deliberative dialogue was quite diverse. The ten participants—five Hispanic, two black, and three white—included teens, a young adult, and middle-aged and retired adults. There were conservatives and progressives within the group that consisted of four males and six females. The group also had participants who were themselves undocumented, which made the dialogue more than just theoretical. The fact that those individuals were willing to reveal this detail about themselves in the context of the dialogue spoke to the high level of trust within the group. It was no surprise, then, that the values of *safety* and *welcoming* were among the common ideals they identified.

This is not to say that there was agreement about what steps to take regarding the issue of immigration. For example, while all of them agreed that writing letters to their senators was a good next step, at least one of them said they would be writing to advocate for stronger immigration laws. Ian admitted that this was difficult for him to hear. At the same time, the fact that the group shared their stories and experiences with each other with a willingness to listen humanized the issue and created a sense of community he had not yet witnessed within the congregation.

Communal Prophetic Proclamation

For his follow-up sermon, Ian focused on John 10:11–18 where Jesus compares himself to a "good shepherd." He used this image to theologically frame the deliberative dialogue as being guided by Christ's presence.

> In the end we did not agree on what action steps to take, but we had found common values in the presence of Christ: safety, structure, welcoming others, justice and fairness. They all play a role in God's kingdom, even if we understand them differently.

> *Al final no estábamos de acuerdo en los siguientes pasos a tomar, pero encontramos valores comunes en la presencia de Cristo: la seguridad, la estructura, el dar la bienvenida y la justicia. Todo esto juega un papel importante en el reino de Dios, incluso cuando no todos están de acuerdo.*

In this sermon, Ian did offer prophetic discernment based on one of the verses in the text: "I have other sheep that do not belong to this fold" (John 10:16). He acknowledged that while this may not sound like good news to some, Jesus' words have implications for how we approach the issue of immigration.

> There are those who we do not consider part of our flock, part of our community, who come from different countries, speak different languages and practice different religions. But they are still counted as part of God's flock. This verse brings good news to us! . . . The Good Shepherd calls us out of our comfort zone to find safety and justice while also welcoming the stranger in our midst.

> *Incluso aquellos a quienes no consideramos parte de nuestro rebaño, parte de nuestra comunidad, que provienen de diferentes países, hablan diferentes idiomas y practican diferentes religiones, todavía se cuentan como parte del rebaño de Dios. ¡Este versículo nos trae buenas noticias! . . . El Buen Pastor nos llama a salir de nuestra zona de confort para buscar seguridad y justicia, y en medio de eso también dar la bienvenida al extraño.*

He then described the complex realities of trying to live out God's purposes on this issue by underscoring the tensions recognized by the dialogue participants:

> What we discerned together is that there are laws and policies currently in place that do not serve the purposes of the Good Shepherd. Rather than gathering the vulnerable sheep together in safety, they tear families apart and attempt to send young adults back to countries that they have never known. We also recognized that there is still much sin and pain in the world. So safety was of immense importance to some people who believe that strong laws protecting the sheep already in the fold must be enforced.

> *Juntos, descubrimos que hay leyes y políticas que no cumplen con los propósitos de Buen Pastor. Leyes que, en vez de unir y dar seguridad a las ovejas más vulnerables, separan familias e intentan enviar a jóvenes a países que apenas conocen. También hablamos de lo lleno que está el mundo de maldad y pecado. Por eso el reforzar la seguridad para las ovejas que ya están en el rebaño fue un tema bastante importante para algunos.*

Ian concluded by affirming Christ's presence in the midst of the dialogue and the church itself, which can offer a model of what healthy dialogue looks like among faithful people about difficult issues.

> It is a calling to work for justice and peace. A calling to talk about what justice and peace mean to the world today. Christ the Good Shepherd is present. His rod and staff are leading us, all of us—native born and immigrant, English speaker and Spanish speaker, Democrat and Republican, Christian and other religions. Jesus intends to lead us beside still waters, accompany us through valleys of death, protect us from those who would harm us, and set out the table of abundance for us all. Let us go boldly forth, proclaim the calling of Christ, and gather the sheep into the Shepherd's fold. Amen.

> *Es un llamado a trabajar por la justicia y la paz. Un llamado a hablar sobre el significado real de justicia y la paz en el mundo de hoy. Cristo está presente, avancemos con valentía a proclamar el llamado de Cristo. Su vara y su bastón nos guían a todos—los estadunidenses e inmigrantes, los que hablan inglés y los que hablan español, demócratas y republicanos, cristianos y los de otras religiones. Jesús quiere guiarnos en las aguas mansas, acompañarnos en los valles de muerte, protegernos de los que quieren hacernos daño y poner la mesa de abundancia para todos. Sigamos con valentía y confianza, proclamando el llamado de Cristo, reuniendo a las ovejas en el redil del pastor. Amén.*[12]

Reflecting on the sermon-dialogue-sermon process, Ian said, "I felt like the sermons and dialogue were life-giving. Constructive and respectful dialogue is something around which to build a ministry career." He said that one of his most important learnings was that he was not going to change people's minds to think the same way he did about these issues. In the same way, he knew that those who were more conservative than he were not going to completely change his mind either. However, he said, "They did change the way that I saw them. It is my hope that they were also changed by the stories they heard from other members of the group." As Katie Day writes, "When we come together in trust and openness to real dialogue, we will change to some degree in the encounter."[13] Ian found this to be the case in his congregation and realized the role he has in the process: "What I can do is open up the lines of communication and give people an avenue to express themselves in productive ways that mean something to the life of the church."[14]

In this way, he challenged Day's critique that "For many congregations, just talking is considered enough. We feel as if we have actually done something just by discussing it."[15] The current reality of our political discord is such that even having respectful dialogue must be counted as a victory. As Ian said:

> To be able to foster a community in which racism and immigration are discussed regularly is, in my opinion, to see the kingdom of God on earth. If each person in the dialogue is allowed to acknowledge and keep their own dignity, and if it does not turn into a debate, these dialogues become one of the most holy times in the church's life. In this conversation is where God is found. Of course, one would love these discussions to lead to next steps, but even if they do not, the (almost) sacrament of community is being shared in a way that personalizes Jesus by personalizing the neighbor.[16]

"ELEPHANT TRAINERS"

Recall from the beginning of this chapter the image of "the elephant in the sanctuary"—the controversial public issue that lumbers around the church while people pretend not to see it and hope that it doesn't do too much damage. These case studies have shown us good examples of "elephant trainers"— preachers who courageously and deftly handled the topic of immigration in their preaching and deliberative dialogues. Each preacher was attentive to their context, employed the dialogical lens for exegeting scripture, and preached a Prophetic Invitation to Dialogue sermon that welcomed people to a deliberative dialogue on the topic of immigration. Then, they facilitated that dialogue with an eye and ear toward how the congregation weighed the pros and cons of each approach, found common values, and identified possible next steps. In their follow-up sermons, the Communal Prophetic Proclamation, they used a conversational preaching approach to interpret the discernment of the group within scriptural and theological images and frameworks.

In reflecting on the sermon-dialogue-sermon process, Lucas McSurley shared the two insights he gained:

> [First], I realized that most people genuinely want to be in loving relationship with others. Although they may struggle with how to go about that, their heart is most often in the right place. Another important thing I learned was that authentic relationship takes time. I came into the deliberative dialogue extremely ambitious, thinking we would solve immigration issues in one afternoon. But while dialogue is sometimes a slow process, it is also critical to establishing and maintaining healthy relationships. People left that conversation with a deep desire to continue to be engaged with one another. Day uses the language of "thick" trust and "thin" trust.[17] Thick trust was certainly at work during the deliberative dialogue because they were moving from acquaintance relationships into more invested relationships where a deeper sense of trust is apparent.[18]

For Ian McMichael, the sermon-dialogue-sermon process showed him that "the church has something to offer society. The church preaches Christ crucified and risen and claims that the entire history of the world is changed because of this." It is precisely this world-changing love of Christ that authorizes, encourages, and calls the church—and preachers—to address the issues that affect the lives of people and communities. "If we do not let the issues of society inform, at least in some ways, the way that we preach and teach," Ian realized, "we completely miss the ways in which we can show society a new path of reconciliation and grace."[19]

What we can see in these sermons is the kind of bridge-building Ian described in his Prophetic Invitation to Dialogue sermon. Ronald J. Allen says that this kind of homiletical bridge-building is essential in our polarized society. In terms of the deliberative dialogue process, this approach "can give the preacher a better (if partial) understanding of how those on the other side of the bridge see the world as they do, and why they do so. The preacher might then be able to find points of identification between the issues at stake and the concerns and values of people locked into their own enclaves." Further, states Allen, because the preacher names those points of identification within the congregation, he or she can then offer

> corrective guidance less from an adversarial position and more from the standpoint of what community members can do together to improve the situation of all. The sermon can have more a tone of invitation than condemnation or threat. The preacher can invite people onto the pathway of blessing for all even while alerting them to the consequences of not following that path.[20]

In the last chapter, we'll explore this image of bridge-building in more detail. But next we'll look at several other case studies involving different justice issues, including health care, end-of-life decisions, climate change, and hunger. The same challenges of threading the needle and bridge-building are present for these preachers as they choose their scripture texts, the paths of prophetic preaching to follow, and the rhetorical techniques to effectively convey the gospel message. We'll see that while the topics may be different, the same principles of dialogue, relationship, trust, and love guide the process.

• *10* •

Case Studies, Part 2

Four Journeys into the Purple Zone

In his book, *The Roundtable Pulpit*, John McClure explains the preacher's role as a *public theologian* for the congregation and why this role is vital to the ministry of the church: "Public theologians assert that the central task of the church's ministry is to 'resist the gravitational pull of privatization' and reconnect the gospel message with the public realm . . . According to Parker Palmer, we cannot be spiritually alive unless we venture into the public realm and encounter the strangers who live there."[1] In the previous chapter we saw four examples of preachers as public theologians connecting the gospel message to the issue of immigration. In this chapter, we'll see examples from four preachers who received training in Purple Zone preaching and applied it to the topics they chose for their sermon-dialogue-sermon process. The topics are health care, end of life, climate change, and hunger, and each case study shows the sermon-dialogue-sermon process used in a different ministry context.

THE COMPLEXITIES OF HEALTH CARE

Background

Andrew Shue is a "blue" pastor in a "red" congregation in North Carolina. The membership is almost entirely white/Caucasian with an average age of fifty-five. He estimates his congregation to be about 80 percent Republican and 20 percent Democrat, ranging from lower-middle-class to affluent. At the time when he took a class with me on preaching in the Purple Zone, he had already worked diligently to help the congregation become more aware of racial issues and how they affect their community, their church, and their own personal lives, so he wanted to choose a justice issue that he had not yet addressed in the congregation. At the time of the course (June 2017), the country was embroiled in intense debates about health care. Because his church holds a health fair in their community every year, they already had some awareness of the complexities involved in medical care, so Andrew chose to use the NIFI issue guide "Health Care: How Can We Reduce Costs and Still Get the Care We Need?"

Prophetic Invitation to Dialogue Sermon

In his Prophetic Invitation to Dialogue sermon, Andrew opened with a description of the controversial movie *John Q* in which the title character takes an emergency room hostage because his son was denied necessary medical treatment by the insurance company. While acknowledging the fictitious nature of the story, Andrew posed the question: "Why is it that so many of us cannot get the medical care we need?" He then recounted some key statistics about the cost of medical care and lack of access for many people. Drawing on his experience with them as their pastor he recalled, "I've been with some of you as you've had to make some of these difficult decisions about health care." In this way, he aligned with his listeners by recounting his relationship with them as their pastor, instead of positioning himself over or against them.

Andrew emphasized that while "John Q" was physically taking the ER hostage, a system of economic injustice had already taken it hostage. At that point he asked: "What should be the church's response to the injustices of the health care system? What responsibilities do we have as Christians to address this issue?"

He then turned to the story in Mark 2:1–12 of the paralyzed man let down through the roof by his friends in order to see Jesus. There were many barriers in the way of his healing. Would he even get access to Jesus' healing power? Andrew then drew parallels to the John Q story and the realities of our contemporary struggle with the politics of health care:

> The desperation of the friends of this paralyzed man mirrors the desperation of John Q. They are determined to help someone who is very sick. John Q's story should trouble us, as should this story from Mark. When we look at healthcare, we of course recognize that it is a complicated and divisive issue. We fight along partisan lines. But in the meantime, people continue to suffer.

Andrew then recounted a desperate health situation faced by his wife and how the church had come through for them by, in a sense, "tearing the roof off" to make sure they received the care they needed.

If the church can come through for my family, I know we can at least have a conversation about how we might come through for others as well. We, like the friends of the paralyzed man, need to tear the roof off and figure out a way to get people the care they need.[2]

His final move in the sermon was to highlight the dialogical nature of the text, the way the different characters had so many different perspectives—from the crowd, to the Pharisees, to the disciples, to the paralyzed man and his friends, to Jesus himself. Each of them had a stake in the outcome, and Jesus fully engaged them all, especially the man in need of healing. Just as the friends discussed among themselves how best to get their friend to Jesus, so, too, can the church engage in dialogue about how to get people the medical care they need. Andrew ended by inviting the congregation to stay after the service for the deliberative dialogue on health care.

Deliberative Dialogue on Health Care

Andrew was surprised at the number of people who stayed after the service for the dialogue because his congregation had not taken part in such a discourse before and he was not sure if people would respond to the invitation. The group of nearly twenty people represented a good cross-section of the congregation. What surprised Andrew even more was how readily people shared their struggles with medical bills or stories of family members who went without the care they needed. "I witnessed a level of sharing that I had not seen among them before," he said later when we debriefed the session. "Discussing the three approaches opened them up to think about possibilities they hadn't considered before. They started to realize how much they value personal relationships—even across party lines. One of our members is a local politician, and he was so impressed by the session, he took pictures of our note sheets to show others." At the end of the dialogue, they arrived at a number of common values surrounding the issue of health care, including *affordability*, *competition in the marketplace*, and *freedom of choice*. They also stressed the importance of people being attentive to their own health needs, taking responsibility for their well-being.

Communal Prophetic Proclamation Sermon

For his Communal Prophetic Proclamation sermon after the dialogue, Andrew chose John 5:1–18, the man healed at the pool at Bethesda, as his text. He began by reminding the listeners of the previous week's story of Jesus healing the paralytic lowered down through the roof and how this text extended the invitation to dialogue about health care. In this sermon, notice how Andrew interweaves the deliberative dialogue with this week's text about the healing waters.

Sermon Excerpt

> In this paragraph and the next, Andrew takes a "pollinating" approach by describing what happened in the dialogue and naming the wariness expressed by some parishioners about engaging the issue.

After church, almost twenty people gathered together to talk about this issue. In this group, we had a variety of people representing a broad political spectrum. We focused on three key ideas of how we might tackle this issue:

1. As a nation and individuals, we need to live within our means.
2. Make health care more transparent, accountable, and efficient.
3. Take responsibility for lowering health care costs by focusing on wellness.

For each of these responses, we talked about the pros and the cons. This could have turned into a heated discussion. However, instead of arguing, we ended up with an incredibly productive session. No, we did not fix the world's problems. No, we did not come up with a new health care proposal for our government. Instead, we had a truly wonderful dialogue where we thoroughly looked at ways we can respond to this issue.

Before we started this dialogue, I know some thought, "Health care? This is not an issue for us to talk about." Our scripture reading today shows us otherwise. There are countless stories of how Jesus provided healing. Here again, we have the same question asked as last week. How will healing come to a sick person?

> Here Andrew is "rooting" in the scripture passage and connecting it to the issue of health care.

Today we have a healing story in the Gospel of John, which is set by the Bethesda pool. According to scholars, people believed the angel of the Lord would stir the waters at this pool. The first person to enter the pool after this stirring would be healed. At this pool, there is a man who has some type of lifelong illness. He is desperate for healing but has no one to help him make his way into the pool. Jesus encounters this man and in a remarkable move, initiates the healing! This is a contrast to our story last week, where the friends of the paralytic man initiated the healing. Jesus engages the man—talks to him directly and offers healing. Just like last week in Mark's text, we again hear the commandment to "pick up your mat and walk!" And just like last week, the man is healed! Within this conversation there is new life.

> In this paragraph and the next, Andrew again turns to "pollinating," highlighting the common values among the politically diverse group.

What we came to realize in our deliberative dialogue is that difficult conversations about these issues of life and death need to happen in the church, even if they are challenging to our systems and structures. We must think about where Jesus would stand on our issues. We must have conversations about the difficult topics so we can understand how we can respond.

In our deliberative dialogue last Sunday, we identified many important values that transcended the red-blue divide. We value life, equality, children, personal relationships, competition in the marketplace, affordability, quality, accessibility, and freedom of choice. Our group was especially concerned about people being proactive about their own health.

> "Fruiting" is the emphasis of this final part of the sermon. Andrew pivots from the issue of health care to highlight how Jesus' healing power was experienced through the dialogue itself. Thus, he offered an expanded vision of what healing can look like for a congregation as well as the larger society.

I mentioned last week how I had support when my wife was sick. That was just one instance. Think of the number of people this church feeds when they are dealing with health challenges. How many visits and calls are made? When people are sick, this church responds! So, how can we expand our support model?

Those healing waters of the Bethesda pool drew people in. Here at this church, we provide care for those in need, and that draws people in as well. Those who are in need must be brought to the healing waters. It is our joy to bring people here. They need healing, which can be individual, communal, and spiritual.

What does it mean to be church? It means to circle around that water pool, just like those in need at Bethesda. There are healing waters here in this church as well—but only if we seek the presence of Jesus! What we discovered is that Jesus' healing isn't just for individuals—it can be for a whole community.

As we continued our dialogue around the healing waters, we recognized that we can, indeed, talk about difficult issues. Our deliberative dialogue was just a sneak peek into the kingdom of God. We have many people hurting and suffering. If a group of twenty people from across the political spectrum can experience those healing waters, maybe there is hope for our nation as well. Together we can come to the healing waters, help those in need, and experience the healing God can provide.

END-OF-LIFE ISSUES

Background

When Rachel McConnell-Switzer worked with the sermon-dialogue-sermon process, she was serving a congregation in Louisiana made up of middle- to upper-middle-class members who were mostly white/Caucasian. Politically, the members were conservative with a few moderates. For her issue, Rachel chose the issue guide "End of Life: What Should We Do for Those Who Are Dying?" because of the increasing number of older members and because some parishioners had already faced difficult decisions for their loved ones.

Prophetic Invitation to Dialogue Sermon

Rachel's Prophetic Invitation to Dialogue sermon focused on John 3:1–17, the conversation between Jesus and Nicodemus. Her sermon highlighted the dialogical nature of the text, especially the aspect of difficult questions:

> This is what the text about Jesus and Nicodemus models for us: an encounter that moves beyond the surface level into the challenging questions that lead to deeper relationships and understanding of our faith. In the upcoming months we are going to have an opportunity to do this—to engage with one another about an issue that needs to be addressed. It's one that some of you may already have dealt with and others will probably deal with in the future. I'm going to host a dialogue on end-of-life issues, that is, how we make decisions with those who are dying. It's a conversation that will require us to follow the Jesus and Nicodemus model of listening and asking questions.[3]

Deliberative Dialogue on End-of-Life Issues

Rachel reported that the group of fifteen who attended the session were a bit hesitant at first to open up about how end-of-life issues had impacted them personally. But after she shared her own personal experience about a loved one's death, others opened up and were willing to enter a more vulnerable space. "I learned that while folks may not bring up these kinds of issues in everyday conversations, they are definitely thinking about them and willing to engage if given the right opportunity," she said in reflecting on the session.

As they took stock of their discussion about the three options, their group saw a number of areas where they found common ground. They valued individuals having *autonomy* and *having agency to make their own choices*. At the same time, *family* and the *sanctity of life* itself were strong values. As you'll see in the sermon, sometimes those values were in tension. Yet in her recounting of the dialogue, Rachel used an apt metaphor of Jesus stilling the stormy waters.

Communal Prophetic Proclamation Sermon

In her Communal Prophetic Proclamation, Rachel focused on Mark 4:35–41. You'll see how she integrates the different components of the deliberative dialogue into the sermon, using a pastorally prophetic approach to describe what happened and frame it biblically and theologically.

Sermon Excerpt

> Notice how Rachel uses the image of the boat on calm water as a metaphor for deliberative dialogue.

Sometimes, like Jesus' disciples, we're offered the chance to step onto the boat. We take that first step when the waters are calm, knowing they may not always be that way. Here at our church, we had a chance to enter the boat on calm waters when I invited everyone to engage in a deliberative dialogue on end-of-life issues. Because this can be a topic fraught with emotions and because we often have a lot tied up in our own experiences with death, I wasn't sure we were going to have a very good turn-out, but we had fifteen people come to the conversation.

We talked about end-of-life issues from three perspectives. 1. Maintaining Quality of Life (that is, prioritizing comfort over longevity for a terminally ill person); 2. Preserving Life at All Costs (that is, doing everything we can to keep a person alive); and 3. My Right, My Choice (that is, terminally ill people have a right to choose when their lives end if they know that increased pain and suffering is all that awaits them in this life).

> Here she names the tension that was present in the dialogue but frames it within the story of Jesus and the disciples on the boat. In this way the "pollinating" and "rooting" paths overlap and intersect.

As we entered into conversation, it became clear that our values didn't align in every aspect of end-of-life issues. There were a few moments when the waters got a little rough. There may even have been a moment or two when people in the group felt the kind of frustration the disciples must have experienced when they said to Jesus, "Teacher, don't you care that we're drowning?" Yet, somehow, we left that conversation with a better understanding of the issue at hand and a clearer understanding of our shared values, even when we didn't agree on everything. That's where we saw Jesus. That's the moment we knew that though we were many, we were still united.

> The "pollinating" aspect of this sermon is nuanced in that she named the points about which the group disagreed and juxtaposed them against the common values they identified. She also made a clear theological claim about Christ being present in the midst of the "stormy" waters.

We might not agree on how long a person should prolong their life if they're in chronic pain; we might not agree on whether quality of life or longevity matters more; we might not agree on whether or not a person should be able to choose how long they live if they know they have a terminal illness. BUT we can agree on the importance of autonomy and personal choice, sanctity of life, faith and prayer in the midst of it all, and the importance of family and faithful preparation for the end. That is where we experienced Christ, in naming those shared values. That is where we found Jesus standing in the midst of the storm, calming the waters saying, "Silence. Be still." The waters of dialogue may have been rough at times, but Jesus offered peace and stillness in the midst of it.

> Notice that Rachel's prophetic exhortation to not ignore end-of-life issues is rooted in the church's identity as "a Pentecost people filled with the Holy Spirit."

As a Pentecost people filled with the Holy Spirit, we are not promised life without hardship. We are not promised life without storms. But as a people filled with the Holy Spirit, we know that we do not find peace by ignoring the storm. We do not find peace by ignoring end-of-life issues. If you've not experienced grief and loss yet in your life, there will be a point at which you do. We do not find peace by refusing to recognize our grief. Instead, we find peace in the midst of it because we're filled with the very same Spirit that Christ sends all his disciples. We are afforded peace in the midst of our most violent and deadly storms.

> The "leafing" aspect of the sermon is evident here where she tells of the opportunity for another dialogue and the plan for a lawyer to talk about preparing for end-of-life issues.

As we continue to confront our own mortality and our own grief, in the upcoming months our church is going to offer a chance to have some conversation about how to be faithful to our families and loved ones in end-of-life planning. This is something our dialogue group decided would be a good next step for us as a community—a way for us to continue the conversation and live into the things we value. We also plan on having a lawyer come and talk about some ways we can better prepare for the end of life. The purpose of this session will be to help our families begin to talk to one another about such things and to prepare for decisions that may need to be made in the future.

> Here, Rachel utilizes a technique known as "bookending"—recapitulating a theme or image from the opening of the sermon again at the end. Her pastoral prophetic proclamation assures the listener of Christ's presence in the midst of the storms they encounter, thus ending with the "fruiting" aspect of prophetic preaching.

Yes, talking about end-of-life issues may be difficult for some of us, but this is an opportunity to step in the boat while the water is still calm, which is what we see Jesus' disciples modeling for us. We step in the boat during calm waters, knowing that sooner or later a storm will hit, and remembering that we will meet Jesus in the midst of it all, trusting that we will indeed know peace again. Amen.[4]

THE CHALLENGE OF CLIMATE CHANGE

Background

TJ Lynch served as a seminary intern at a church in Colorado when taking the "Preaching in the Purple Zone" course. A large, affluent, and well-educated congregation, the racial makeup of the church is white/Caucasian with a political spectrum that TJ estimated to be around 20 percent conservative, 20 percent progressive, and 60 percent moderate. He chose the topic of climate change because he felt it was an issue that was not on the radar of the congregation and needed to be brought to their attention.

Prophetic Invitation to Dialogue Sermon

For his Prophetic Invitation to Dialogue sermon, TJ preached on Matthew 21:33–46, the parable of the vineyard and the wicked tenants. He framed his sermon around the question, "If Earth is God's vineyard and we are the tenants called to care for it, how are we doing?" Keeping in mind the Purple Zone of his congregation, he was intentional about creating a sermon that was courageous enough to name the issue while prudent enough to avoid inflammatory rhetoric.

Sermon Excerpt

> Notice how the beginning of the sermon catches the listener's attention with humor and a description of TJ's budding interest in oenophilia (love of wine). This creates a natural connection to the lectionary text assigned for that day.

Recently, I have become enthralled with the world of wine. [Pause for dramatic effect.] No, no . . . not like that. A few weeks ago, I had the privilege of experiencing a six-course tasting/pairing menu at the only 5-star restaurant in Columbus, Ohio. We were served by the top wine sommelier in the country for the year 2016. After this experience I began watching documentaries about wines, and what I found was that the more I learn about the actual science and process of producing wine, the more fascinated I become.

So naturally, with my recent obsession, our Gospel texts the last three weeks have really caught my attention because they all include parables about a vineyard! This week we read the parable about a landowner who plants a vineyard and rents it out to some farmers.

> After recounting the story in the parable, TJ provides some biblical "rooting" in the Old Testament to give the listeners important background on the significance of the vineyard in scripture.

Isaiah 5:1–7 is clear that the "vineyard" is a metaphor for the people of Israel and that God is the caretaker of this vineyard. Even though this vineyard was planted on luscious, fertile soil, and even though the caretaker took very good care of said vineyard, it still only produced "wild grapes." Because of these wild grapes, the caretaker says, "You know what, I'm just not going to care for it anymore!" "For the vineyard of the Lord of hosts is the house of Israel, and the people of Judah are his pleasant planting; he expected justice, but saw bloodshed; righteousness, but heard a cry!"

> Here TJ uses the "flowering" path to introduce the issue of climate change. Notice how he connects the issue to a topic in which he and the listeners are already invested—the wine. And then notice how he frames the question about caring for Earth using the language of the parable as well as creating an emotional connection to the geographical context of the congregation.

I've been thinking about this as I continue learning more about wine. Did you know that as the climate continues changing all around us, this can have serious repercussions on the vineyards, which can have disastrous effects on the wine? Vineyards around the world are dealing with water deficits, increasingly warmer temperatures, and severe weather events, all of which have a negative impact on the quality and quantity of wine. So this got me thinking, what if Earth is God's vineyard and we are the tenants?

You might agree with me when I say it is hard to be here in Colorado for any period of time and not fall in love with God's Creation, to not fall in love with the beauty and splendor. I mean we are surrounded by it! Every day I drive to work, I come up that hill and my eyes are met with the foothills of the Rocky Mountains. Lauren and I love to take our dog Bexley down to the South Platte River Basin and just walk along the flowing river. Many of us have gone up into the mountains to experience the breathtaking beauty of the changing aspen trees.

> TJ continues on the "flowering" path by providing key facts about the warming planet.

The more I fall in love with Creation the harder it is not to read a passage such as today's without raising the question of Earth being God's vineyard and us being the tenants. Sure, we may not have literally stoned, beaten or killed anyone, but what about the pain or hurt we bring upon this planet on a daily basis? The facts are alarming:

- Earth's temperature has risen about two degrees since the late 19th century, largely because of the increased carbon dioxide and other human-made emissions in the atmosphere. Sixteen of the seventeen warmest years on record occurred since 2001.
- Our oceans are warming, wreaking havoc on fish populations and coral reefs.
- The Greenland and Antarctic ice sheets are decreasing in total mass. NASA showed that Greenland lost nearly 60 cubic miles of ice between 2002 and 2006, while Antarctica lost 36 cubic miles.

> Anticipating that there may be some in his congregation who might dismissively label him an "environmentalist," he makes his argument for addressing climate change based on caring about *people* as well as the planet.

I'm not an environmentalist, but I'm really concerned about climate change, and not just because of the grapes in the vineyard but because of the people, too. We might not be physically beating people up like those tenants, but our carbon output is contributing to storms that are, literally, killing people, destroying their homes and businesses, and, yes, devastating the agriculture as well.

If Earth is God's vineyard and we are the tenants, how are we doing? Check out the news any given day and you'll hear of another "natural" disaster. Just in the last few months we've had Hurricanes Harvey, Irma, Maria, in addition to devastating wildfires out west. Summers are getting longer and hotter. Nations around the world are seeing record temperatures. Weather is becoming more and more unpredictable. And these are all just weather-related effects. Let us not forget that thousands of our brothers and sisters in Haiti still do not have access to clean drinking water, and millions of people around the world are starving due to lack of food and nutrition. As much as people like to label so many of these things as "natural," the fact is, it's not natural at all. It's not what God intended for the vineyard, the garden of Earth.

> At this point, the sermon takes on a more prophetic tone, "rooting" in the theological claim about God's intentions for creation, and Jesus' intention for the vineyard.

God has created this beautiful vineyard. It's been planted on rich, fertile soil. But over and over and over again we fail to take proper care of it. We fail to make choices that consider the long-term effects of our actions. We fail to care for

Creation. Not only that, but we fail to care for each other. We let hate overpower love. We let darkness overcome the light.

That's why God sent Jesus, the Son of God, God in the flesh. He is God's perfect image of who we were created to be: taking care of Creation, taking care of each other, and drawing all things into this incredible way of life simply through love. "But when the tenants saw the son, they said to themselves, 'This is the heir; come, let us kill him and get his inheritance.'" And that's just what they did. They seized Jesus, they threw him out of the vineyard, and killed him. All Jesus was doing was loving people, loving God's Creation; he was doing what God created us all to do. But they nailed him to that cross because he threatened the power structures the world has established. He challenged the economic inequities and the institutional evil within the religious and ruling classes, and they killed him for it.

> Here TJ poses a series of provocative questions. In a typical sermon, the preacher would then follow up with answers. But see what he does instead in the next paragraph.

The question we must ask is, can we see ourselves in today's parable of the wicked tenants? If so, what are we doing about it? As we consider this parable, and think about our role in the vineyard, I wonder if we might consider a new ending? Is there a way we can stop, take a step back and consider what we might do differently as tenants of God's vineyard? What are the choices we have before us for addressing our changing climate? What options do we have for helping to restore the vineyard of Earth?

> He gives a clear invitation to the dialogue, noting that he does not have the answers but wants to explore the questions with the congregation. Thus, he is "pollinating," inviting people into the conversation, as well as "leafing"—giving people a chance to respond to the questions he has posed.

I would love for us as a church to talk about this, because I don't have the answers, but I'm really interested in the questions and how each of us approaches them. So this Wednesday we are going to have an open dialogue about this very topic: how can we become better stewards of this earth? How can we become better caretakers of our rivers and streams, our local wildlife, our local ecosystems? How can we become better at caring for each other?

> In this paragraph, TJ reminds them of the "rooting" sermon he had preached, making the case that the church can—and should—courageously address important social issues.

Remember a few weeks ago when I said there would be times when I'll have to preach about difficult issues? Climate change is one of those topics. People have different thoughts and opinions. But this is exactly why we, the church, need to discuss it. We were baptized with God's love that empowers us to tackle these issues with good will and good faith.

| Bringing the sermon to a close, he reminds them of two core values—the love of Christ and their baptismal identities. | It starts with love. At our baptism, that water covers our head and we're marked and sealed with the cross of Christ forever . . . When love is the basis for our care of creation we don't abuse the environment, we |

don't neglect the cries of the Earth. We make choices that lead to a safe and peaceful world for all people.

| The conclusion continues with a sacramental framing, bringing the sermon full circle with a clever pivot back to wine and the communion table. By reminding them of these core values, he winds up on the "fruiting" path. | Would you like to know what my favorite wine is? It's right there. [Turns and points to the communion table.] Not because it's 1941 Inglenook Cabernet Sauvignon. Not because the sweetness, acidity, and body are perfectly harmonized. It's because that is the wine that Christ gives, full of forgiveness, grace, hope. When we come together and drink from this cup, we are all drawn together in faith, filled |

up and sent out to draw all people and all Creation back to God. May we leave here today as a people united, producing the fruits of the kingdom. It all starts with love.

Deliberative Dialogue on Climate Change

While TJ received many positive comments about this sermon, he also fielded negative feedback from a parishioner who disputed the existence of human-caused climate change. Nevertheless, he welcomed this parishioner to the dialogue, trusting that with the guidance of the ground rules and the wisdom of the group, this parishioner would be heard, but also be encouraged to listen.

As it turned out, this is what happened. He used the NIFI issue guide, "Climate Choices: How Should We Meet the Challenges of a Warming Planet?" which is nonpartisan in its approach to addressing global warming. Twelve people—five men and seven women—ranging in age from twenty-nine to sixty attended the session. TJ noted that given the topic, it worked well for him *not* to be an expert on climate change. He was able to approach the facilitation without an agenda and without feeling he had to convince anyone. He found the biggest challenge was keeping the group on task, especially when one or two individuals started going off on tangents. Nevertheless, he used techniques of redirection to keep the group on task.

The "a-ha" moment for the group was the realization that all three options—reduce carbon emissions, prepare and protect communities, and accelerate innovation—needed to happen and that this issue was not an either-or scenario. Reflecting on the dialogue, TJ noted: "With all three approaches, the core common value throughout the conversation kept coming back to our identity as God's children. The recurring theme was that caring for Creation and being conscious of the effects that our choices have on the climate is part of who we are called to be as Christians."

For TJ, having the time for an open, honest conversation about a tough issue was helpful not only for him in a pastoring role but also for his preaching. "What I love about the sermon-dialogue-sermon process is that it allows the listeners to talk through the concerns and questions they may have. This allows them to see that the sermon and dialogue aren't about proving each other right or wrong. Rather, it's about talking about difficult topics because we love each other, we love all of God's Creation, and we love God's mission to which we've been called."[5]

Communal Prophetic Proclamation Sermon

TJ's follow-up sermon happened to fall on Christ the King Sunday, which for that lectionary year meant that the Gospel reading was Matthew 25:31–46, the parable about the sheep and the goats. He began by posing a question to expand their understanding of "the least of these":

> If you're anything like me, when I think of the "least of these," I automatically think of the poor, the sick, the homeless, the outcast, the bullied, the addicted, etc. But let me ask you this: Do you think it would be fair to include God's Creation—the natural world—on this list of "the least of these"?

He then briefly recounted the discussion around the three options for approaching climate change and described the outcome of the dialogue:

> What this dialogue did for me was two things. First, as a growing and emerging leader in the church, it was wonderful to see that it is possible for people to come together as brothers and sisters, each with our own differing opinions, and have a conversation about a difficult, even controversial, topic. We had folks on far opposite sides of the political spectrum who were able to walk away open to new and different ways of thinking. We had someone who admittedly came having no interest in the topic, but purely to support my internship learning. Yet, this person left that night saying how appreciative they were to learn about the different approaches to addressing climate change. They had never realized the impact they could have on climate change and were thankful for the opportunity to learn through the dialogue.
>
> The second thing this dialogue did for me was that it made me realize HOW MUCH OF A GOAT I AM!

TJ went on to describe how he has been guilty of not recognizing Christ suffering in the midst of a suffering planet. In fact, the very beauty he was privileged to enjoy in Colorado blinded him to the environmental blight visited on so many millions of people around the world. By admitting his own culpability on this justice issue, he avoided coming off as holier-than-thou over and against his listeners. Instead, he modeled what it looks like to be open to the prophetic word of God and how it can change one's perspective. He then posed the question of what it looks like to tend to God's Creation as one of "the least of these."

> Our group realized that taking care of God's Creation looks like being mindful of the choices we make, and the lifestyle we choose to lead, and the consequences that has on the Earth and all of God's beautiful Creation. This includes the impacts that affect us and those that might affect others. Caring for "the least of these" happens when we have intentional conversations, like we did around climate change, setting our differences aside and having healthy dialogue over different, viable options like reducing our carbon output, responding to the horrible effects communities are already facing, or being on the leading edge of coming up with solutions.

Toward the end of the sermon, he described his "God-sized dream" of humanity putting an end to climate change and the pain inflicted on God's Creation. Yet, he admitted:

> There are times that this seems really daunting and I feel completely alone in this mission. Thanks be to God that every time I come to the communion feast I am reminded that I'm not alone at all. In fact, I'm joined by the saints here at this church, and saints around the world who are committed to this task of caring for the least of these. Despite all the things that divide and separate us, Jesus fills us with his very presence. He opens our eyes and transforms us from goats into sheep to be sent out into the world, caring for the least of these in the human and Creation communion together.

In his conclusion, he returned to the theme of Christ the King Sunday, placing the topic of climate change within a larger theological context:

> I truly believe that not only can we address changing climate, but that together we can change the world. The Reign of Christ is in our midst. And his presence among us, in us, through us, and through all of Creation is, indeed, changing the world.
>
> I can already tell that Jesus is changing me and changing our congregation here. Can you see it? The sheep are on the rise!⁶

HUNGER: MOVING BEYOND—AND DEEPER INTO— THE CHURCH FOOD PANTRY

Background

Brooke Baker was serving as a student pastor in a congregation in Ohio at the time she took the "Preaching in the Purple Zone" course with me. The church was 80 percent white/Caucasian and 20 percent African American and Latinx in a mixed white-collar and blue-collar community. The church had a thriving food pantry that had been serving those in need for over two decades, but Brooke wanted to challenge them to consider *why* the food pantry was needed in the first place. In other words, she wanted to encourage them to think about the systemic issues that create the conditions whereby people find themselves unable to get the food they need for themselves and their families.

Prophetic Invitation to Dialogue Sermon

She began her Prophetic Invitation to Dialogue by describing the well-stocked pantry in her family's kitchen growing up and how her father always made sure that they gave some away to the pantry at church. This led to her description of the congregation's food pantry and acknowledging the good work they had done feeding so many people over the years. But then she asked a counterintuitive question:

> What if we could serve *fewer* people? I know what you're thinking: "What are they teaching her at that seminary? Serve fewer people? But the need is so great!" Yes, the need is great, but what if we could do something to decrease the *need*? What would happen if we addressed why people are hungry?

After listing the many and varied reasons for hunger in the United States, she drew on the parable of the sower and the seeds in Matthew 13:1–9, 18–23, to make the case that the church's food pantry has been planted in "good soil." But she challenged them to think about planting new seeds for ministry by addressing the systemic reasons for hunger in their community. She invited them to a deliberative dialogue after the worship service to discuss how they might address the larger issues of hunger and think about what it would entail to decrease the need for their food pantry.

Deliberative Dialogue about the Church's Food Pantry

Brooke's deliberative dialogue was different from most of the other examples in this book because she chose to create her own issue guide entitled, "How

Can We Decrease the Need for Our Food Pantry?" She looked at model materials from other groups in the Kettering network to design a one-page, double-sided "placemat" version of the issue guide. One column had introductory and background information with key statistics about hunger in their area, noting how unemployment and underemployment play a significant role as contributing factors. The other three columns listed three approaches: 1) Direct action in helping unemployed and underemployed people find sustaining jobs; 2) Advocate for raising the minimum wage; and 3) Search for ways to decrease "food deserts."[7] As with other issue guides, each option had a description of the approach and a list of potential actions, as well as concerns and trade-offs.

There were fifteen participants in the deliberative dialogue that Brooke facilitated—nine females and six males, all white/Caucasian. They ranged in age from mid-forties to seventies and eighties. While the congregation is politically liberal, Brooke was surprised at the pushback she received when presenting the options to the group because it revealed the hidden biases they held about the very people they served in the pantry. The participants insisted that none of the options would work because those who come to the pantry don't even have the life skills to work in the first place. Brooke perceived a great deal of "victim-blaming" coming from the group. As well, there was resistance to sharing personal stories about how hunger had affected their own lives (mostly because none of them had experienced it themselves). Neither were they able to get to the "shared values" part of the dialogue. Instead, the consensus was that most of the people who came to the food bank either did not want to work or could not work because of past criminal records or disabilities.

Perhaps the most biting comment was, "You don't get this, Brooke. You don't know these people. You haven't done your homework."

While the deliberative dialogue did not meet her expectations or proceed in the way she had hoped or anticipated, Brooke saw the experience as a learning opportunity. When she and I debriefed, she admitted that, in fact, she had not yet had a chance to visit the food pantry because they were only open at times when she had to work at her full-time job. I suggested that in preparation for her follow-up sermon, she might consider taking a day off to go to the food pantry and see what goes on for herself. Doing so would indicate her willingness to take the critique of the group to heart and to learn from them what they were trying to tell her—that she needs to understand the people about whom she is speaking and for whom she is advocating. My hunch, I told her, is that she may discover more than what she—and they—bargained for.

This is exactly what she did. Brooke went to the food pantry the next week. That experience—along with the deliberative dialogue—directly shaped her Communal Prophetic Proclamation sermon. Let's analyze how she used the image of the mustard seed in Matthew 13:21–22, 44–52, to frame the narratives about the deliberative dialogue and her visit to the food pantry. As you'll see, the result is a nuanced yet profoundly prophetic sermon she titled, "It's Not What It Looks Like."

Communal Prophetic Proclamation Sermon Excerpt

> Notice how Brooke puts a face on the issue of hunger and poverty. In fact, she describes three different encounters with people at the food pantry. Thus, she is following the "flowering" path by raising awareness of how hunger affects real people.

I spent some time in the food pantry this week and I'd like to introduce you to some of the people I met and talked with. I'm using pseudonyms to protect their privacy. Anita arrived with her paperwork in hand. It's July and the volunteers have posted all month long in both English and Spanish that people must bring proof of the ages of the people they are claiming in their household to receive food. Anita had her own ID, and ID for her six children and husband. Anita was organized, efficient, and had it all together so that she could feed her family for another month. As I listened, she explained to me that her brother-in-law had been living with them for the last four months because "he isn't well." I asked some questions about whether he was physically or mentally unwell and she explained physically, but went on to share that she had a son who struggled with mental illness. So she is managing a household of nine people, two with special needs. I realized that just because she relies on our food pantry doesn't mean she doesn't have organizational skills to manage her family and all that is involved in helping them to survive. It's not what it looks like.

Another person I met was Sandra. She showed up having forgotten that she had already visited the food pantry this month. But the volunteers told her they could provide a rescue bag for her and she was grateful. Sandra was tearful as she talked to me about where she lived and how her hands hurt. But she was quick to tell me that when she wakes up and her hands feel okay, she likes to go do something. She shared with me that she likes to volunteer at St. Matthias in their food program because she can give back as well as receive food. Sandra shared that she has some mental health issues, but she wants to work when she is able. It's not what it looks like.

Katrin and her husband Juan arrived to get food for themselves and three children under the age of 12. Juan was in his 70s and Katrin was in her 60s. They were clearly raising grandchildren. Juan hung back, not interacting with anyone. I don't know why. I could speculate—pride, language barrier, something else on his mind—but I don't really know. Katrin was more than willing to talk to me. I was limited in that I could only speak to her in English—not her first language. I wonder what answers I might have heard had I been able to speak to her in her native language? But she confirmed that it was her three grandchildren, that her husband was retired, but still worked some odd jobs. When I asked about the parents she assured me they were around, but then said it was only her and Juan in the house. When we finished our conversation, she hugged me, gave me a kiss on my cheek and went on her way with Juan and the food to feed their family. It's not what it looks like.

> By acknowledging the critique she heard from the deliberative dialogue, and how she responded to it, she is following the "pollinating" path.

Two weeks ago, I gave a sermon about our food pantry and asked you to think about what we might do next to address why there was a need for our food pantry. Fifteen people came to have a discussion about the pros and cons of different ways to approach the issue of hunger so that we could reduce the need for our food pantry. Some of you were rightfully critical—in the kindest of ways—that perhaps I didn't have a good grasp of what the clientele of the food pantry was really like. Hence, my visit to the food pantry this week. I still don't have a good grasp, but I certainly have a *better* grasp.

> Notice her repeated use of the phrase, "It's not always what it looks like." This is called a "through-line" because it provides a running thread that gives both cohesiveness and a unifying theme.

We came up with pros and cons for each of the approaches and then looked at what were some of the themes that were similar in all of the areas. One of the pros in each of the approaches was to be able to empower the people visiting the food pantry. One of the cons was the sense that many of them didn't really have a desire to work or learn new skills, or perhaps they were unable to because of physical or mental illness or disabilities. But what I learned in my brief visit is that it's not always what it looks like.

Our gospel reading this morning uses lots of metaphors to describe the kingdom of heaven: seeds, yeast, treasure, merchants, and fishermen. But the message is the same—God is able to take the most unlikely things, help them to grow, and thus bring in the kingdom of heaven. Two weeks ago, we talked about the fertile soil to help things grow and I acknowledged that our church had planted its community food pantry in very good soil. But I asked you to consider if it was time to plant new seeds.

178   *Preaching in the Purple Zone*

> Here she is firmly "rooting" in the biblical text, using the seed image to reframe her original question from the first sermon and the deliberative dialogue.

What I heard from the deliberative dialogue is that we need to nurture the seeds we have and those seeds that are found in the people who use our food pantry. We need to nurture those seeds because we are followers of Christ. And Christ teaches us that when we nurture those seeds we bring the kingdom of heaven. When we do that we are changed, the seeds are changed, and we all get to experience the kingdom of heaven. But here's the thing—it is not that the seeds need to be changed; the seeds need to be nurtured. So how do we do that? Here are a couple of things I learned from the deliberative dialogue and from my brief time at the food pantry.

> In this section, Brooke deftly fuses two paths—"pollinating" and "leafing." The action she recommends is *listening* to the people in the food pantry. This is a prophetic move in that it challenges the assumptions made about them by those who volunteer in the pantry.

First—and I believe most importantly—we need to listen to the people who are using the pantry. Many of you could tell me stories about the people who use our pantry and I certainly learned about some of them by asking a few questions and then listening to their responses. But there seems to be so much more we could learn through listening to their stories that would help them to feel more empowered. Simply telling our stories and having someone listen gives each of us a sense of empowerment.

> One of the interesting features about this sermon is its *chiastic* form in which she begins with the three examples, brings them to the central point of *listening*, and moves back out through the three examples to draw out the implications.

Imagine if we nurture that seed of empowerment in Anita, with her stack of her family's IDs, how she might feel and how it might change her life. Instead of seeing someone dependent, maybe we could see someone who could use her organizational skills in a job to help support her family. Maybe it's not that she doesn't want to work, but that no one has ever empowered her to be able to work. Maybe Sandra with her mental health challenges can't work every day, but what if she was empowered to have some place to volunteer when she felt up for it? This might help her feel a sense of pride and accomplishment.

> Here, Brooke adds yet another layer of "pollinating" and "leafing" by suggesting serving those who come to the food pantry in their native language. Thus, both dialogue and action are taken to another level.

Second, what if we nurtured the seeds of hearing their stories or offering assistance in their native languages? Anita and Katrin and Juan did not speak English as their primary language. During the summer we are fortunate to have someone volunteering who is fluent in Spanish, but then school starts and she returns to her job as a teacher. The only person who can speak to them in their native language is our building manager who has other responsibilities. Anita and Katrin were perfectly capable of sharing their stories with me, but how much more empowered might they feel if they could have spoken in their native language? Perhaps it's not that they don't want to share more with the volunteers, but they could better do it in their native language.

> Instead of lambasting those who took part in the dialogue for their prejudices and lack of compassion, she models what it looks like to be open to changing one's mind. Thus, listeners can identify with her instead of feeling judged by her.

Through our deliberative dialogue, and through my conversations with the people at the food pantry, I've learned that sometimes my first impressions about people are wrong. And I've learned to wonder instead of making assumptions. Because sometimes, it's not what it looks like.

> She ends on the "leafing" path by offering a concrete action of inviting food pantry visitors to participate in a deliberative dialogue. What better way to embody the compassionate spirit of Christ—listening and learning from them, just as Brooke listened and learned from the participants in the deliberative dialogue and the people in the food pantry? The ending talks about God planting seeds—even as the sermon itself is planting seeds as well!

I'm learning that as Christians, we are called to look at the situations of poverty, hunger, immigration, and so many other issues not just through human eyes, but through God's eyes. And I'm learning that maybe there is more we can do with this God-centered vision. Maybe we can invite our visitors to the food pantry to participate in a future deliberative dialogue with us? Maybe we can listen to them as a group, as a church, as members of the Body of Christ?

God is indeed planting seeds here in this place. Let's keep our eyes open to see what happens next! Amen.[8]

PREACHERS-AS-TEACHERS IN ACTION

While the preachers in these four case studies each had a different topic to address in their sermon-dialogue-sermon process, they are all examples of what Richard Voelz might envision for the preacher-as-teacher model which we learned about in chapter 2. Recall that Voelz suggests reviving the image of the preacher-as-teacher as a way to circumvent the risk of splits in the relationship between the pastor and her parishioners. Embracing the identity of preacher-as-teacher involves being a reflective practitioner, empowering others to engage in critical thinking, and teaching toward transformation. Each of these four preachers—as well as the ones in the previous chapter—demonstrated what it looks like to equip their congregations for the political and cultural struggles within the Purple Zones of their churches and beyond.

Andrew's sermon-dialogue-sermon process on health care was a model of being a reflective practitioner. He took into account not just the complexities of the issue but his own family's struggle, as well as his role as pastor to a congregation that wrestles with navigating the health care system of our country. Rachel empowered her congregation to engage in critical thinking about end-of-life issues and used a gospel story to help them navigate the "stormy waters" of tension when it came to competing values. TJ's case gave us a glimpse of what it looks like to address a social justice issue—climate change—in a congregation that had not really discussed it before. His prophetic invitation and communal prophetic proclamation sparked a transformation in the congregation's self-understanding of their role in caring for God's creation.

Finally, Brooke's case showed us a way to handle a dialogue that doesn't go as we had planned or would have hoped. Not only did she demonstrate what it looks like to discover the "contested spheres" of cultural, socioeconomic, and racial-ethnic tension around issues of hunger, she modeled a pastoral-prophetic "intervention." She did this by being open to critique and self-reflection, learning more about the people whose lives are affected by intersections of injustice, and employing the biblical theme of seed-planting to effect an "emancipatory practice" within her sermon. In this way, she fused both the pastoral and prophetic voice in her preaching, building a bridge that connected her listeners with the people they serve in their food pantry.

This bridge-building is both co-creative and co-relational because it strengthens the Body of Christ by bringing the gospel into the lives of the people, their congregation, those they serve, and the wider community. In the final chapter, we'll learn more about this idea of bridge-building as we encounter the work of Dale Andrews and other homileticians who have thought deeply about what it means to preach "prophetic care."

• *11* •

Building Bridges in the Purple Zone

Where Do We Go from Here?

PREACHING PROPHETIC CARE

On Wednesday, November 9, 2016, Dale P. Andrews, Distinguished Professor of Homiletics, Social Justice and Practical Theology at Vanderbilt Divinity School, and I sat with students at Wake Forest University School of Divinity the morning after the presidential election. It was supposed to be a conversation about the intersections of race and environmental justice. We were there for the school's Prophetic Ministry Week and were prepared to talk with them about what prophetic preaching looks like in the face of eco-racism and related issues. But that morning as tears flowed and audible sobs were heard throughout the room, the feelings of shock, confusion, and utter despair meant that we needed to process with these theologically trained students—some of whom were preparing for ordained ministry—what had transpired for our nation.

"How are we supposed to go into our churches on Sunday morning?" they asked. "What are we supposed to say and do? How can we face those who are going to gloat over this victory? How are we going to endure the pain of those who are devastated by the outcome? What does it look like to be church in the midst of all this?" These were the kinds of questions they were asking.

Dr. Andrews astutely reminded the students that this is exactly why they are called to be a Christian, to preach, to minister. "For such a time as this," he said, invoking Mordecai's words to Esther when she was faced with going into a place of potential danger for herself, carrying the burden of her people's safety in her hands (Esther 4:14). In other words, this is exactly the time when pastors are needed. We must preach that God is already at work—even when the underhanded politics of Haman are threatening us. God is already in the tomb even after it appears sealed forever. Jesus has already gone ahead to Galilee to meet you. The Spirit is already at work in ways that may not yet be evident. You are called to be a pastoral presence and to use all of your skills of reflective listening, empathy, and attentive presence.

As we spoke to the students, I advised them that ensuring people's safety is top priority. Given the rhetoric of the man who was then president-elect, a significant portion of this country was now experiencing alarm and legitimate fear about their physical and emotional safety, or for the safety of their family members, friends, fellow students, and coworkers. Women, people of color, immigrants and their children, people of differing sexual orientations, people with disabilities, those who rely on health care from the Affordable Care Act, and Muslims were among those desperately worried about their safety and health as the new administration was coming into power.

"If you are a pastor or leader of a congregation," I said, "you must clearly state that no kind of hateful rhetoric or disparaging remarks about those who are now threatened will be tolerated in God's house of worship. The church is called to be a place of refuge. And if you are a Christian, you are part of the Body of Christ, which means that you are to refrain from that kind of talk even outside of the church. You represent Christ in the world. Behave in a manner that reflects the One whom you worship."

For those brief hours, Dr. Andrews and I counseled the students on how to preach what he aptly called "prophetic care"—a way of understanding prophetic preaching as an *expression of pastoral care*. Rather than seeing the two aspects of ministry in contrast or even opposition to each other, he saw pastoral care and prophetic proclamation as inextricably fused. When pastors care for their people, they call out sin (including systemic sin) for the way it harms individuals, families, communities, the nation, and the planet. And when they are prophetic, it springs from their deep and empathetic—even suffering—love for God's people. All of this is done, he explained, in the spirit of *bridge-building*—seeking ways to span the seemingly uncrossable polarizations between people of different political orientations, religions, races, ages, genders, physical/mental abilities, and socioeconomic strata.

As I listened to and watched Dr. Andrews interacting with these students, I knew I was at the feet of a master. He had a mesmerizing ability to simultaneously comfort the afflicted while challenging them to take up their crosses and follow Jesus. It was like watching a living manifestation of the Chinese principle of yin and yang. Just as the dark and light are balanced with the two halves each containing a kernel of the other, Dale's teaching helped us understand that the pastoral and prophetic are both interdependent and arising from each other. Prophetic care means that the dual callings of confronting sin while also extending loving concern are complementary, interconnected, and interrelated. That day reminded me what the Purple Zone is truly about.

Seven months later, we mourned the untimely death of Dr. Andrews. Yet his work as a homiletician, teacher, minister, and social justice activist, along with his legacy of prophetic care, was immediately preserved and re-seeded into a collection of essays by scholars and practitioners who understood the importance of his bridge-building work. The collection of twenty-nine essays became the edited volume, *Preaching Prophetic Care: Building Bridges to Justice, a Festschrift in Honor of Dale P. Andrews.*[1]

In this final chapter of *Preaching in the Purple Zone*, the concept of bridge-building will be the metaphor for my concluding thoughts about the sermon-dialogue-sermon method. I will begin by setting out some keys to faithful prophetic preaching and dialogue, but we will also consider what to do when the sermon-dialogue-sermon method fails. Not all bridges work, and despite our best efforts, some structures will collapse, or at least need repair or restructuring. I will offer some reflections and suggestions for when this happens in a congregation.

Sometimes, however, the bridges lead to even more connections than we had originally intended. We will look at two examples of clergy who have used the sermon-dialogue-sermon method and deliberative dialogue forums in an expansive way beyond their own congregations. Their bridge-building efforts suggest that the Purple Zone can extend from a single church into partnerships with other congregations and even the secular community.

Before concluding the chapter, I will offer some suggestions for future research. These are based on questions that have come up for me while teaching and writing about the sermon-dialogue-sermon method, as well as from the questionnaire "Preaching About Controversial Justice Issues." My hope is that the work done here will spark ideas for other research projects and bridge-building efforts to enable the Purple Zone to deepen and expand.

BRIDGE-BUILDING IN THE PURPLE ZONE

Recall from chapter 1 that approximately 80 percent of preachers who have addressed a controversial justice issue in their preaching have experienced some kind of negative feedback. Look again at table 1.3 on page 24 to see the ways in which this pushback is experienced. Knowing the reality of our country's polarization, atmosphere of toxic rhetoric, and the risks that come with entering the Purple Zone, these responses should come as no surprise.

This is why it's all the more important that our preaching be both pastoral *and* prophetic. As O. Wesley Allen recommends: "The order should almost always be a movement from pastor to prophet instead of the other way around. If we sound off as a prophet without our congregation (or members of it) knowing and trusting that we care for them, they will never accept us as either pastor or prophet. If, instead, we first establish a strong pastoral relationship with our congregation (and all of its members), then they will trust us when we claim a prophetic voice, whether they agree with our stance or not."[2]

My goal in this book has been to provide pastors and congregations with keys to effectively address issues of public concern as well as a method for doing so in a way that engages both preacher and listeners in a process of deliberative dialogue. Generally, we can say that the keys to preaching and dialoguing about "hot topics" are: 1) articulating boundaries for civil behavior along with reminders of our trust and respect among those in our churches; 2) encouraging the sharing of stories to humanize the difficult issues with which we are grappling; 3) listening deeply and reflectively; 4) moving beyond negative generalizations and stereotypes about the side with which we disagree; 5) seeing how God is working—even within the complexity of our most difficult issues—to bring about new life and renewed hope.

As for the method, the Purple Zone process involves: 1) using a dialogical lens for interpreting scripture and the Five Paths of Prophetic Preaching; 2) preaching a "rooting" sermon that provides biblical and theological rationale for the church to address issues of public concern; 3) carefully choosing a topic from among the issue guides provided by the National Issues Forums Institute and making a plan for engaging in the sermon-dialogue-sermon process; 4) preaching a Prophetic Invitation to Dialogue sermon that acknowledges the complexity of the issue and holds back on expressing a stance on the issue while inviting people to the dialogue; 5) facilitating the deliberative dialogue on the topic; 6) preaching a follow-up sermon, the Communal Prophetic Proclamation, using the conversational/collaborative preaching approach and rhetorical techniques to incorporate the dialogue into the sermon.

As I stated in chapter 2, preaching in the Purple Zone requires courage because of the risks that come with proclaiming prophetic truths. At the same time, preachers are not expected to be like Jesus and be sacrificed for the gospel. Jesus' death on the cross does not have to be repeated. Of course, many preachers do choose to put their lives and/or careers on the line for the sake of the gospel, and thanks be to God for the sacrifices they have made. But there are many other ways to be faithful proclaimers of the Word as well.

If you are one of those pastors who wants to preach prophetically but hesitant for any of the reasons listed in table 1.3, here are some suggestions that summarize what we've learned in the Purple Zone. This is not a complete list, of course, because this is a work in progress. But whether the issue you're facing as a preacher is on an international, national, local, or congregational level, this list is intended as a word of encouragement and practical advice.

1. **Let the biblical text guide you to lift up the "big questions" that underlie the headlines or controversies.** Remember the Five Paths of Prophetic Preaching and remain *rooted* in biblical witness as the first component of prophetic preaching. Before taking a stand on an issue, articulate the questions that arise from the issues and frame them in biblical and theological terms. Key questions might include:

    What does God want for us?
    Where do we find similar situations in the Bible?
    Where or how do we see the Triune God at work?
    What teachings and actions of Jesus might be helpful here?
    Where/What are signs of hope that the Spirit is showing us?
    What is God calling us to do?
    What kind of Christians shall we be in light of this?[3]

2. **Ask yourself: What is breaking my heart the most right now about what's going on with our nation, our community, and/ or our church?** And then ask: If I were sitting in a pew where the pastor was intending to preach a word of truth, hope, and love, what would I want to hear in the sermon? Remember—you are the first hearer of your sermon. If what you preach is not speaking to your own heart and mind, how can you expect it to reach others? This is not to say that you should get on your soapbox or use the pulpit as therapy. But it's okay to be honest about how you feel. Emotions are messengers. The Bible is replete with examples of God's people being honest about their fears, anger, confusion, and joy about the events of the world around them. God can work with those authentic feelings.

3. **Invite conversation after the sermon.** This book showed one model of using a sermon to invite dialogue (Prophetic Invitation to Dialogue), facilitating a deliberative dialogue about a controversial issue, and preaching a follow-up sermon that incorporates the discernment of the group (Communal Prophetic Proclamation). Even if you do not follow this exact process, there are still ways to invite listeners to engage a topic beyond a single, stand-alone sermon. In your sermon, you can offer an opportunity for a roundtable discussion and/ or Bible study about the issue so that the sermon will not be the final word but a word of invitation for community-building. Be sure to use

ground rules for engagement and brush up on your facilitation skills so that the experience will be healthy and productive. Remember—this is not about having a debate or coercing people to change their minds. It's about transforming the culture of the congregation from one of divisiveness (or avoidance) to one of healthy conversation that enables God's justice to take root and grow.

4. **Find ways to build bridges.** Lift up the core values that different viewpoints have in common. Peace, nonviolence, fairness, safety, meaningful work, and healthy relationships are all common ideals we can share, even as we debate about how best to go about achieving them. When preachers remind their congregations of these values, they help to anchor the community in God's intentions. Raising up the vision of hope, forgiveness, and reconciliation that is given by the prophets and Jesus Christ is a way to elevate the conversation above the partisan fray.

5. **Admit your own complicity and struggles with the issue**. Avoid inadvertently setting yourself above and/or apart from the congregation in self-righteousness. Finger-wagging only creates unnecessary and harmful distance between the pastor and congregation. Instead, share how you have come to change your mind about something, how you were once "blind" but now see. Revealing your humanity and vulnerability can help open space for dialogue and prophetic critique.

6. **Use the power of silence, ritual, prayer, and liturgy to hold these powerful emotions and big questions.** If you are truly averse to speaking about an issue, or you discern that the sermon is not the place to tackle it, at least offer some acknowledgment of the event or issue through prayers or some other aspect of the liturgy. A few minutes of prayerful silence during worship can hold and sanctify all that we bring to it. For example, setting up a table full of candles and inviting everyone to light one can provide both prayerful agency and evoke peace in the midst of a chaotic time.

WHEN BRIDGES FAIL AND REPAIRS ARE NEEDED

Even with your best intentions, there is a risk that simply asking the questions about these issues or naming certain current events in your sermon can cause a swift and negative reaction. What we hoped would be a bridge of connection and healing can sometimes be compromised by structural problems or unstable ground on either side. As Ronald J. Allen observes: "In such cases, even something intended to provide safe passage can itself be dangerous."[4]

For example, I was once at a worship service where a clergy colleague was preaching about the commandment on coveting. The preacher made the observation that much of this country's advertising and economic system is based in a cycle of coveting. A loud voice called out from the pews, "No, it's not!" To my colleague's credit, the sermon continued, despite the fact that the interrupter continued to make audible comments throughout the rest of the sermon. Such an interruption indicated that there are likely deep cracks somewhere in the congregation's bridge that need attention.

In my eighteen years of ordained ministry, and in my forty-plus years of hearing sermons in churches, I had never witnessed this kind of intentional disruption during a sermon. It was disconcerting, to say the least. However, when I posed the question to colleagues and clergy groups on Facebook, asking if others were noticing or experiencing this kind of bold-faced interruption during their sermons, within just a few days I received responses from over thirty pastors. Their stories recounted instances they had encountered in the last two years of parishioners interrupting their sermons with hostile verbal feedback. Though I do not yet have formal data to track this kind of behavior, the anecdotal evidence suggests that while it is not widespread, there has been an uptick in the last two to three years of this kind of pushback against pastors *while they are actually preaching.*

More often, however, the negative responses come *after* the sermon in ways listed in chapter 1. As Lisa Cressman describes it: "Sometimes preaching is more like stirring a nest of fire ants. Many of us only have to offer a social justice sermon for those fears to come pouring out every which direction, ready to defend their innate need to survive."[5] Whether it happens during the sermon,[6] in the greeting line after the service, or in a heated exchange via email or in person days later, here are suggestions for how to handle the surge of energy coming from the person so that you can ground it like a lightning rod or even convert it into something that generates positivity and/or growth going forward.

What to Do If You Are "Attacked" about a Sermon

1. **Breathe and pause.** This sounds like a given, but it's the most fundamental thing to remember when powerful energy is coming at us. Taking one deep breath will center you, give you a moment before responding, and allow you to gather your thoughts.
2. **Say "thank you."** This may sound counterintuitive. Why would you thank someone who has just criticized you? Precisely because

they shared their criticism with you directly instead of taking it to the parking lot, or Sunday brunch, or home to talk about you behind your back. So, whether or not you think the criticism was fair, unwarranted, or spot on, you can respond with something like: "Thank you for sharing your concern with me. You could have left without saying anything to me and stewed about it. You would have been angry with me and I would not have known why, so I appreciate you sharing this with me directly."

3. **Ask to meet with the person.** "I want to hear your concerns when we have uninterrupted time. Can we meet for lunch or coffee? Or can I visit you at your home?" Meeting in person is preferable to an email exchange where body language and in-person communication is missing. Also, if the confrontation happens in person at an inopportune time, asking to meet at a separate time communicates your willingness to engage them and give them your full attention. When choosing a location, it's probably best to avoid meeting at your office. Choose neutral ground or their home. A word of caution, however: if you do not trust the goodwill of this person or are feeling unsafe meeting with this person alone for any reason, ask if a neutral third party can be part of your meeting. The board president, head of the staff-parish relations committee, or another mutually agreed-upon person are all good options.

4. **Ask questions that get to the emotional level, rather than debating content.** "How did you feel when you listened to the sermon? What emotions did you experience?" As we discussed in chapter 2, at the base of every conflict that appears to be about principles there are feelings that are powerful and need to be acknowledged. The person may reiterate the principles and intellectual reasons for their dispute with you. Acknowledge them, and then ask how they came to believe the way they do. Invite them to share their journey with you. In other words, use the skills of facilitating a deliberative dialogue—they can be helpful in one-on-one conversations as well.

5. **Use reflective listening.** Listen to them without trying to defend yourself. Ask clarifying questions. And then paraphrase what you heard them say: "What I hear you saying is . . . Do I have that right?" Assuring the person that they have been heard is critical for establishing trust and maintaining the pastoral relationship.

6. **Identify the common biblical and Christian ground.** "We are both Christians and want to follow God's will. We are both serving this church and want what's best for this congregation. We are both good people who have a heart for following Jesus. Remember, there

are lots of stories in the Bible of God's people disagreeing with each other. It's important to me that I hear those disagreements, and I trust the Holy Spirit to guide us through this."
7. **Thank them for sharing with you and affirm your care for them.** It's a sign of trust that they felt comfortable enough to share their feelings and their story with you. Express your appreciation for their willingness to have this difficult conversation, and clearly state your respect and care for them as their pastor.
8. **See if they are willing to hear *you* on a deeper level as well. If they are open, share what's at stake for you.** "Would you like to know why I decided to preach about this?" Explain how you prayerfully discerned the call to preach on the topic in question. Share how you engaged the Bible, looked at different perspectives, and listened to a variety of voices. Then, depending on the context and timing, you might invite them to the deliberative dialogue, or suggest a community conversation about the topic in the future.
9. **If appropriate, apologize.** If you realize you made a mistake, or hurt the person's feelings, don't be afraid to say you're sorry. For example, I once preached a sermon in which I inadvertently perpetuated some harmful stereotypes about older adults. When a parishioner pointed this out, I realized my mistake, apologized, and thanked her for bringing it to my attention.

    This does not mean, however, that we should apologize if someone is offended by the gospel itself. For instance, I once preached a sermon critiquing our country's obsession with war and violence, drawing on the story of Jesus' warning that "those who live by the sword will die by the sword" (Matthew 26:52). A parishioner who worked for a large military industrial corporation felt that I was lambasting his vocation of protecting the country. We had a long conversation in which he shared his passion for, and belief in, his work. I thanked him for sharing his perspective with me, of which I had not previously been aware, and we talked at length about the meaning of Jesus' words. But I did not apologize for the sermon or for Jesus' teaching.
10. **Return to their feelings and seek a way forward.** "How are you feeling now that we've had a chance to talk about this? How can we move forward from here?"

As you can see, this process is about building trust through pastoral relationships. This trust is built over months and years. If you have shown your love for your congregation through visiting them in the hospital, sending cards of appreciation, speaking kind words, thanking them for their service, taking their kids on youth retreats, visiting their relative in the nursing home—all of this will go a long way toward opening their hearts and minds for what you have to say in your sermon. If they know you love them and that you sincerely have their best interests at heart—as well as the best interest of preaching God's Word—this will help to create the kind of community your sermons proclaim. Even when they disagree with you and squirm when their positions are challenged by the gospel, if they experience Christ's love and a heart of peace from you rather than a heart of judgment, the chances of maintaining those relationships in the Purple Zone increase dramatically.[7]

When the Bridge Collapses

When bridges do collapse, it's important for preachers to acknowledge their feelings about this failure *without directing those feelings toward the congregation in a way that exacerbates divisions or inflames hostilities*. Feelings of frustration, disappointment, depression, and anger are all normal when the work we have done either comes up short or elicits the exact opposite response of what we intended. However, we want to avoid channeling these feelings in a way that compounds the problem. Sermons arising from strongly defensive emotions often result in preaching that comes off as dismissive, self-righteous, blaming, or passive-aggressive. I share Allen's observation that "such anger, blasting at those who frustrated the bridging process, typically only feeds the anger present in the system, and increases the violence of the system. Anger begets anger."[8]

This anger may also be directed at the preacher herself or himself, resulting in hopelessness, self-blame, feelings of personal inadequacy, and even doubts about one's call to preach or be in ministry. If this happens for you, keep in mind Allen's wise words:

> The preacher cannot take responsibility for how people respond to prophetic care expressed in thoughtful and pastoral modes. The recipients of the sermon have the freedom to respond as they will. If they accept the invitation toward a more pastoral world, they may take some tentative steps in that direction and become a part of the transformative process. If they do not accept the invitation born from prophetic care, they may maintain, and even intensify present manifestations of polarity . . . The preacher, however, *is* responsible for framing the sermon in such a way as to minimize unnecessary interference between the speaking and the hearing, and to offer as clearly as possible optimum opportunities for recognizing the value of embracing a pastoral approach to life and for suggesting initial steps on that journey.[9]

As we learned in chapters 4, 5, and 6, there are many ways that a pastor can frame their preaching so as not to unnecessarily wallop sore spots and trigger negative reactions. One way to pick up the pieces after a bridge collapse is for the preacher to say to the congregation something akin to: "'Let me share with you something that touches my heart, that I think will touch your heart, and that we can change together.' This approach does not guarantee a positive outcome, but it attempts to deal with a genuinely prophetic concern in a way that is consistent with the pastoral goal itself."[10]

Granted, the above process assumes the presence of emotionally healthy human beings with the ability to self-reflect and have genuine good will. But sometimes the people involved in the conflict are compromised due to their emotional or mental health or level of maturity. Sometimes they are unable or unwilling to self-reflect, do not have good will toward each other, or are simply opposed to the message of the gospel. Sometimes our listeners include those who are so resistant to hearing perspectives that differ from or challenge their own worldview, there is nothing we can do to engage them in constructive dialogue. If this is the case, the Purple Zone process is, admittedly, much more difficult.

It is also the case that some congregational systems are unable either to engage certain topics or to take part in healthy dialogue. As we discussed in chapter 5, some churches have a history of conflict that renders the system unable to withstand any tension. In other words, the structural supports of the bridge are so unstable that it is not able to bear the weight of any conflict. If the bridge does come crumbling down, Allen suggests that the preacher take "a pastoral pause, a time-out. The preacher can step back to survey the scene of bridge failure, to consider what went wrong and why, and to ponder next steps. Such steps could include renewed (if different) approaches to preaching."[11]

Ultimately, of course, "Preachers do not control the effects of sermons in the genre of prophetic care, nor do preachers know what effects such sermons have over time."[12] Speaking from personal experience, there was a time when a sermon I had preached had long-lasting negative effects on a parishioner who felt insulted and ultimately faded away from the church (though the individual never shared with me what they were angry about). On the other hand, I've also heard from a parishioner who reached out to me years after I had moved on from a congregation and reminded me about a sermon I had preached against the United States entering into the Iraq war. At the time, the person was opposed to the stance I had taken. But years later, in retrospect, the person reflected, "You were right. We never should have gotten into that war. That sermon has stuck with me like a kernel in my shoe." So, "like the seeds growing secretly (Mark 4:26–30), sermons may someday push their way to the surface of personal and social consciousness with a pastoral harvest."[13]

WHEN BRIDGES LEAD TO EVEN MORE CONNECTIONS

While the worst-case scenarios exist and can happen in any congregation, it's also true that clergy who enter the Purple Zone with bridge-building intentions can end up making or discovering even more connections than they had anticipated. Lest we forget the power of the Holy Spirit to "make a way out of no way," as the spiritual goes, I want to lift up two examples of clergy who followed the path into the Purple Zone and found it leading to opportunities for bridge-building where none had existed before. Both pastors chose to reach beyond their individual congregations and find dialogue partners with other churches and even with secular groups. The results of their Spirit-led efforts surprised them and their congregations with renewed hope for healing and excitement for growth.

Two Congregations, One Topic

Karleen Jung is the pastor of a small church in a Kentucky suburban area whose members span the political spectrum from very far left to moderate to extreme conservative. The congregation is middle- to upper-middle-class, white, and made up of mostly middle-aged and retired members. Their ministry includes a well-known and award-winning food pantry that serves over 1,000 people each month. Because many of those who visit the food pantry are undocumented and documented immigrants and refugees, Karleen decided to design a sermon-dialogue-sermon series around the issue of immigration. But instead of preaching in the Purple Zone just in her own church, she reached out to another clergy colleague who also pastors a small congregation in their community. They each decided to preach a four-week sermon series in their congregations on the four chapters of the book of Ruth and co-facilitate a deliberative dialogue on immigration using the NIFI issue guide.

In Karleen's first three sermons, she both "rooted" the issue and offered a Prophetic Invitation to Dialogue. Using the story of Naomi and Ruth to illustrate what life was like for those who were refugees and immigrants, she noted the similarities between their story and the stories of contemporary refugees. In both cases, people are escaping conditions of famine and poverty, vulnerable women are often travelling alone, and newcomers face enormous difficulties in adjusting to life in a land where they are not accepted. In all three sermons, Karleen interpreted the text using a dialogical lens, pointing out the exchange between Naomi and Ruth in deciding how they would respond to the tragedies that had befallen them, as well as the exchange between Ruth and Boaz, who would become her protector and husband. All of this was framed within a key theological concept found throughout the book of Ruth—*hesed*, the Hebrew word for God's steadfast faithfulness and love. She invited the congregation to attend the dialogue on immigration in a spirit of *hesed*, showing loving kindness toward each other (regardless of their political positions), toward their ecumenical partners who would join them for the dialogue, and toward immigrants themselves. (You can read excerpts of Karleen's first three sermons at https://www.thepurplezone.net.)

Karleen and her pastoral colleague chose to call this deliberative dialogue session "Sacred Conversations" and began the event with a potluck meal. Over thirty people attended which surprised Karleen, given the level of resistance she encountered from a number of people who were hesitant to participate when invited. I asked her the reasons for their reticence.

"Some are just conflict-averse and are reluctant to take part in anything that might be contentious," she said, "but many were afraid that the discussion would devolve into a tense conflict. Others said that trying to talk about the issue is a useless proposition because people's minds are already made up. 'I'm just not up for this,' was what I heard from a few folks."

Karleen, her pastoral colleague, and the participants were pleasantly surprised to find out their initial misgivings were unwarranted. After agreeing to the ground rules and beginning with prayer, the group of conservative, progressive, and moderate participants were open in their sharing and felt safe enough to disagree with each other without fear of being attacked or disrespected. They split into two groups to discuss the three approaches to the issue, then reconvened to share what they learned and to discern common values. One of the things the group agreed on is that there should be a path made for citizenship for immigrants with no criminal records. While they disagreed on *how* this should happen, there was no disagreement that when families and parents are desperate, they will do anything for their children and loved ones.

Some in the group worked in businesses that employed undocumented workers and shared the harrowing stories they heard of what some of them had endured in their home countries. They also affirmed the strong work ethic and honor they observed in these employees. Yet everyone agreed that there should be restrictions on immigration and that having open borders is not an option. Through the conversation, a sense of empathy for immigrants became obvious, regardless of people's political positions. "We all agreed that these people are children of God, just like us," Karleen said later in reflecting on the experience. "What really surprised me was the sense of hope that came out of the session, like, we really *can* do this! We can talk about this tough issue. By the end, people were talking about the possibility of tackling another tough topic together in the months ahead."

This feeling of new life coming out of a hopeless situation aligned beautifully with the final chapter of Ruth, which Karleen preached about in her Communal Prophetic Proclamation sermon. Just as God's *hesed* is working behind the scenes in the story of Naomi, Ruth, and Boaz, so does that divine loving kindness enter into and shape our story today in subtle ways. As Karleen described it in her sermon:

> By the end of the dialogue, that hope had turned into something more like joy. As I listened to people laugh and joke with each other, even knowing that they might be in different places politically, there was joy in the knowledge that we were still sisters and brothers in Christ and that God had been at work in our conversation. Bringing hope and joy out of anxiety. Bringing new, collaborative possibilities out of old, divisive ways. Bringing fullness out of emptiness. Bringing life out of death.
>
> And, that, my friends, is what this story of Ruth has been all about—God's *hesed*. How God has worked behind the scenes and through the conversations in this story to bring fullness out of emptiness, especially for Naomi. Hope out of loss. Joy out of bitterness. New life out of death. A grandson, who will be in the ancestral line of the King of Kings—our Savior, Jesus Christ. This is a story for our time. It is a way of being together for our time. It is God's way. A way of love-in-action.[14]

FIVE CHURCHES, A COMMUNITY GROUP, AND A SERIES OF DELIBERATIVE DIALOGUES

Daryl Emowrey pastors a small-town congregation in rural Indiana that is almost evenly split between conservatives, moderates, and progressives. While he had been concerned about the growing negativity within our country's public discourse, he was convinced that the good news of God's love is not only desperately needed in the public square but that it can transform people's understanding of the world and how they interact with each other. "I wanted to find a way to point to the love of God in the public realm, to offer another narrative, another view of reality, that is firmly rooted not in the chaos and turbulence we see in the world but in the sure and steadfast love of God revealed to us through Jesus Christ," he said. However, he didn't want to limit this public engagement to just his own congregation, so he reached out to the churches in his town's ministerium, inviting them and their congregations to participate in a community deliberative dialogue.

Four of the clergy responded enthusiastically, so the interdenominational group arranged to hold a series of deliberative dialogues at a local coffee shop to encourage community participation beyond their churches. They also partnered with a local community action group, thus extending the bridge not just within the faith community but to the secular realm as well. They chose four topics: the opioid crisis, mass shootings, immigration, and energy choices. Prior to the beginning of the dialogue series, in the spirit of the Prophetic Invitation to Dialogue, Daryl and one of the other pastors designed their sermons to introduce the upcoming forums within a scriptural framework. Then at each forum, the sessions began with an optional twenty-minute prayer service to lead into the deliberative dialogue. Attendance at the dialogue forums ranged from 23–37 participants.

Each week when they gathered, they broke into smaller groups for the dialogues, which were facilitated by both clergy and lay leaders. Participants included those who came from all four churches and the community action group, as well as folks who were interested in the particular topic being discussed for that session. The town's mayor even attended one of the sessions, indicating how far-reaching deliberative dialogue can be if given space in the public sphere. According to Daryl, the series created a newfound sense of community among the participants who came from many walks of life and represented a cross-section of different ages, occupations, genders, socioeconomic levels, and religious affiliations.

"The clergy and community leaders were all very pleased with the process," Daryl said. "They felt like it helped set the foundation for our primary goal of getting people together and helping them have a space to develop relationships, to talk about tough issues in a constructive way, and, for the church members, to engage all of that process as a part of their faith lives." He noted that one woman was particularly grateful for the forums. "She appreciated the dialogues because these are issues she wants to know more about, and the people in the forums were willing to share what they know. She felt safe in the group because she could admit her lack of knowledge without being judged or ridiculed for her ignorance. She said it was wonderful to have a place like that, to learn alongside others about the things we might do to address these issues in our community."

This last point about addressing these issues in the community was actually the challenge that emerged for Daryl in reflecting on the process. How to follow up on the next steps that were raised during the final stages of each deliberative dialogue was a lingering question. This has, in fact, been a concern for many of the students and pastors I have trained in the sermon-dialogue-sermon method—how to follow through on the good ideas that emerge from the dialogues. The pastor may feel the burden to ensure that the fruits of the dialogue do not simply wither on the vine. This requires communication, organization, and the possibility of recruiting individuals to share in the ministry tasks. All of this can be overwhelming for clergy who are already burdened with too many expectations for their ministry.

What Daryl learned from the process is that helping people connect with each other via email and social media was key to keeping the community conversation going beyond the single deliberative dialogue event. He also noted, depending on the availability and agreement of the groups assembled, that rather than doing four dialogues on four separate topics back-to-back, he would recommend focusing on one issue over the course of several weeks. This would lend itself better to the sermon-dialogue-sermon process and allow the discussion to unfold over a longer period of time with more opportunity for follow-up.

Overall, Daryl found the process of facilitating dialogue with his fellow clergy colleagues to be a blessing. "I thoroughly enjoyed the process," he said. "It was an opportunity to get to know new people and to find ways for our community to engage difficult issues in respectful and healthy ways. I also greatly enjoyed working with the clergy group. They made the process possible *and* joyful. All of the leaders were able to help create a welcoming and inviting atmosphere for people to share their thoughts and opinions in a safe yet challenging way. Participants kept telling us that this is what our society needs; this is what we need to keep doing."

UNANSWERED QUESTIONS AND SUGGESTIONS FOR FUTURE RESEARCH

As we come to the end of this book, I realize that we are really at the *beginning* of this journey into the Purple Zone. The inquiry into how preachers handle sermons about controversial issues that led me into this project is now opening up even more questions. Also, in talking with students and colleagues about my research and the sermon-dialogue-sermon method, many of them have raised questions for me to consider. Here are just a few lines of inquiry and possible research questions:

- **What are options for pastors wanting to extend engagement with a topic beyond a single application of the sermon-**

dialogue-sermon process? After the deliberative dialogue and follow-up sermon, what's next? Should the pastor start the process again with the same issue but with a different group? Or are there ways to build upon the work already done? Could the sermon-dialogue-sermon process become part of a larger cycle wherein the pastor preaches another Prophetic Invitation to Dialogue sermon that references the deliberative dialogue and Communal Prophetic Proclamation sermon that came before? Perhaps this second cycle could revisit the work the congregation has done on the next steps and reassess where they go from here. If so, when should the cycle start again—six months, a year? Should the leaders develop their own issue guide focused on their particular situation?[15] As I continue to work with clergy and lay leaders in the Purple Zone, these are questions I'll be exploring through blog posts on my website, https://www.thepurplezone.net.

- **What effects does the sermon-dialogue-sermon process have over the long term?** While I have trained over thirty students and clergy in the sermon-dialogue-sermon method and nearly all of them have found the process to be productive and life-giving to their preaching and congregations, we don't know what effects this method has beyond a single application. Does the sermon-dialogue-sermon method really make a difference in terms of transforming the culture of a church? For that matter, what effect does the method have on people's lives beyond the parish? Ethnographic research and longitudinal studies will be needed to test what effects this approach to preaching can have in a congregation and in parishioners' lives over an extended time of six months, a year, and even longer.

- **How can *laity* within congregations practice living in the Purple Zone?** As I mentioned in the introduction, this book is designed not just for preachers but for their congregants as well. After having gone through a deliberative dialogue, folks often ask how they can take the principles of dialogue into their everyday life. How can they foster healthier dialogue that would impact their congregation, community, family, schools, and places of employment? Thus, another area of research could be to follow individuals from different walks of life who commit to living out the principles of deliberative dialogue and positive civil engagement to see how they make connections between their faith and their life beyond the church. Look for blog posts that address these questions on my website, https://www.thepurplezone.net.

- **How can we encourage people to participate in dialogue who are suspicious of the process?** Sometimes the very people that should be at the table are the very ones who are absent. People refuse to engage in dialogue for any number of reasons. For more conservative folk, there is sometimes a suspicion that dialogue itself is part of a "liberal agenda" to change their minds. Alternatively, some folk in marginalized populations or those who are wary of power dynamics among the participants may refuse to participate if they feel they are not safe.[16] This is an ongoing question for the Kettering Foundation and NIFI, and one that we continue to wrestle with in the research exchanges.

- **What are the unique challenges for *female* preachers in the Purple Zone?** One group of pastors I trained in the sermon-dialogue-sermon method was a cohort of early-career United Methodist female clergy in Louisiana.[17] Questions that we continually explored revolved around the unique experience of being female while preaching prophetically in a congregation. Issues such as authority, identity, sexuality, embodiment, authenticity, boundaries, voice, and self-care all impact female clergy in ways that are different from their male counterparts. In my research from the "Preaching Controversial Justice Issues" questionnaire, I will explore the differences that gender and sexual orientation make when it comes to tackling issues of public concern in the pulpit. It would also be worth undertaking an ethnographic study to talk to female clergy in order to understand how they negotiate these challenges while preaching in the Purple Zone.

- **What are the unique challenges for *clergy of color* and/or *congregations of color* in the Purple Zone?** You may have noticed that nearly all the case studies and sermon examples in this book came from students and clergy who are white and are serving white congregations.[18] In one sense, this is not surprising, given that mainline Protestant churches in the United States are generally comprised of white members, and Black/African American clergy comprise less than 10 percent of the roster in most mainline Protestant denominations. Nevertheless, this is all the more reason why research into the Purple Zone needs to extend beyond a white/Caucasian population. Political differences are not limited to white congregations. Neither should we make the mistake of assuming that all Black churches are monolithic in their members' politics or stances on issues. A more fine-grained approach is needed for exploring the Purple Zone for clergy of color serving white or multicultural congregations; clergy of color serving Black, Hispanic, Korean, African, or other ethnic congregations; and white clergy serving multicultural congregations.

- **What is the Purple Zone like for congregations in other countries?** While my research is situated among mainline Protestant congregations in the United States, this country is certainly not the only one experiencing polarization, divisiveness, and extremism. However, the culture and context of other nations would certainly impact the contours of the Purple Zone (not to mention that the symbolic colors of "red" and "blue" would not carry the same meaning outside the United States). Also, the relationship between church and state, a preacher's ability to speak freely about issues of public concern, and the particularities of the political situations of different countries would require a modified set of questions and lines of inquiry. Nevertheless, my hunch is that the principles of the sermon-dialogue-sermon process and the deliberative dialogue format would be adaptable to churches in other countries. At the same time, there are likely preaching practices in other countries that might inform Purple Zone preaching in the United States. I welcome and encourage research studies and teaching projects that both incorporate the foundations of Purple Zone preaching in other countries and exchange ideas to enhance Purple Zone bridge-building stateside and in international contexts.

All of this is to say that the Purple Zone is at the seedling stage of research. My hope is that this study will inform the work of other scholars and spark more inquiries into the unique challenges of preaching into the vicissitudes of church and culture in the years to come.

KEEPING THE LONG GAME IN MIND

As we have seen, the task for preachers in this divided time of political discord requires sustained efforts toward prophetic care and bridge-building in congregations and communities. A token sermon here and there with a nod toward justice for God's people and creation would be a disservice to one's pastoral call and the gospel of Jesus Christ. In his book *Preaching in the Era of Trump*, O. Wesley Allen observes: "The true power of the pulpit is less in the individual sermon and more in the cumulative effect of preaching to the same congregation week in and week out over the course of years. We must offer our hearers multiple experiences of an issue over time if we hope for it to take hold in them."[19] The sermon-dialogue-sermon method within the Purple Zone offers a way for preachers and parishioners to have these multiple experiences with an issue over time.

It is my hope that this method is one tool that clergy will find helpful for integrating dialogue and preaching with the kind of prophetic care Dale Andrews had in mind. As Ted Smith describes it:

> In the dialectic Andrews envisions, neither the prophetic nor the pastoral disappears into the other. And neither approach must compromise its deepest commitments. Rather, dialogue elucidates the prophetic dimensions already present in the best pastoral practice. And dialogue pushes prophetic theology toward practice in ways that help it fulfill its own telos of making change in the real world. The two approaches remain distinct, even as they require one another for fulfillment.[20]

Thinking back to that fateful day following the 2016 presidential election when Dr. Andrews and I talked with the students about how the church could move forward in the midst of the onslaught of injustice to come, he reminded them that because they are called by God into ministry: "You don't have the luxury of absence." I added that on the day after Jesus' crucifixion, the women did something that we need to do. They showed up. The women were confused and anguished perhaps angry, and certainly in deep grief. But they went to the tomb because they were faithful. They went to perform the rituals—the sacred actions and words—that were part of their people's faith for centuries. We, too, are called to show up. The dialogue is only possible if the preacher shows up in the Purple Zone with their whole selves and brings all of their "people skills," exegetical tools, theological rigor, pastoral sensitivities, and heart for the gospel.

To quote Mother Teresa, we are not called to be "successful," we are called to be faithful. That faithfulness is aided, in part, by the actions and words of our worship—the rituals and sermons that are designed to hold the vast range of feelings and experiences of the congregation. We can rely on the ancient pattern of worship that is so ingrained in us—gathering, hearing God's word, breaking bread and sharing wine, and sending out into the world. We enter the Purple Zone sustained by divine love, knowing that "there is no fear in love. But perfect love drives out fear" (1 John 4:18a). Let the liturgy and the Word of God minister to you and your congregation. Let it gather in all who will come. And trust that the Spirit of God through the compassion and justice of Jesus Christ will indeed be in our midst to show us the way forward.

Appendix A

Sample Newsletter Article Announcing Deliberative Dialogue

MARK YOUR CALENDAR—DELIBERATIVE DIALOGUE
ON [TOPIC] PLANNED FOR [DATE]

What is the role of the church when faced with controversial issues? How can people of faith address the topic of [SUBJECT]? Join us on [DAY, DATE, TIME] for a nonpartisan deliberative dialogue on [ISSUE] to help our church discuss how we can faithfully engage this issue in the midst of a divided political culture. Our goal is to have a wide range of people from different ages, backgrounds, experiences, and political standpoints in this process, so we hope that you'll attend to share in the dialogue. Copies of the issue guide from the National Issues Forums Institute (part of the Kettering Foundation) will be available in [LOCATION]. With the guidance of the Holy Spirit, we can discern how God is at work in the midst of this complex issue, identify our common values, and suggest ways we can move forward together in faith.

Appendix B

Options for Planning One, Two, or Three Sessions for the Deliberative Dialogue

As mentioned in chapter 7, the deliberative dialogue can be conducted in one, two, or three sessions, depending on the availability and schedule of the congregation, facilitator, and participants. Ideally, the process should happen in a 90- to 180-minute single session. This allows for continuity and maintains momentum, allowing the process to unfold without interruption.

However, if that amount of time is not feasible (such as when the sessions are planned during the one hour of time allotted between or after services during Sunday School on Sunday mornings), then splitting up the sessions is another option. The disadvantages to such an arrangement are that you may not have all the same participants each time, and it may be difficult to maintain a sense of cohesion from week to week. However, there may be an advantage to having two or three sessions in that more people may become involved over the course of time. In any case, you'll need to build in time at the beginning of the second and/or third session to review what happened in the previous one. This will be helpful for past participants and bring new participants up to speed on what occurred. Also, remember to save the large sheets of paper from week to week because they will contain a written record of what was discussed. This will be a helpful reference and visual reminder that can maintain continuity from week to week.

ONE SESSION

Introduce the topic.
Establish ground rules.
Share how this issue impacts you personally.

Evaluate the pros and cons of the three options to identify common themes and shared values.

Reflect on the pros and cons of the three options to identify common themes and shared values.

Suggest and discuss next steps for taking action.

TWO SESSIONS

Session One

Introduce the topic.

Establish ground rules.

Share how this issue impacts you personally.

Evaluate the pros and cons of the three options to identify common themes and shared values.

Session Two

Quick review of the topic.

Quick review of ground rules.

Reflect on the pros and cons of the three options to identify common themes and shared values.

Suggest and discuss next steps for taking action.

THREE SESSIONS

Session One

Introduce the topic.

Establish ground rules.

Share how this issue impacts you personally.

Session Two

Quick review of the topic.

Quick review of ground rules.

Deliberate the pros and cons of the three options.

Session Three

>Quick review of the topic.
>Quick review of ground rules.
>Reflect on the pros and cons of the three options to identify common themes and shared values.
>Suggest and discuss next steps for taking action.

Appendix C

"Cheat Sheet" Questions for Facilitating Deliberative Dialogue

Generally, avoid questions that lead to yes-or-no answers. Frame open-ended questions.

- Could you share a story to illustrate that point?
- I understand you do not like that position, but what do you think people who favor it deeply care about?
- How would someone make a case *against* what you said?
- What is there about this approach that you just cannot accept?
- How may your ideas affect other people?
- Can someone suggest areas that we seem to have in common?
- Would someone identify the values that seem to be clashing? What is really happening here?
- Who should we include in this dialogue that is not already represented?
- If we followed this course of action, what would be the effects on your life?
- What values might people hold who support this position?
- Can anyone envision how their life would change if this approach became national policy?
- What negative consequences might take place if this action were pursued, or what might be foreseeable downsides to this course of action?
- Would you give up [A] in order to achieve [B]?
- What are the consequences of what you said? Do they make a difference?
- How might your concerns differ if you were (poor/wealthy)?
- How do you separate what is a private matter from a public matter in this issue?

Notes

INTRODUCTION

1. John Blake, "Do You Believe in a Red State Jesus or a Blue State Jesus?", CNN, November 2, 2012, accessed July 13, 2016, http://www.cnn.com/2012/11/02/politics/red-blue-state-jesus.

2. Leah D. Schade, *Creation-Crisis Preaching: Ecology, Theology, and the Pulpit* (St. Louis, MO: Chalice Press, 2015).

3. Katie Day, *Difficult Conversations: Taking Risks, Acting with Integrity* (Alban Institute, 2001), 3.

4. Day, *Difficult Conversations*, 5, 9.

5. David Buttrick, "A Fearful Pulpit, a Wayward Land," in *What's the Matter with Preaching Today?*, ed. Mike Graves (Louisville, KY: Westminster/John Knox, 2004), 44.

6. Leonora Tubbs Tisdale, *Prophetic Preaching: A Pastoral Approach* (Louisville, KY: Westminster/John Knox, 2010), xiii, 3.

7. Ronald J. Allen, John S. McClure, and O. Wesley Allen, *Under the Oak Tree: The Church as Community of Conversation in a Conflicted and Pluralistic World* (Eugene, OR: Cascade Books, 2013), xvi.

8. Ronald J. Allen, "Building Bridges: Pastoral Care for the World in a Prophetic Mode," in *Preaching Prophetic Care: Building Bridges to Justice, Essays in Honor of Dale P. Andrews*, ed. Phillis-Isabella Sheppard, Dawn Ottoni-Wilhelm, and Ronald J. Allen (Eugene, OR: Pickwick/Wipf and Stock, 2018), 52.

9. Allen, "Building Bridges," 52.

10. Tisdale, *Prophetic Preaching*, xiii.

CHAPTER 1: PREACHING ABOUT CONTROVERSIAL JUSTICE ISSUES

1. I calculated my optimal sample size (1,051) based on information collected from the statistics and research departments of eight mainline Protestant denominations to

arrive at an estimate of the total number of pastors currently serving congregations. While I received responses that represented over sixteen different denominations, I calculated my sample pool (67,701) based on the number of active, nonretired clergy currently serving congregations in eight denominations in the United States: United Methodist, Presbyterian Church–USA, Episcopal, Lutheran (ELCA), American Baptist, United Church of Christ, Disciples of Christ (Christian Church), and Reformed Church in America. The number of responses (1,205) exceeded the optimal sample size needed for a statistically accurate sampling at a confidence level of 95 percent with a 3 percent margin of error. It is important to note that not all questions were completed by all participants, so the confidence level and margin of error is adjusted accordingly for each question.

2. Leonora Tubbs Tisdale, *Prophetic Preaching: A Pastoral Approach* (Louisville, KY: Westminster/John Knox, 2010), 10–20.

3. Survey questions included all of these demographic subgroups, as well as education level, bilingual and immigration status, age, and ministerial status. These demographic markers as they relate to a preacher's willingness to address controversial justice issues will be addressed in a later work.

4. Duncan Forrester, *Christian Justice and Public Policy* (Cambridge/New York: Cambridge University Press, 1997), 38, referencing the work of Barbara Wootton, *The Social Foundations of Wage Policy: A Study of Contemporary British Wage and Salary Structure* (London: Allen & Unwin, 1962).

5. Richard B. McBrien, "Social Justice: It's in Our Bones," unpublished address cited by Ann Patrick, *Liberating Conscience: Feminist Explorations in Catholic Moral Theology* (New York: Continuum, 1997), 99.

6. Daniel Maguire, *The Moral Care of Judaism and Christianity: Reclaiming the Revolution* (Minneapolis, MN: Fortress, 1993), 211.

7. James Luther Mays, "Justice: Perspectives from the Prophetic Tradition," *Interpretation: A Journal of Bible and Theology* 37, no. 1 (1983): 8.

8. Mays, "Justice," 7.

9. Mays, "Justice," 7.

10. Walter Brueggemann, *Money and Possessions*. Interpretation: Resources for the Use of Scripture in the Church series (Louisville, KY: Westminster/John Knox, 2016), 15.

11. Brueggemann, *Money and Possessions*, 104.

12. Stephen C. Mott, "Justice," *Harper's Bible Dictionary*, 1st ed., Paul Achtemeier, ed. (New York: HarperCollins, 1985), 519–20.

13. Cynthia Moe-Lobeda, *Resisting Structural Evil: Love as Ecological-Economic Vocation* (Minneapolis: Fortress Press, 2013).

14. When discussing the term "prophetic," Tisdale clarifies that she is not speaking of preaching that predicts the future in apocalyptic terms. Rather, she is interested in the type of preaching that is "cutting edge and future oriented (yet not future predicting), and that addresses public and social concerns" (*Prophetic Preaching*, 3). While she includes definitions of "prophetic preaching" by other scholars, she resists offering her own definition. Instead, she offers "seven hallmarks of prophetic preaching" to help readers understand what makes proclamation "prophetic" (see pages 3–10). This will be discussed further in chapter 3.

15. The following is a sample of other questions I intend to pursue through an examination of the data generated by the questionnaire: Are clergy in conservative congregations more or less willing to preach about controversial justice issues? How does the setting of a congregation (rural, urban, suburban) affect the kinds of issues clergy are willing to preach about? Are clergy in certain denominations more likely to address controversial justice issues than others? Does the size of a church—or the size of its budget—have an effect on a minister's willingness to tackle tough topics in the pulpit? Are female preachers more or less likely than their male counterparts to address controversial issues in the pulpit? How do the factors of race, language, and immigration status within a congregation impact a preacher's choice of topics for preaching? Do clergy feel they have been sufficiently prepared by their seminary education to preach about controversial justice issues? What guidance are clergy seeking as they navigate ministry in light of the increasing divisiveness of U.S. politics, and the divides within their congregations? These questions and more will be addressed in a future book using information from the survey.

16. Many respondents took care to note that their sermon subjects are not necessarily driven by current events, but by the lectionary readings assigned for the day. Many preachers follow the Revised Common Lectionary and stated that they will only preach about a specific topic if it is applicable to the biblical text. Other respondents noted that they do not decide what they will preach about until that week but will often mention current issues as they pertain to the biblical text. Ultimately, many survey respondents indicated that they are intent on keeping their focus on the scriptures. As one respondent said, "The top topic I intend to preach on is the gospel reading of the day. If it leads me to preach on any of these [issues] (and often it does), I will go there." See chapter 5 for a more detailed discussion about lectionary preaching versus topical sermons.

17. How do these data compare to other surveys of preachers? According to Guthrie, research conducted by Stark and Glock in the early 1970s indicated that nearly one-third of preachers claiming a liberal political position remained silent on social issues (Rodney Stark, Bruce D. Foster, Charles Y. Glock, and Harold Quinley, "The Sounds of Silence," *Psychology Today* 3, no. 11 (1970): 38–41, 60–61, as described by Guthrie, 82). However, Guthrie also notes that, "Koller and Retzer replicated this study a decade later (1980), challenging what they perceived to be a liberal bias in the first study's design. They surveyed 232 Protestant clergy in North Carolina asking them about their sermon topics on controversial issues, and their attitudes toward preaching. Their survey showed that preachers ten years into their ministries and in this more conservative context were in fact more likely to preach on social issues. Four out of five believed it was part of their duty to speak about such issues from the pulpit, and only 13% had not preached on any of the topics in a list of twenty key issues of the day," (Doug Guthrie, "The Sounds of Silence Revisited," *Sociological Analysis* 41, no. 2 (2007): 82–83, 155–161, referencing Norman B. Koller and Joseph D. Retzer, 1980).

18. In a later word, I will be delving further into the data set to explore this aspect of race within the survey respondents and how this (along with other demographic factors) affected responses.

19. How is this concern different from "pastoral concern for parishioners" or "fear of being disliked"? Tisdale does discuss the pastor's concern of not compounding parishioners' hurts and griefs by preaching "bad news." Likewise, she addresses the personal discomfort pastors feel when they are rejected. However, she does not touch on the ways in which a pastor's ability to effectively minister may be compromised. This includes, but is not limited to, parishioners not calling the pastor when there is a pastoral need (care of the sick, funerals, weddings, etc.), parishioners not trusting the pastor to lead, experiencing a chilling effect on pastoral encounters during visitations, or parishioners refusing to volunteer in the church to avoid working with the pastor.

20. Leah D. Schade, "9 Reasons You Need to Preach about Charlottesville and White Supremacy," EcoPreacher at Patheos, August 15, 2017, http://www.patheos.com/blogs/ecopreacher/2017/08/9-reasons-preach-charlottesville-white-supremacy.

21. Deliberative dialogue is a process developed by researcher Scott London and used by organizations such as the National Issues Forums Institute and the Kettering Foundation which involves face-to-face interactions of small groups of diverse individuals exchanging and weighing ideas and opinions about a particular issue. This process will be discussed at length in chapters 5, 6, and 7.

CHAPTER 2: BEYOND "POLITICAL"

1. H. Richard Niebuhr, *Christ and Culture* (New York: Harper & Row, 1951).

2. Quoted in Robert Benne et al., "'Two Kingdoms' as Social Doctrine," *Dialog* 23, no. 3 (Summer 1982): 210.

3. For a comprehensive and detailed look that the dynamics of women in ministry, see Karoline Lewis, *She: Five Keys to Unlock the Power of Women in Ministry* (Nashville, TN: Abingdon, 2016).

4. David Odom, "Cultivating Trust Is a Crucial Task for Leaders," *Faith and Leadership*, Duke Divinity School, July 24, 2018, accessed September 2, 2018, https://www.faithandleadership.com/dave-odom-cultivating-trust-crucial-task-leaders.

5. Ellen Ott Marshall, *Christians in the Public Square: Faith that Transforms Politics* (Eugene, OR: Wipf and Stock, 2008), xx.

6. Lucas McSurley, unpublished sermon, October 2017. Used with permission.

7. Robert Driesen, "Difficult Conversations and a New Way of Talking," unpublished speech delivered at Bishops Retreat with Rostered Leaders of the Upper Susquehanna Synod, State College, Pennsylvania, April 25, 2016. Used with permission.

8. Audrey Borschel, *Preaching Prophetically When the News Disturbs: Interpreting the Media* (St. Louis, MO: Chalice, 2011), 12.

9. Borschel, *Preaching Prophetically When the News Disturbs*, 13.

10. Leonora Tubbs Tisdale, *Prophetic Preaching: A Pastoral Approach* (Louisville, KY: Westminster/John Knox, 2010), 43.

11. Richard Voelz, forthcoming work to be published by Abingdon, 2019.

12. Voelz, forthcoming, chapter 1.

13. Voelz, forthcoming, chapter 1.

14. Voelz, forthcoming, chapter 1.

15. Voelz, forthcoming, chapter 1.
16. Voelz, forthcoming, chapter 1.
17. Voelz, forthcoming, chapter 1.
18. O. Wesley Allen, *Preaching in the Era of Trump* (St. Louis, MO: Chalice, 2017), 25–26.
19. Allen, *Preaching in the Era of Trump*, 47.

CHAPTER 3: HOMILETICAL FOUNDATIONS FOR PURPLE ZONE PREACHING

1. Karl Barth, quoted in *Time* Magazine, May 31, 1963.
2. Kenyatta R. Gilbert, *The Journey and Promise of African American Preaching* (Minneapolis, MN: Fortress, 2011), 11.
3. Gilbert, *Journey and Promise*, 81.
4. Gilbert, *Journey and Promise*, 12.
5. Dawn Ottoni-Wilhelm, "God's Word in the World: Prophetic Preaching and the Gospel of Jesus Christ," in *Anabaptist Preaching: A Conversation Between Pulpit, Pew, and Bible,* ed. David B. Greiser and Michael A. King (Telford, PA: Cascadia, 2003). Quoted in Tisdale's *Prophetic Preaching*, 5.
6. Ottoni-Wilhelm, "God's Word in the World."
7. Leonora Tubbs Tisdale, *Prophetic Preaching: A Pastoral Approach* (Westminster/John Knox, 2010), 3.
8. Tisdale, *Prophetic Preaching*, 10.
9. David Schnasa Jacobsen, "*Schola Prophetarum*: Prophetic Preaching Toward a Public, Prophetic Church," *Homiletic* 34, no. 1 (2009): 15.
10. Jacobsen, "*Schola Prophetarum*," 12.
11. National Council of Churches, quoted in *Preaching Prophetically When the News Disturbs: Interpreting the Media*, Audrey Borschel (St. Louis, MO: Chalice, 2011), 7; citing William J. Nottingham, *The Practice and Preaching of Liberation* (St. Louis, MO: CBP Press, 1986), 26.
12. Clark M. Williamson and Ronald J. Allen, *A Credible and Timely Word: Process Theology and Preaching* (St. Louis, MO: Chalice, 1991), 42.
13. Dennis Ngien, "Theology of Preaching in Martin Luther," *Themelios* 28.2 (Spring 2003), http://www.biblicalstudies.org.uk/pdf/themelios/luther_ngien.pdf.
14. Richard Lischer, *A Theology of Preaching: The Dynamics of the Gospel*, rev. ed. (Eugene, OR: Wipf and Stock, 2001), 9.
15. John S. McClure, *Other-Wise Preaching: A Postmodern Ethic for Homiletics* (St. Louis, MO: Chalice, 2001), 136.
16. McClure, *Other-Wise Preaching*, 139.
17. McClure, *Other-Wise Preaching*, 137.
18. McClure, *Other-Wise Preaching*, 137.
19. Lischer, *A Theology of Preaching*, 21.
20. Gilbert, *Journey and Promise*, 15.
21. Gilbert, *Journey and Promise*, 57.
22. Fred Craddock, *As One Without Authority* (Nashville, TN: Parthenon, 1979), 55.

23. Lucy Atkinson Rose, *Sharing the Word: Preaching in the Roundtable Church* (Louisville, KY: Westminster/John Knox, 1997).

24. John S. McClure, *The Roundtable Pulpit: Where Leadership and Preaching Meet* (Nashville, TN: Abingdon, 1995); Ronald J. Allen, *Interpreting the Gospel: An Introduction to Preaching* (St. Louis, MO: Chalice, 1998); O. Wesley Allen Jr., *The Homiletic of All Believers* (Louisville, KY: Westminster/John Knox, 2005).

25. Rose, *Sharing the Word*, 4–5.

26. Jacobsen, "*Schola Prophetarum*," 19.

27. Rose, *Sharing the Word*, 128.

28. Rose, *Sharing the Word*, 123.

29. Ronald J. Allen and O. Wesley Allen, *The Sermon without End: A Conversational Approach to Preaching* (Nashville, TN: Abingdon, 2015), 102.

30. Ronald J. Allen, "Building Bridges: Pastoral Care for the World in a Prophetic Mode," in *Preaching Prophetic Care: Building Bridges to Justice, Essays in Honor of Dale P. Andrews* (Eugene, OR: Pickwick/Wipf and Stock, 2018), 48, footnote 3.

CHAPTER 4: FIVE PATHS OF PROPHETIC PREACHING IN THE PURPLE ZONE

1. Leah D. Schade, *Creation-Crisis Preaching: Ecology, Theology, and the Pulpit* (St. Louis, MO: Chalice, 2015), chapter 2.

2. See *The Green Bible* (New York: HarperCollins, 2008) for passages about nature marked in green ink to understand the full scope of biblical references to Creation.

3. See Walter Brueggemann, *Money and Possessions*. Interpretation: Resources for the Use of Scripture in the Church series (Louisville, KY: Westminster/John Knox, 2016).

4. For an excellent study on this process of deliberation, see Luke Timothy Johnson, *Scripture and Discernment: Decision Making in the Church* (Nashville, TN: Abingdon, 1983).

5. The dialogical lens I am describing is not to be confused with Martin Buber's *dialogical hermeneutic*. See Steven Kepnes, *The Text as Thou: Martin Buber's Dialogical Hermeneutics and Narrative Theology* (Bloomington, IN: Indiana University Press, 1992).

6. David Lose, "Preaching as Conversation," in *Under the Oak Tree: The Church as Community of Conversation in a Conflicted and Pluralistic World*, ed. Ronald J. Allen, John S. McClure, and O. Wesley Allen Jr. (Eugene, OR: Cascade Books, 2013), 87.

7. John S. McClure, *Other-Wise Preaching: A Postmodern Ethic for Homiletics* (St. Louis, MO: Chalice, 2001).

8. Ian McMichael, unpublished sermon, February 2018. Used with permission.

9. Daniel Gutman, unpublished sermon, February 2018. Used with permission.

CHAPTER 5: PREPARING FOR THE SERMON-DIALOGUE-SERMON PROCESS

1. Julie Cory, unpublished sermon, June 2018. Used with permission.

2. "About the NIF," National Issues Forums Institute, accessed July 7, 2018, https://www.nifi.org/en/home.

3. See also, Martín Carcasson, "Tackling Wicked Problems through Deliberative Engagement," Colorado State University Center for Public Deliberation, October 2013, accessed August 6, 2018, https://cpd.colostate.edu/wp-content/uploads/sites/4/2014/01/tackling-wicked-problems-through-deliberative-engagement.pdf.

4. It is possible to create your own issue guide, but the process is labor-intensive. Nevertheless, the NIFI has personnel and resources who can guide you through the process. Examples of issue guides created by local communities are available on the NIFI website.

5. Aimee C. Moiso, "Standing in the Breach: Conflict Transformation and the Practice of Preaching," unpublished paper presented at the 2018 Academy of Homiletics.

6. For resources on conflict management, try the following: Arbinger Institute, *The Anatomy of Peace: Resolving the Heart of Conflict*, 2nd ed. (Oakland, CA: Berrett-Koehler, 2015); Kendra Dunbar et al., "Conflict Transformation," JustPeace UMC (United Methodist Church), https://justpeaceumc.org/category/conflict-transformation; Speed Leas, "Levels of Conflict," Center for Congregational Health, https://cntr4conghealth.wordpress.com/2011/09/01/levels-of-conflict-by-speed-leas; Carolyn Schrock-Shenk, *Making Peace with Conflict: Practical Skills for Conflict Transformation* (Herald Press, 1999). See also Ellen Ott Marshall, *Christians in the Public Square: Faith that Transforms Politics* (Eugene, OR: Wipf and Stock, 2008). Ellen Ott Marshall, ed., *Conflict Transformation and Religion: Essays on Faith, Power, and Relationship* (New York: Palgrave Macmillan/Springer Nature, 2016).

7. Moiso, "Standing in the Breach."

8. See chapter 4 of Lucy Atkinson Rose's book, *Sharing the Word: Preaching in the Roundtable Church* (Louisville, KY: Westminster/John Knox, 1997), for an extended discussion of what it means to consider those who are not "at the table" in our roundtable pulpits.

9. David G. Buttrick, *Homiletic: Moves and Structures* (Philadelphia: Fortress, 1987), 405–48.

10. Ronald J. Allen, *Preaching the Topical Sermon* (Louisville, KY: Westminster/John Knox Press, 1992), 5.

11. Allen, *Preaching the Topical Sermon*, 11.

12. Allen, *Preaching the Topical Sermon*, 3.

13. The conversational *approach* to preaching is not to be confused with the conversational *style* of preaching, whereby a preacher assumes a less formal, more conversational tone of voice or mode of delivery.

14. Ronald J. Allen and O. Wesley Allen Jr., *The Sermon without End: A Conversational Approach to Preaching* (Nashville, TN: Abingdon, 2015), 104.

15. Allen and Allen, *The Sermon without End*, 105.

CHAPTER 6: PREACHING SERMON 1

1. Ronald J. Allen, "Building Bridges: Pastoral Care for the World in a Prophetic Mode," in *Preaching Prophetic Care: Building Bridges to Justice, Essays in Honor of Dale P. Andrews*, ed. Phillis-Isabella Sheppard, Dawn Ottoni-Wilhelm, and Ronald J. Allen (Eugene, OR: Pickwick/Wipf and Stock, 2018), 54.

2. O. Wesley Allen Jr., *Preaching in the Era of Trump* (St. Louis, MO: Chalice), 27.

3. In his book, *The Roundtable Pulpit: Where Leadership and Preaching Meet*, John McClure suggests that the preaching ministry is an act of hospitality wherein "the preacher is a *host* who welcomes to a roundtable strangers who bring various gifts into the community." Just as the table is at the heart of Christian hospitality, so the preacher strives to "keep the pulpit and the Lord's table in as close proximity as possible" (29).

4. Linda Clader, *Voicing the Vision: Imagination and Prophetic Preaching* (Harrisburg, PA: Morehouse, 2004), 6.

5. Paul Scott Wilson, *The Four Pages of the Sermon* (Nashville, TN: Abingdon Press, 1999).

6. Joanna Samuelson, unpublished sermon, October 2017. Used with permission.

7. Laura Ferree, unpublished sermon, March 2018. Used with permission.

8. Leslie Stephens, unpublished sermon, April 2018. Used with permission.

9. TJ Lynch, unpublished paper, December 2018. Used with permission.

10. J. Philip Wogaman, *Speaking Truth in Love: Prophetic Preaching to a Broken World* (Louisville, KY: Westminster/John Knox, 1998), 19, quoted in Tisdale, *Prophetic Preaching: A Pastoral Approach* (Louisville, KY: Westminster/John Knox, 2010), 43.

CHAPTER 7: DELIBERATIVE DIALOGUE IN THE PURPLE ZONE

1. Michael D. Regan, "What Does Voter Turnout Tell Us about the 2016 Election?," PBS *NewsHour Weekend*, November 20, 2016, accessed September 20, 2018, https://www.pbs.org/newshour/politics/voter-turnout-2016-elections.

2. Dana Horrell, "Holding a Forum on a Difficult Public Issue," Faithful Citizen (blog), March 24, 2018, accessed July 29, 2018, http://faithfulcitizen.net/holding-a-forum-on-a-difficult-public-issue.

3. Gregg Kaufman and the Kettering faith-based research team have developed faith-based leader guides for several of the NIFI issue guides to enable houses of worship to more easily adapt the materials to their faith-based setting. Visit http://www.thedeliberativevoice.com and click "Contact" to submit an inquiry.

4. Other organizations include Sustained Dialogue Institute (https://sustaineddialogue.org), Better Angels (https://www.better-angels.org), National Institute for Civil Discourse (https://nicd.arizona.edu), and Teaching Tolerance (https://www.tolerance.org), to name a few.

5. Roger Willer, "Community of Moral Deliberation and an Emerging Responsibility Ethic," *Journal of Lutheran Ethics*, April 4, 2014, accessed July 29, 2018, https://www.elca.org/JLE/Articles/56.

6. Joanna Samuelson, unpublished paper, December 2017. Used with permission.

7. Katie Day, *Difficult Conversations: Taking Risks, Acting with Integrity* (Alban Institute: 2001), 47.

8. Two other sources for ground rules I've found helpful are "Touchstones for Creating Safe Spaces" by the Center for Courage and Renewal (https://www.couragerenewal.org/PDFs/HHD/Touchstones-for-Creating-Safe-Spaces-HHD-guide.pdf) and "Invitation to Brave Space" by Mickey ScottBey Jones (http://www.mickyscottbeyjones.com/invitation-to-brave-space).

9. See Martín Carcasson, "Tackling Wicked Problems through Deliberative Engagement," Colorado State University Center for Public Deliberation, October 2013, 11, accessed August 6, 2018, https://cpd.colostate.edu/wp-content/uploads/sites/4/2014/01/tackling-wicked-problems-through-deliberative-engagement.pdf.

10. Horrell, "Holding a Forum."

CHAPTER 8: PREACHING SERMON 2

1. John S. McClure, *The Roundtable Pulpit: Where Leadership and Preaching Meet* (Nashville: Abingdon, 1995), 47.

2. See chapter 3 for a fuller discussion on the way in which conversational preaching influences this approach.

3. McClure, *Roundtable Pulpit*, 9.

4. McClure, *Roundtable Pulpit*, 11.

5. McClure, *Roundtable Pulpit*, 20.

6. McClure, *Roundtable Pulpit*, 20.

7. Kenyatta R. Gilbert, *The Journey and Promise of African American Preaching* (Minneapolis: Fortress, 2011), 81.

8. McClure, *Roundtable Pulpit*, 24.

9. McClure, *Roundtable Pulpit*, 22.

10. McClure, *Roundtable Pulpit*, 49–50.

11. Ronald J. Allen and O. Wesley Allen, Jr., *The Sermon without End: A Conversational Approach to Preaching* (Nashville: Abingdon, 2015), 105.

12. O. Wesley Allen Jr., *Preaching in the Era of Trump* (St. Louis, MO: Chalice, 2017), 19.

13. McClure, *Roundtable Pulpit*, 56.

14. McClure, *Roundtable Pulpit*, 57.

15. See *Preaching Prophetic Care: Building Bridges to Justice, Essays in Honor of Dale P. Andrews,* ed. Phillis-Isabella Sheppard, Dawn Ottoni-Wilhelm, and Ronald J. Allen (Eugene, OR: Pickwick/Wipf and Stock), 2018.

16. Leonora Tubbs Tisdale, *Prophetic Preaching: A Pastoral Approach* (Louisville, KY: Westminster/John Knox, 2010), 43.

17. Tisdale, *Prophetic Preaching*, 43.

18. McClure, *Roundtable Pulpit*, 57. Citing David J. Hesselgrave, "Gold from Egypt: The Contribution of Rhetoric to Cross-Cultural Communication," *Missiology: An International Review* 4 (1976): 95.

19. McClure, *Roundtable Pulpit*, 73.

20. McClure, *Roundtable Pulpit*, 58. To aid in including the "actual talk" of the dialogue, McClure provides helpful rhetorical strategies for recreating the dynamics of the dialogue in his chapter, "The Language of Collaboration: What It Sounds Like."

21. Gregg Kaufman, a research associate with Kettering Foundation and the National Issues Forums Institute whom I mentioned in chapter 7, has developed faith-based leader materials for a few of the NIFI issue guides, including gender-based violence and the opioid epidemic. At the time of this writing, he is working with a

team of fellow research associates to develop future materials to be used by faith groups to facilitate deliberative dialogues in their settings. Visit http://www.thedeliberative voice.com and click "Contact" to request more information.

22. See chapter 5 for an explanation of how to preach using a topical sermon.
23. See *Preaching Prophetic Care*, ed. Sheppard et al.
24. Laura Ferree, unpublished sermon, April 2018. Used with permission.
25. Colleen Bookter, unpublished sermon, May 2018. Used with permission.
26. McClure, *Roundtable Pulpit*, 58.
27. Allen, *Preaching in the Era of Trump*, 54.

CHAPTER 9: CASE STUDIES FROM THE PURPLE ZONE, PART 1

1. O. Wesley Allen, *Preaching in the Era of Trump* (St. Louis, MO: Chalice, 2017), 23.
2. Allen, *Preaching in the Era of Trump*, 24.
3. Allen, *Preaching in the Era of Trump*, 24.
4. The Marshall Islands are an island nation east of the Philippines being swallowed up by rising sea levels due to climate change. The Compact of Free Association has allowed for Marshall Islands refugees to migrate visa-free to the United States. It was created as a favor after Marshallese land was used as a site for nuclear testing which resulted in contamination and disease after dozens of U.S. nuclear bomb tests were conducted there in the 1940s and 1950s.
5. Daniel Gutman, unpublished sermon, April 2018. Used with permission.
6. For more information on the Sanctuary Movement, visit: https://www.sanctuarynotdeportation.org.
7. Gordon W. Lathrop, *Holy Ground: A Liturgical Cosmology* (Minneapolis, MN: Fortress, 2009), 30–33, 38, 108, 133, 135, 142.
8. John McClure, *The Roundtable Pulpit: Where Leadership and Preaching Meet* (Nashville: Abingdon, 1995), 57.
9. Lucas McSurley, unpublished sermon, October 2017. Used with permission.
10. Lucas McSurley, unpublished sermon, December 2017. Used with permission.
11. Ian McMichael, unpublished sermon, March 2018. Used with permission.
12. Ian McMichael, unpublished sermon, April 2018. Used with permission.
13. Katie Day, *Difficult Conversations: Taking Risks, Acting with Integrity* (Alban Institute, 2001), 55.
14. Ian McMichael, unpublished paper, May 2018. Used with permission.
15. Day, *Difficult Conversations*, 61.
16. McMichael, unpublished paper.
17. Day, *Difficult Conversations*, 30.
18. Lucas McSurley, unpublished paper, December 2017. Used with permission.
19. McMichael, unpublished paper.
20. Ronald J. Allen, "Building Bridges: Pastoral Care for the World in a Prophetic Mode," in *Preaching Prophetic Care: Building Bridges to Justice, Essays in Honor of Dale P.*

Andrews, ed. Phillis-Isabella Sheppard, Dawn Ottoni-Wilhelm, and Ronald J. Allen (Eugene, OR: Pickwick/Wipf and Stock, 2018), 55.

CHAPTER 10: CASE STUDIES, PART 2

1. John S. McClure, *The Roundtable Pulpit: Where Leadership and Preaching Meet* (Nashville, TN: Abingdon, 1995), 13–14.
2. Andrew Shue, unpublished sermon, June 2017. Used with permission.
3. Rachel McConnell-Switzer, unpublished sermon, March 2018. Used with permission.
4. Rachel McConnell-Switzer, unpublished sermon, May 2018. Used with permission.
5. TJ Lynch, unpublished paper, December 2017. Used with permission.
6. TJ Lynch, unpublished sermon, December 2017. Used with permission.
7. Food deserts are neighborhoods or communities where it is difficult to buy affordable or good-quality fresh food. Food deserts result from a dearth of grocery stores or farmers markets within an easily traveled distance for local residents. In these areas (which can be in rural, suburban, or urban areas), the main food sources tend to be convenience stores, gas stations, or fast food restaurants.
8. Brooke Baker, unpublished sermon, July 2017. Used with permission.

CHAPTER 11: BUILDING BRIDGES IN THE PURPLE ZONE

1. *Preaching Prophetic Care: Building Bridges to Justice, Essays in Honor of Dale P. Andrews*, ed. Phillis-Isabella Sheppard, Dawn Ottoni-Wilhelm, and Ronald J. Allen (Eugene, OR: Pickwick/Wipf and Stock, 2018).
2. O. Wesley Allen, *Preaching in the Era of Trump* (St. Louis, MO: Chalice, 2017), 26.
3. An excellent book for helping preachers articulate what it looks like to be our best selves in times of crisis is Margaret J. Wheatley's, *Who Do We Choose to Be?: Facing Reality, Claiming Leadership, Restoring Sanity* (Oakland, CA: Berrett-Koehler, 2017).
4. Ronald J. Allen, "Building Bridges: Pastoral Care for the World in a Prophetic Mode," in *Preaching Prophetic Care*, 55.
5. Lisa Cressman, *Backstory Preaching: Integrating Life, Spirituality, and Craft* (Collegeville, MN: Liturgical Press, 2018), 99.
6. There are, of course, many variables involved in instances of hostile sermon interruptions. Is the person a member or a visitor? Does the person have a history of inappropriate behavior? Is this interruption part of a pattern of behavior? Is there a threat to anyone's safety? Steps 1, 2, and 3 above can happen fairly quickly in the moment during a sermon. The remaining steps would, of course, happen after the service. It is prudent to have ushers trained for how to handle situations that may escalate.
7. An excellent book for helping people work through conflicted situations is Arbinger Institute's *The Anatomy of Peace: Resolving the Heart of Conflict* (Oakland, CA: Berrett-Koehler, 2015).

8. Allen, "Building Bridges," 57.
9. Allen, "Building Bridges," 57.
10. Allen, "Building Bridges," 57.
11. Allen, "Building Bridges," 58.
12. Allen, "Building Bridges," 58.
13. Allen, "Building Bridges," 58.
14. Karleen Jung, unpublished sermon, August 2018. Used with permission.
15. Recall that two of the preachers discussed in this book did develop their own materials (see Jenny Perkins' story in chapter 9 and Brooke Baker's story in chapter 10). The Kettering Foundation and National Issues Forums Institute have resources and offer assistance for groups looking to create their own issue guides. Visit https://www.nifi.org.
16. For example, the basic assumption of deliberative dialogue—that citizens can gather together in a civil way to talk and solve problems—assumes that all parties are on equal ground. This is not always the case, especially if the participants are an employer and employee, for example. The person in the subordinate position may not feel comfortable challenging someone who is in a position of power over them. Or as a friend once said to me, when it comes to certain people's attitudes toward other-than-white, male, heterosexual folks, "You can't expect me to dialogue with someone who wants to take away my rights, wants me silenced, wants me deported, jailed, or even dead." This is a reality for many which cannot be minimized and must be taken seriously as we pursue the process of deliberation.
17. This training was made possible through the Perkins Center for Preaching Excellence, Perkins School of Theology at Southern Methodist University, under the direction of Alyce McKenzie.
18. All but a few of the students and clergy I trained in the initial courses were white/Caucasian. One of the exceptions was Tiffanie Postell, an African American pastor who served an African American church in Louisiana. She chose to preach on the issue of hunger in her community and utilized the NIFI issue guide "Land of Plenty" for her deliberative dialogue. In the dialogue, the older participants shared stories of how families used to engage in food sharing in past generations. This became an important communal memory for the group. The common value of working together to solve a problem came to the fore and confirmed Tiffanie's hunch that education and sharing narratives could help bridge the generational gap in her congregation.
19. Allen, *Preaching in the Era of Trump*, 20.
20. Ted A. Smith, "Truly More Than Just: On the Bridge Between the Pastoral and the Prophetic," in *Preaching Prophetic Care*, 38–39.

Selected Bibliography

Achtemeier, Paul, ed. *Harper's Bible Dictionary*, 1st ed. New York: HarperCollins, 1985.
Allen, O. Wesley Jr. *The Homiletic of All Believers*. Louisville, KY: Westminster/John Knox, 2005.
———. *Preaching in the Era of Trump*. St. Louis, MO: Chalice, 2017.
Allen, Ronald J. "Building Bridges: Pastoral Care for the World in a Prophetic Mode." In *Preaching Prophetic Care: Building Bridges to Justice, Essays in Honor of Dale P. Andrews*, edited by Phillis-Isabella Sheppard, Dawn Ottoni-Wilhelm, and Ronald J. Allen. Eugene, OR: Pickwick/Wipf and Stock, 2018.
———. *Interpreting the Gospel: An Introduction to Preaching*. St. Louis, MO: Chalice, 1998.
———. *Preaching the Topical Sermon*. Louisville, KY: Westminster/John Knox, 1992.
Allen, Ronald J., and O. Wesley Allen Jr. *The Sermon without End: A Conversational Approach to Preaching*. Nashville, TN: Abingdon, 2015.
Allen, Ronald J., John S. McClure, and O. Wesley Allen Jr., eds. *Under the Oak Tree: The Church as Community of Conversation in a Conflicted and Pluralistic World*. Eugene, OR: Cascade Books, 2013.
Arbinger Institute. *The Anatomy of Peace: Resolving the Heart of Conflict*, 2nd ed. Oakland, CA: Berrett-Koehler, 2015.
Benne, Robert, et al. "'Two Kingdoms' as Social Doctrine." *Dialogue* 23, no. 3 (Summer 1982): 210.
Blake, John. "Do You Believe in a Red State Jesus or a Blue State Jesus?" CNN, November 2, 2012. Accessed July 13, 2016. http://www.cnn.com/2012/11/02/politics/red-blue-state-jesus.
Borschel, Audrey. *Preaching Prophetically When the News Disturbs: Interpreting the Media*. St. Louis, MO: Chalice, 2011.
Brueggemann, Walter. *Money and Possessions*. Interpretation: Resources for the Use of Scripture in the Church series. Louisville, KY: Westminster/John Knox, 2016.
Buttrick, David G. "A Fearful Pulpit, a Wayward Land." In *What's the Matter with Preaching Today?*, edited by Mike Graves. Louisville, KY: Westminster/John Knox, 2004.

———. *Homiletic: Moves and Structures*. Philadelphia: Fortress, 1987.
Carcasson, Martín. "Tackling Wicked Problems through Deliberative Engagement." Colorado State University Center for Public Deliberation. October 2013. Accessed August 6, 2018. https://cpd.colostate.edu/wp-content/uploads/sites/4/2014/01/tackling-wicked-problems-through-deliberative-engagement.pdf.
Clader, Linda. *Voicing the Vision: Imagination and Prophetic Preaching*. Harrisburg, PA: Morehouse, 2004.
Craddock, Fred. *As One Without Authority*. Nashville, TN: Parthenon, 1979.
Cressman, Lisa. *Backstory Preaching: Integrating Life, Spirituality, and Craft*. Collegeville, MN: Liturgical Press, 2018.
Day, Katie. *Difficult Conversations: Taking Risks, Acting with Integrity*. Alban Institute, 2001.
Forrester, Duncan. *Christian Justice and Public Policy*. Cambridge/New York: Cambridge University Press, 1997.
Gilbert, Kenyatta R. *The Journey and Promise of African American Preaching*. Minneapolis, MN: Fortress, 2011.
Guthrie, Doug. "The Sounds of Silence Revisited." *Sociological Analysis* 41, no. 2: 82–161.
Horrell, Dana. "Holding a Forum on a Difficult Public Issue." Faithful Citizen (blog). March 24, 2018. Accessed July 28, 2018. http://faithfulcitizen.net/holding-a-forum-on-a-difficult-public-issue/.
Jacobsen, David Schnasa. "*Schola Prophetarum*: Prophetic Preaching Toward a Public, Prophetic Church." *Homiletic* 34, no. 1 (2009): 12–21.
Johnson, Luke Timothy. *Scripture and Discernment: Decision Making in the Church*. Nashville, TN: Abingdon, 1983.
Kepnes, Steven. *The Text as Thou: Martin Buber's Dialogical Hermeneutics and Narrative Theology*. Bloomington, IN: Indiana University Press, 1992.
Lathrop, Gordon W. *Holy Ground: A Liturgical Cosmology*. Minneapolis, MN: Fortress, 2009.
Lewis, Karoline M. *She: Five Keys to Unlock the Power of Women in Ministry*. Nashville, TN: Abingdon, 2016.
Lischer, Richard. *A Theology of Preaching: The Dynamics of the Gospel*, rev. ed. Eugene, OR: Wipf and Stock, 2001.
Maguire, Daniel. *The Moral Care of Judaism and Christianity: Reclaiming the Revolution*. Minneapolis, MN: Fortress, 1993.
Marshall, Ellen Ott. *Christians in the Public Square: Faith that Transforms Politics*. Eugene, OR: Wipf and Stock, 2008.
———. *Conflict Transformation and Religion: Essays on Faith, Power, and Relationship*. New York: Palgrave Macmillan/Springer Nature, 2016.
Mays, James Luther. "Justice: Perspectives from the Prophetic Tradition." *Interpretation: A Journal of Bible and Theology* 37, no. 1 (1983).
McBrien, Richard B. "Social Justice: It's in Our Bones." Unpublished address. Cited by Ann Patrick. *Liberating Conscience: Feminist Explorations in Catholic Moral Theology*. New York: Continuum, 1997.

McClure, John S. *Other-Wise Preaching: A Postmodern Ethic for Homiletics.* St. Louis, MO: Chalice, 2001.

———. *The Roundtable Pulpit: Where Leadership and Preaching Meet.* Nashville, TN: Abingdon, 1995.

Moe-Lobeda, Cynthia. *Resisting Structural Evil: Love as Ecological-Economic Vocation.* Minneapolis, MN: Fortress, 2013.

Moiso, Aimee C. "Standing in the Breach: Conflict Transformation and the Practice of Preaching." Unpublished paper presented at the 2018 Academy of Homiletics.

Ngien, Dennis. "Theology of Preaching in Martin Luther." *Themelios* 28.2 (Spring 2003). http://www.biblicalstudies.org.uk/pdf/themelios/luther_ngien.pdf.

Niebuhr, H. Richard. *Christ and Culture.* New York: Harper & Row, 1951.

Odom, David. "Cultivating Trust Is a Crucial Task for Leaders." *Faith and Leadership*, Duke Divinity School. July 24, 2018. Accessed September 2, 2018. https://www.faithandleadership.com/dave-odom-cultivating-trust-crucial-task-leaders.

Ottoni-Wilhelm, Dawn. "God's Word in the World: Prophetic Preaching and the Gospel of Jesus Christ." In *Anabaptist Preaching: A Conversation Between Pulpit, Pew, and Bible*, edited by David B. Greiser and Michael A. King. Telford, PA: Cascadia, 2003.

Rose, Lucy Atkinson. *Sharing the Word: Preaching in the Roundtable Church.* Louisville, KY: Westminster/John Knox, 1997.

Schade, Leah D. *Creation-Crisis Preaching: Ecology, Theology, and the Pulpit.* St. Louis, MO: Chalice, 2015.

———. "9 Reasons You Need to Preach about Charlottesville and White Supremacy." EcoPreacher at Patheos. August 15, 2017. http://www.patheos.com/blogs/ecopreacher/2017/08/9-reasons-preach-charlottesville-white-supremacy.

Smith, Christine. *Preaching as Weeping, Confession and Resistance: Radical Responses to Radical Evil.* Louisville, KY: Westminster/John Knox, 1992.

Smith, Ted A. "Truly More Than Just: On the Bridge Between the Pastoral and the Prophetic." In *Preaching Prophetic Care: Building Bridges to Justice, Essays in Honor of Dale P. Andrews*, edited by Phillis-Isabella Sheppard, Dawn Ottoni-Wilhelm, and Ronald J. Allen. Eugene, OR: Pickwick/Wipf and Stock, 2018.

Tisdale, Leonora Tubbs. *Prophetic Preaching: A Pastoral Approach.* Louisville, KY: Westminster/John Knox, 2010.

Voelz, Richard. Forthcoming. Abingdon, 2019.

Willer, Roger. "Community of Moral Deliberation and an Emerging Responsibility Ethic." *Journal of Lutheran Ethics.* April 4, 2014. Accessed July 29, 2018. https://www.elca.org/JLE/Articles/56.

Williamson, Clark M., and Ronald J. Allen. *A Credible and Timely Word: Process Theology and Preaching.* St. Louis, MO: Chalice, 1991.

Wootton, Barbara. *The Social Foundations of Wage Policy: A Study of Contemporary British Wage and Salary Structure.* London: Allen & Unwin, 1962.

Scripture Index

OLD TESTAMENT

Genesis
  2:15 — 60
  chapter 11 — 62
Exodus
  1:15–2:10 — 137
  3:1–17 — 39
  5:1–12 — 137
  5:18–21 — 137
  chapter 18 — 62
Numbers
  21:4–9 — 144
Deuteronomy
  4:6 — 97
  7:2–5 — 63
  10:19 — 62
Joshua
  chapter 22 — 62
Ruth, Book of — 128, 192–194
  chapter 2 — 63
1 Samuel
  3:1–21 — 150–151
1 Kings
  17:17–24 — 60
Ezra/Nehemiah — 62
Esther
  4:14 — 6, 181
Psalms
  8 — 61
  23 — 128
  51 — 92–93
  112 — 16
  134 — 136
Isaiah
  1:17 — 16
  chapters 4–6 — 63
  5:1–7 — 168
  9:1–7 — 151
Jeremiah
  22:3 — 16
Amos
  5:18–24 — 129
Habakkuk
  2:6–8 — 61

NEW TESTAMENT

Matthew
  5:21–37 — 44
  5:43–48 — 95, 130
  10:16 — 25, 44
  12:25 — 6
  13:1–9 — 18–23, 129, 174
  13:21–22 — 44–52, 176

15:21–28	88	5:1–18	161–163
16:2	60	6:15–16	40
21:33–46	167	10:11–18	130, 134, 154–155
22:15–22	33, 90, 142		
22:39	35	Acts of the Apostles	62
25:31–46	172	4:32–35	129
25:40	99	16:11–15	40, 73–75
26:52	189	Romans	
Mark		2:15	35
Bartimaeus	149	13:1–7	33
1:9–15	67–70	1 Corinthians	
1:21–28	131	chapter 12	99
2:1–12	60, 160–161	Galatians	
4:26–30	192	3:28	130
4:35–41	165	5:19–23	102
7:24–30	88	Hebrews	
10:46–52	147	5:5–10	153
Luke		10:16	35
1:51–53	61	13:2	63
3:7–14	63	1 John	
5:17–39	60	3:16–24	134, 136
John		4:18a	12, 200
3:1–17	164	Revelation	
3:11–21	146	22:2	60

Index

accountability, 34, 48, 61, 68, 110
advocacy, 4, 82, 100, 111, 138, 148, 149
agape love. *See under* love
Allen, O. Wesley, 5, 45–46, 57, 84, 86, 121, 140, 141, 184, 199
Allen, Ronald J., 5, 9, 83, 51, 55, 57, 84, 85, 121, 157, 187, 190–191
Andrews, Dale P., 11, 125, 133, 180, 181–183, 199–200
anger, 4, 13, 19, 20–23, 30, 36, 38, 102, 118, 121, 125, 185, 190. *See also* emotion(s); fear(s)

baptism, 67–70, 74, 96, 171; of Jesus, 44, 67–68, 70
Bartimaeus, 147–149
Beloved Community, 35. *See also* Realm of God
Bible: choosing passages for Purple Zone preaching, 83–84, 127–130; conflict and, 79–81; contemporary issues and, 13, 26, 34–35, 38, 41, 43, 47, 51–53, 60–65, 88–92, 185 (*see also* sermons); dialogical lens and, 65–70, 76, 88–92 (*see also* dialogical lens); justice and, 16–18, 120 (*see also* justice); lectionary and, 83–84; politics and (*see* political, politics); "rooting" prophetic preaching in, 60–65, 88–92, 131 (*see also* "Five Paths of Prophetic Preaching"); topical preaching and, 83–84, 127–130. *See also* Scripture Index
Body of Christ, 10, 12, 43, 81, 85, 94, 101, 179, 180, 182; "white blood cells" and, 12, 101
bridge, bridge-building, 11, 133, 153, 157, 158, 180, 181–183, 186, 192, 195, 199; bridge failure, repairs, 186–192
"burning bush," 38–40

call, calling. *See* God, call of
Christ. *See* Jesus Christ
Christ and Culture (Niebuhr H. Richard), 8, 29, 31–33
Christianity: first-century, 2, 68, 73–75, 129; history of controversies, 2; history of deliberation, 62
Christians: attitude toward culture (*Christ and Culture*, Niebuhr, H. Richard), 31–35; authorized and called to address public issues, 41–42, 47–49, 51–52, 62, 84, 90, 95–96, 98, 118, 160, 172, 179, 181–182; first-century, 2, 68, 73–75, 129; modeling community, 95–96, 119–120; red state–blue state, 1–2; response to

227

228 Index

climate change, 167–173; response to end-of-life issues, 164–167; response to gender-based violence, 137–139; response to gun violence, 94–96, 130; response to health care, 159–163; response to hunger issues, 174–179; response to immigration, 143–158, 192–194; response to mental health issues, 92–94, 126, 130, 134–137; response to opioid crisis, 108–110, 132–133; theological beliefs about conflict, 79–81, 188
Christian faith, 51–52
Christian identity, 31–35, 39, 51–52, 62, 68, 73–75, 95–96, 118, 181–182, 185
church(es): African American, Black church, 33, 48, 198, 220n18; "being the church," 11, 39, 67, 73, 74 77, 82, 88, 94, 139–140, 146, 163, 181–182; "bridge-building" within, 183–196; case studies of sermon-dialogue-sermon used in (*see* sermon-dialogue-sermon method or process); conflict and, 79–81 (*see also* conflict); conversational/collaborative approach within, 55–57, 62–63, 86–88, 119–121; culture and, 31–33, 133, 197, 199 (*see also* church and society); dialogue and, 44, 45, 67, 70, 75–83, 86–88, 98–99, 100–103, 108, 111–112, 117–118, 120, 124, 128, 134–137, 148, 150–151, 155–156, 160, 163, 165, 166, 170, 174–179, 180–189, 192–196, 201 (*see also* conversation); discernment and (*see* community, discernment); divisiveness, polarization and, 5, 10, 23, 24, 71, 74, 81, 82, 98, 127, 191 (*see also* divisive, divisiveness; polarization); early and historical, 2, 73–75; engagement with contemporary issues and, 5, 7, 18–19, 22, 24, 26, 27, 29, 33–34, 38, 39, 41–44, 49, 52, 53, 60, 63, 65, 67, 70, 71, 74–83, 88, 93–95, 98–106, 108, 112, 120, 124, 127, 133–137, 139–140, 142, 145, 147–149, 150–158, 159–160, 163, 165, 166, 170, 173, 174–179, 184, 192–196, 199, 201; food pantry in, 174–179, 192; God working through, 132, 136, 152, 31–35, 39–40, 49, 64, 65, 127, 132–133, 194; healthy, 10–12, 14–15, 25, 27, 45, 71, 75–76, 79–80, 82, 90, 96, 98, 100–102, 146, 155, 157, 173, 186, 191, 196; Hispanic, Spanish-speaking, 150–152, 152–156; immigration and (*see* immigration); mission and, 49, 119, 121, 123, 126, 136, 140, 149, 172; politics and, 29–35, 48, 181–183 (*see also* politics); public square and, 4–5, 8, 15, 39, 42–43, 44, 47–48, 50, 51, 92, 100, 130, 159, 183, 195, 198–200; "Purple Zone church" (*see* Purple Zone); preparing for Purple Zone preaching in, 43–46; red-blue divide within (*see* "red-blue divide"; *see also* congregation(s), divided); research about, 20–26, 35; "sanctuary church," 147–150; "schools of democracy," 100–101; sermon-dialogue-sermon method benefitting, 8, 11–12; state and (including: separation of), 8, 29, 30, 33–35, 45, 199; society and, 9, 31–35, 38, 39, 42, 43, 46, 48–49, 53, 60, 63, 67, 70, 75, 98–101, 112, 118, 133, 137, 157, 159, 173, 183, 194–195; transforming through Purple Zone preaching, 64–65; trust within (*see* trust); worship in (*see* worship)
citizen(s), "citizen-believers," 27, 31, 37, 77, 91, 93, 97–99, 117–118
civic engagement, 97–100
civil discourse, 8, 84, 99, 117. *See also* church, and dialogue; deliberative dialogue; public deliberation, dialogue, discourse

Index 229

clergy, 2–4, 7–8, 11, 13–15, 18–25, 30, 33, 40–41, 43–45, 47, 54, 57, 59, 75, 79, 86, 99–100, 104–105, 119, 142, 187, 192, 195–199, 209–210n1, 211n15, 211n17; female, 198; of color, 20, 198, 220n18 (*see also* Black, African American church); preaching and (*see* preaching); white, 20. *See also* pastor(s); preacher(s)

climate change (*see also* global warming), 3, 11, 19, 27, 38, 59, 60, 79, 105, 125, 158, 159, 167–173, 180, 218n4

collaboration, 10, 48, 55, 81, 99, 104, 111, 119–121, 124–126, 139, 150, 184, 194. *See also* preaching, collaborative

collaborative preaching. *See* preaching, collaborative

covenant, 17, 94, 107

common good, 10, 17, 38, 51, 64, 71, 118

common ground, 5, 106, 110–114, 122–123, 164, 188

common values, 8–10, 66, 67, 77, 102, 110–114, 118, 122–123, 127, 138, 146–148, 151, 154, 156, 161, 163, 164, 166, 171, 186, 193, 201, 204, 207, 220n18

Communal Prophetic Proclamation sermon, 10, 76, 77, 88, 96, 98, 108, 110, 112, 119–140, 147, 180, 184, 185, 194, 197; examples of, 149–150, 151–152, 154–156, 161–163, 165–167, 172–173, 176–179. *See also* sermon-dialogue-sermon method or process

community: building, restoring, or transforming, 3, 10–12, 37–40, 55–57, 62, 64, 75, 86–88, 95–101, 107–112, 119–121, 129, 143–158, 159–180, 185, 189–190, 192–196, 216n3, 220n18; church working with secular community, 11, 27, 37, 53, 55–57, 82, 86–88, 95–101, 103, 107–112, 129, 141–142, 143–158, 159–180, 183, 185–186, 192–196; discernment of, 9, 47–48, 53, 55–57, 62, 64, 67–70, 77, 86–88, 95–101, 107–112, 120–121, 124, 129, 131–134, 143–158, 159–180, 192–196, 220n18 (*see also* church, and dialogue; church, and engagement with contemporary issues; church, and public square; church, and society; deliberative dialogue; public deliberation, dialogue, discourse); health, safety and well-being of, 13–14, 95–101, 107–112, 117–118, 143–158, 163, 192–196; identity, 6, 37–40, 55–57, 107–112; Jesus and his, 6, 8, 40–41, 48, 62, 67–70, 81, 87–88, 90–92, 129–131 (*see also* Jesus Christ); justice within, 14, 16–17 (*see also* justice); of faith, 2, 4, 19, 49, 84, 120, 143, 152, 152 (*see also* houses of worship); preacher articulating discernment of, 124–127, 143–158, 159–180, 192–196, 216n3; problem-solving within, 37, 64, 78, 97, 102, 106, 118, 215n3, 220n16, 220n18

compassion, 37, 49, 73, 75, 92, 110, 118, 120, 125, 141, 179

complexity, 10, 15, 44, 64, 77, 85, 135, 142, 184,

conflict, ix, 7, 9, 15, 21–22, 24, 43, 46, 65, 66, 67, 78, 79–81, 82, 89, 92, 96, 100, 112, 115, 121, 133, 188, 191, 193; management, resources for, 215n6, 219n7; mediating within deliberative dialogue, 115; "theology of," ix, 9, 79–81. *See also* church: divisiveness, polarization and

congregation(s). *See* church(es)

context, contextualizing: congregational, 9–10, 48–49, 78–79, 96, 144, 152–156, 159, 168, 199; deliberative dialogue and, 78–79, 96, 107–108, 111, 120, 122, 153; preaching and,

8–10, 19, 23, 49, 52, 57, 63, 66, 69, 75, 78, 85, 93, 110, 120–121, 139, 144, 145, 153–156, 159, 168, 173, 199, 211n17. *See also* framing, reframing, frameworks; perspective, perspectives
controversial justice issue(s), 13–27, 75, 102, 141; preaching about (*see* sermon(s): social issues); survey (*see* Preaching Controversial Justice Issues survey)
conversation(s), vii, 6–7, 25, 36–41, 43–45, 48, 51–53, 55–57, 63–71, 78–79, 82, 84, 86, 88–96, 102, 119–121, 126, 133–138, 145, 153, 156, 161–166, 170–173, 179, 185, 188, 193–196; about contemporary issues and faith, 61–65, 92–94, 133–138, 161, 166, 170, 185–186, 188–189, 193–194; difficult, vii, 93–96, 106, 161, 163, 172–173, 189 (*see also* Day, Katie); healthy, 10, 11, 45, 71, 75–76, 79, 90, 96, 98, 100, 146, 155, 173, 186, 196–197; Jesus in (*see* Jesus, in conversation); roundtable (*see* Roundtable Pulpit); within deliberative dialogue, 102–118; within scripture, 67–71, 76, 145–146. *See also* church, and dialogue; church, healthy; "Five Paths of Prophetic Preaching," "pollinating"; deliberative dialogue; "dialogical lens," public deliberation, dialogue, discourse
conversational preaching. *See* preaching, collaborative/conversational
courage, 6, 7, 19, 42–43, 44, 50, 68–69, 73, 74, 75, 156, 167, 170, 184
Craddock, Fred, 53–55
Creation, 3, 17, 19, 44, 59, 60, 62, 167–173, 180, 199, 214n2. *See also* climate change; Earth; environmental issues
Creation-Crisis Preaching (Schade, Leah D.), 3, 59–60

critical thinking, critical pedagogy, ix, 42–43, 56, 180
cross, crucifixion. *See* Jesus, cross
culture, 31–33, 51, 74, 112, 131, 143, 152, 199; divided, vii, 2, 74, 201; of the church, 10, 71, 75, 90, 98, 133, 186, 197. *See also* Christ and Culture (Niebuhr, H. Richard)
curious, curiosity (being, having), 2, 88, 115. *See also* wonder

Day, Katie, vii, 4, 106–107, 156–157
deliberative dialogue, viii, 8, 10, 25, 37, 43, 50, 65–67, 76–84, 85–96, 97–118, 119–140, 188–189, 191, 197, 201, 212n21, 217n21, 220n16; case studies and examples of, 146–147, 148–149, 151, 153–154, 161, 164–165, 171–172, 174–176, 192–196, 220n18; facilitating, moderating, 104–117, 203–207; ground rules and, 106–107; explanation of process, 103–111, 203; house(s) of worship and, 99–100, 117, 216n3 (*see also* community, of faith); inviting people to participate in, 103, 220n16; issue guides (*see* National Issues Forums Institute); Kettering Foundation and (*see* Kettering Foundation); mediating conflict within, 115; National Issues Forums Institute and. *See* National Issues Forums Institute (NIFI); politics and, 97–102, 108–111, 117, 122, 127, 137–138, 147, 150, 152–153, 161–164, 167, 172, 175, 192–196, 201; preparing for, 73–84, 103–104, 203–207; questions for reflecting on, 122–123; recorder, 104; sermon incorporating (*see* Communal Prophetic Proclamation); timekeeping, 104. *See also* church, and dialogue; church, and engagement with contemporary issues; church, and public square; church, and society;

community, discernment; public deliberation, dialogue, discourse; sermon-dialogue-sermon method
dialogue, 7, 9–11, 37, 53–56, 62, 64–69, 73–84, 88–96, 97–118, 119–140, 141–158, 183–184, 186, 192–194, 198, 200; healthy, 15, 25, 45, 75–76, 79–80, 155, 173, 186, 196–197; Jesus engaging in (*see* Jesus, in conversation or dialogue); preaching and, 9, 11, 43, 50, 52–53, 185, 199–200, 217n20; organizations for, 216n4. *See also* church, and dialogue; deliberative dialogue; discourse; public deliberation, dialogue, discourse; *Roundtable Pulpit* (McClure, John)
democracy, 99–100, 112
"dialogical lens," 9, 44, 57, 63, 65–67, 69, 83, 89–92, 123, 129, 156, 184, 193, 214n5 (*see also* Bible)
discern, discernment, 4, 9–10, 25, 26, 38, 51, 53, 57, 62–65, 75–77, 81–82, 85, 87–88, 90, 97, 99, 101–102, 114, 120, 123–124, 132–133, 139, 141, 143, 146, 148, 150, 154–156, 185–186, 189, 193, 201
discourse (civil, political, public) 2, 8, 12, 26, 36, 38–40, 45, 49, 53, 75, 84, 91, 97–99, 112, 117, 145, 161, 194. *See also* church, and dialogue; church, and engagement with contemporary issues; church, and public square; church, and society; community, discernment; public deliberation, dialogue, discourse
diversity, 8, 10, 37, 41, 56, 82, 86, 95, 103, 108, 111, 120–121, 127, 136, 138, 143, 147, 151, 163, 212n21
divisive, divisiveness, 2, 4, 10–11, 13–14, 46, 71,73, 74, 79, 86, 90–91, 94, 98, 101, 121, 133, 153, 160, 186, 194, 199, 211n15. *See also* church: divisiveness, polarization in; polarization; political, politics

Earth, 6, 17, 38, 51, 52, 60, 105, 167–173. *See also* climate change, Creation, environmental issues
ecology, ecological issues. *See* climate change; Creation; Earth
emotion(s), 8, 18, 21, 29–30, 35–36, 66, 82, 87, 115, 134, 135, 165, 168, 182, 185–186, 188, 190, 191
empathy, 36, 115, 125, 182, 193. *See also* compassion
empower, empowerment, 36, 41–42, 49–50, 75, 95, 98, 101, 106, 119, 120, 148, 170, 177, 178–180
end-of-life issues, 11, 158, 164–167
environmental issues, 2, 3, 38, 47, 59, 60, 100, 105, 167–173, 181. *See also* climate change; Creation; Earth
equality, 6, 17, 47, 74, 92, 130, 163, 220n16; inequality, 17, 91
ethical, ethics, 9, 15, 35, 46, 48–51, 52, 61, 84, 101, 121, 140; morals/morality and, 26, 51, 100, 115. *See also* justice

faith: action and (or, life and), 63, 70, 90, 92, 96, 101, 107, 120, 128, 130, 146, 148–150, 155, 166, 195, 197, 200; Christian, 51, 52, 54, 63, 67, 73–74, 80, 92, 96, 115, 129, 138, 142, 146, 155, 166, 171,184, 197, 200; communities of; people of, 2, 4, 27, 34, 37, 42, 43, 49, 56, 62, 65, 67, 71, 74, 84, 90, 100, 120, 129, 132, 138, 143, 152, 195, 200, 201, 217n21; faithfulness of God, 193–194; politics and, 1, 4, 31, 33, 34, 39, 42, 61, 74, 90, 115, 138, 148–150, 155, 195, 201; fear(s), 5, 6, 12, 66, 85, 89, 93, 121, 129, 133, 135, 139, 145, 182, 185, 193, 200; clergy and, 14–15, 20–25, 29, 93, 212n19; preaching that addresses and names, 129, 135, 139, 145, 187; "fight or flight," 36, 42, 98, 115

"Five Paths of Prophetic Preaching," 9, 57, 59–71, 88–89, 130–134, 137, 184, 185; diagram, 59; examples of sermons using, 69–70, 92–94, 135–137, 137–139, 144–146, 162–163, 165–167, 167–171, 176–179; flowering and, 59, 61–64, 69–70, 88, 93, 131–132, 135, 137, 144, 168–169, 176; fruiting and, 59, 64–65, 69, 70, 88, 92, 94, 131, 133, 136, 139, 163, 167, 171; leafing and, 59, 63–64, 88, 94, 131, 132–133, 136, 138, 145, 166, 170, 178, 179; pollinating and, 62–63, 64, 65, 69, 70, 88, 93–94, 131, 132, 135, 138, 144, 146, 162–163, 165–166, 170, 177–178; rooting and, 50, 60–65, 67, 69–70, 76, 77, 88, 93, 121, 131, 133, 135, 138, 139, 145, 162, 165, 166, 168–170, 178, 184–185, 192

framing, reframing; frameworks: deliberative dialogue and, 106, 112, 115, 117, 143, 195, 207; sermons and, 10, 11, 27, 39, 45, 49, 84, 85, 90, 92, 94, 95, 123, 129, 131, 137, 139, 145, 148–149, 152, 154, 156, 165, 167, 168, 171, 176, 178, 185, 190–191, 193; politics, 8, 29, 38, 98; biblical, ethical, theological 49, 60–62, 75, 84, 85, 92, 94, 95, 123, 129, 131, 137, 139, 145, 148–149, 152, 154, 156, 165, 167, 168, 171, 176, 178, 185, 193, 195

freedom, 40, 51, 68, 120, 130, 143, 144, 161

gender issues, 15, 149, 198, 217n21; gender-based violence, 130, 137–139. *See also* clergy, female
Gilbert, Kenyatta R., 48–49, 53, 120
global warming. *See* climate change
God: active, present in the world, 10, 12, 16, 31–35, 39–40, 49, 52, 61, 62, 64, 65, 66, 68, 69, 75, 79–81, 89–94, 107, 118, 120, 123, 127–130, 132–134, 136–137, 141–142, 144, 150–152, 167–172, 177, 179, 181, 184–186, 193–194, 200, 201; burning bush and, 38–40; call of, ix, 11, 24, 40, 67, 73, 90, 120, 130, 150–151, 200; children of; people of, 13, 14, 17, 38, 42, 43, 53, 61, 63, 94, 129, 130, 139, 153, 172, 182, 185, 189, 193, 199; conflict and, 79–81 (*see also* conflict); commandments of (*or* Ten Commandments) 34, 63; Creation and 167–173 (*see also* Creation); dialogue and, 67–70, 88–94, 129–130, 185–186; faith in (*see* faith); grace of (*see* grace); healing and, 92–94 (*see also* healing); household of, 56; judgment of, 14; justice and, 16–17, 56–57 (*see also* justice); kingdom of (*see* Kingdom of God); law of, 34–35; love of, 12, 16, 17, 50, 56, 94, 96, 136, 141, 193–194 (*see also* love); Moses, Israel, and, 38–39, 145–146; people of (*see* God, children of); preaching about, 45–46, 50, 56–57, 60–65, 177, 179, 193–194; Samuel, Eli, and, 150–151; shepherding, 134–137, 154–156; society, church and, 16–17, 32–35, 47, 60–65, 88–94, 132, 151–152, 185–186; speaking through preachers, prophets, church, 14, 16; Spirit of *See* Holy Spirit; trusting, 4, 75, 134 (*see also* trust); will of, 41, 53, 69, 80, 143, 188; Word of (*see* Word of God); worshiping (*see* worship). *See also:* theology, theological
Good Shepherd. *See* God, shepherding; Jesus, Good Shepherd
gospel (*or* Good News), 34, 41, 43, 52, 57, 75, 83, 87, 100, 120–121, 126, 141, 154, 180, 184, 189–191, 194, 199, 200; preaching, proclaiming the, x, 3, 34, 37, 54, 56, 63, 75, 83,

87, 120–121, 126, 141, 146, 158, 159, 180, 184; prophetic dimensions of, 41, 48, 52, 124–125, 159; Prosperity Gospel, 31; Social Gospel Movement, 32, 100. *For* Gospels of Matthew, Mark, Luke, John, *see* Scripture Index
government. *See* church, state and (*including*: separation of); political, politics
grace, 31, 45, 52, 67, 75, 157, 171; proclaiming God's, 46, 52, 70
guns, gun control, gun violence, 4, 5, 19, 47, 82, 94, 95–96, 118, 130, 141. *See also* National Issues Forums Institute (NIFI), issue guide: gun violence, mass shootings

healing, health, 5, 11, 12, 35, 37, 43, 65, 93–95, 102, 118, 120, 133, 139, 162–163, 192; stories in Bible about, 60, 88, 147–149, 160–163; Jesus and, 40, 51, 60, 147–149, 160–163; church and (*see* church, healthy); mental (*see* mental health). *See also* Body of Christ, "white blood cells" and
health care, 47, 60, 117–118, 129, 158, 159–163, 180, 182. *See also* National Issues Forums Institute (NIFI), issue guide: health care
Hispanic, Spanish-speaking churches. *See* churches, Hispanic, Spanish-speaking; immigration
history, 34, 43, 57, 62, 79, 80, 81, 100, 107, 143, 147, 152, 157; church, 57, 100, 107, 143, 191; congregation's, congregational, 44, 79, 81–82, 147; God's people, of, 13, 16; human, 34, 62, 80, 157; national, 2, 14; personal, 152, 219n6; Holy Spirit, 5, 49, 50, 68, 70, 74, 81, 107, 115, 166, 200; activity of, 66, 68, 70, 74, 81, 85, 87, 89, 90, 91, 95, 102, 115, 118, 120, 123, 127–128, 133,

146, 182, 185, 192, 200; guidance of, 6, 10, 12, 53, 57, 75, 107, 111, 115, 119, 127–128, 135–136, 146, 185, 189, 192, 200, 201; gift of, 10, 85, 102, 166; inspiring preacher, preaching, 54, 120, 179; working within congregation, 37, 81, 85, 87, 90, 95, 102, 107, 111, 115, 118, 123, 127–128, 133, 135–136, 146, 166, 182, 185, 200
homiletic theory, homiletics, 9, 47–57, 182–183; contemporary issues and, 48, 51, 98, 157; conversational preaching (*see* preaching: collaborative, conversational); ethics and, 9, 66; New Homiletic, 53–54. *See also* preaching; sermons
hope, 40, 48, 49, 50, 52–53, 67, 90, 111, 120, 123, 134, 144, 146, 163, 171, 184–186, 192–194
Horrell, Dana, 98, 118
hospitality, 6, 63, 73–75, 94, 141, 216n3
humility, 37, 50, 86
hunger, 41, 100, 129, 158, 159, 174–179, 180, 220n18. *See also* National Issues Forums Institute (NIFI), issue guide: hunger

ideology, 5, 52, 138
immigration, 5, 11, 19, 27, 47, 62–63, 69, 70, 79, 82, 100, 118, 128, 141–158, 179, 182, 192–194, 195, 210n3, 211n15. *See also* National Issues Forums Institute (NIFI), issue guide: immigration
injustice. *See* justice, injustice and
integrity, 6, 73, 75, 83, 120
"issues of public concern," ix, 7, 8, 9, 14, 21, 29, 33, 34, 38, 43, 45, 52, 57, 60, 71, 83, 87, 121, 123, 130, 184, 198, 199; Bible and, 60–65 (*see also* Bible); Church and (*see* church, and engagement with contemporary issues)

Jacobsen, David Schnasa, 50, 56
Jesus Christ, 12, 25, 31, 33, 40–41, 49, 51, 87, 99, 120, 123, 126, 141, 155, 156, 182, 184–186, 194, 199, 200; baptism of, 44, 67–70; "bridge-builder," 153; calming storm, 165–167; casting out demons, 131; climate change and, 60, 169–170, 173; conversation or dialogue (engaging in), 40–41, 43, 48, 62, 68, 81, 88, 90–92, 94, 127, 129, 131, 142, 146, 147–148, 153, 161–162, 164, 189; cross, crucifixion, 41, 51, 70, 146, 170–171, 182, 184, 200; engaging with public issues, 8, 26, 40–41, 43, 47–48, 60, 62, 68, 90–92, 94, 130, 142, 153, 164, 189; faith in, 27; Good Shepherd, 130, 134–137, 152, 154–155; healing, 60, 147–149, 160–163; love of, 3, 130, 146, 190; political, 8, 35, 40–41; politics and, 1; red-state, blue state, 1–2, 43 (*see also* "red-blue divide"); resurrection of, 12, 38, 40, 51, 53, 120, 149; taxes and, 142; teacher, 42–43. *See also* Christ and Culture
John the Baptist, 35, 63
joy, 35, 52, 102, 120, 163, 185, 194, 196
justice: Bible and, 16–18, 27, 51, 61, 67, 74, 85, 120, 129, 168; biblical concepts of *mishpat* and *tsĕdaqah* (justice and righteousness), 16–18, 27, 120; God, Jesus, and, 14, 16–17, 27, 34–35, 40, 45, 49, 56, 62, 65, 67, 90, 92, 120, 129, 133, 168, 185–186, 199–200; definition of, 8, 15–19, 35; economic, 61, 160; injustice and, 5, 16–17, 18, 33, 51, 53, 61, 73, 74, 85, 160, 180, 200; King, Martin Luther Jr. and, 32; "least of these" and, 52, 62, 99, 172–173, 200; morality and, 15; Paul of Tarsus and, 74; preaching and, 2–3, 5–8, 10, 13–27, 29–30, 35, 45, 49–50, 53, 55–56, 61–62, 65, 69–70, 75, 82, 90, 92, 100, 120, 123, 129, 133, 141, 154–155, 160–161, 180, 185, 187, 199, 211n15 (*see also* preaching); righteousness (*see* justice, biblical concepts of); survey, "Preaching about Controversial Justice Issues" (*see* Preaching Controversial Justice Issues survey); worship and, 16. *See also* injustice

Kaufman, Gregg, viii, 99, 143, 147, 216n3, 217n21
Kettering Foundation, Charles F., viii, 10, 98–101, 175, 198, 201, 212n21, 217n21, 220n15; *See also* National Issues Forums Institute (NIFI)
King, Martin Luther, Jr., 32
Kingdom of God (*also* Kingdom of Heaven; Realm of God; Reign of God; Household of God; Beloved Community; Peaceable Community), 8, 16, 32, 33, 35, 40–42, 46, 49, 52, 56, 57, 64, 68, 69, 132–133, 154, 156, 163, 171, 173, 177–178. *See also* Two Kingdoms

laity, lay leaders, 8, 11, 27, 56, 99, 106, 120, 195, 197
leaders, leadership, 14, 26, 36–37, 42, 44, 80, 86, 90, 97, 99, 100, 105, 106, 118, 119–121, 140, 150, 172, 182, 195–196, 197
"least of these." *See* justice, "least of these"
lectionary, 26, 44, 83, 128, 134, 142, 167, 172, 211n16
liberate, liberation, 16, 40, 43, 50, 130, 137, 139; liberation theology, 52, 66
listen, listening, 3, 5, 6, 9, 36–37, 51, 54, 56–57, 65, 69, 70, 73–75, 84, 86–88, 96, 100, 102, 107, 109, 117, 121, 125, 148–149, 150–151, 154, 164, 171, 176, 178–179, 182, 184, 188–189

liturgy, 186, 200
love, 12, 16–17, 35, 37, 40–43, 51, 62, 67, 69, 95–96, 102, 125, 129–130, 136–137, 144, 147, 158, 170–171, 172, 182, 185, 189–190, 194, 200; *agape*-love, 37, 41–42, 96, 125; Christ's (*see* Jesus Christ, love of); enemies and, 95, 130; God's (*see* God, love of); neighbor-love, 18, 35; speaking truth in love (*see* truth: speaking truth in love)
Luther, Martin; Lutheran theology, 8, 32, 33–34, 52, 120. See also "Two Kingdoms" doctrine
Lydia of Thyatira, 9, 73–75

marginalized, margins, 34, 52, 56, 98, 198
Marshall, Ellen Ott, ix, 37, 215n6
McClure, John S., 5, 10, 44, 52, 55, 66, 119–121, 124–127, 150, 159, 216n3, 217n20
mental health, mental illness, 27, 92–94, 110, 126, 130, 134–137, 176, 177, 178. *See also* National Issues Forum (NIFI), issue guides: mental health, mental illness
Miriam, 130, 137–139
mission. *See* church, mission and
Moiso, Aimee, ix, 79–81
model, modelling: Bible as modelling dialogue, 62, 67, 73, 76, 88, 129, 164, 167; church as, 45, 95–96, 155; deliberative dialogue and, 104, 115, 125; Jesus as, 48, 81, 87–88, 131, 164, 167; Lydia of Thyatira as, 9, 73–75; preachers, preaching as, 81, 84, 87, 121, 173, 179, 180; sermon-dialogue-sermon as, 37, 141, 180, 185
Moses, 38–39, 62, 137, 144–146

narrative, 16, 54, 65, 66, 68, 108, 111, 176, 194, 220n18. National Issues

Forums Institute (NIFI), viii, 10, 76, 77, 98–99, 101–102, 104, 106–107, 110, 112, 184, 198, 201, 212n21, 217n21, 220n15; issue guides, 76–78, 90, 92, 99, 102, 106–107, 110, 214n3, 216n3, 217n21, 220n15, 220n18: climate change, 171–172 (*see also* climate change; environmental issues; Creation); economic issues, 90; end-of-life, 164–167; faith-based, 143–144; gender-based violence, 137–139 (*see also* gender issues: gender-based violence); gun violence, mass shootings, 94–96, 130 (*see also:* guns, gun control, gun violence); health care, 160–162 (*see also*, health care); immigration, 142–143, 146–147, 192–194 (*see also* immigration); mental health, mental illness, 92–94, 126, 130, 134–137 (*see also,* mental health, mental illness); opioid crisis, 108–110, 132–133, 217n21. *See also* deliberative dialogue; Kettering Foundation
Nazi(s), neo-Nazis, 23, 34
neutral, neutrality, 30, 87, 188; deliberative dialogue and, 104–105, 108; preaching and, 122. *See also* nonpartisan
Nicodemus, 146, 164
Niebuhr, H. Richard. *See* Christ and Culture
nonpartisan, 7, 10, 14, 201; Jesus as, 40; National Issues Forums Institute issue guides and, 10, 99, 106, 171. *See also* neutral, neutrality

oikos ("house"), 6, 56
opioid addiction crisis, 108–110, 131–133, 195, 217n21. *See also* National Issues Forums Institute (NIFI), issue guides: opioid epidemic
oppression, 14, 16, 17, 34, 40, 42, 51, 52, 68, 91, 139

partisan, partisanship, 10, 33, 37, 39, 61, 108, 160, 186. *See also* nonpartisan
pastoral, pastoral care, pastoral relationships 5–6, 15, 19, 21–22, 25, 30, 36, 42, 48–50, 53, 56, 76, 85–86, 94, 182, 184, 188–192, 199–200, 212n19
Paul of Tarsus, 33, 73–75, 102
peace, peacemaking, 51, 69–70, 79, 92, 94, 102, 148, 155, 166–167, 171, 186, 190, 215n6, 219n7
"Peaceable Community." *See* Kingdom of God
perspective, perspectives: biblical, theological, and contemporary issues, 4–5, 26, 43–44, 49, 60–64, 85–88, 142, 161; conflicting, 4–5, 19, 95, 187–190; deliberative dialogue and, 103, 108–117, 123, 147, 151–153, 165; preaching that incorporates different perspectives, 10, 43–45, 60–64, 84–88, 95, 108–111, 121, 161, 173, 189, 191. *See also* context
polarization, 5, 85, 90, 97, 111, 157, 182, 183, 190, 199. *See also* church, churches: divisiveness, polarization; political, politics
policy. *See* public policy
political, politics: Bible and, 38, 40–41, 61, 66–69, 73–75, 77, 90–92, 129, 142–158, 159–180, 181; church and, 2, 4–5, 8, 13, 27, 29–46, 56, 68–71, 74, 77, 86, 92, 100–102, 134, 137, 142–158, 159–180, 181–182, 192–193, 198–200, 201; clergy and, 15, 22–27, 29–46, 86, 159–180, 192–196, 198–200, 211n15, 211n17; definition, 8, 29–31, 37–40; deliberative dialogue and (*see* deliberative dialogue); divided, 86, 91, 92, 199, 201, 211n15; divisive (*see* divisive, divisiveness); faith and (*see* faith, politics and); national, 1–2, 5, 97–102, 211n15; red-blue, 1–2, 27, 39, 71, 159, 199 (*see also* "red-blue divide"); Jesus and, 1, 8, 40–41, 68–69, 90–92, 153–155, 160–163 (*see also* Jesus Christ); Lydia and (*see* Lydia of Thyatira); partisan, nonpartisan, 7, 10, 14, 33, 37, 39, 40, 61, 99, 106, 108, 160, 171, 186, 201; Paul of Tarsus and (*see* Paul of Tarsus); polarized; (*see* polarization); preachers and, 13, 19–27, 29–46, 68–71, 85–92, 134–140, 142–158, 159–180, 192–196; preaching and, 4–8, 13, 19–27, 29–46, 52, 68–71, 85–92, 126–127, 129, 134–140, 142–158, 159–180, 192–196, 198–200, 211n15 (*see also* preaching, prophetic); sermons, 8, 13, 19–27, 29–46, 68–71, 85–92, 126–127, 129, 134–140, 142–158, 159–180, 192–196
poverty, 41, 148, 176, 179, 192
power: abuse of, 14, 17, 34, 35–36, 40, 63, 68, 91; accountability and, 17–18, 34, 35–36, 49, 91; God and, Holy Spirit and, 40, 50 52, 192 (*see also* God; Holy Spirit); differentials in society, 19, 80, 198; differentials between clergy/preachers and parishioners, 35–36, 80, 220n16; equality and, 6, 91; exercising, 41; Jesus and, 8, 40–41, 90–92, 160, 163, 170 (*see also* Jesus Christ); levels of, 41; political, politics and, 40, 68, 97 (*see also* political, politics); powers and principalities (also "the powers"), 6, 8, 51, 68, 170; preaching and, 53, 84, 199; shared, 120; speaking truth to power, 40, 49, 141; those in positions of, 17–18, 34, 35–36, 40–41, 48, 68, 80; those without, 56, 80; trust and, 36–37 (*see also* trust); wealth and, 6, 69, 91
pray, prayer, praying, 1, 6, 73, 74, 130, 136, 166, 186, 189; deliberative dialogue and, 106, 107, 112, 115, 193, 195

preacher, preachers: accused of violating separation of church and state, 33–35; advice for preaching prophetically, 181–186, 199–200; as "elephant trainers," 141–142, 156–158; as host of "potluck of ideas," 86–88, 216n3; as "Lone Ranger," 50–51; as prophets, 45–46, 48–50, 53, 85–86, 124; as public theologians, 48, 119, 159; as teacher, 9, 42–43, 48, 179–180; as "threading the needle," 142–144, 158; attending to the margins, 52–53; avoiding controversial justice issues, 10, 21, 71, 90, 98, 133; collaborative (*see* sermons); contemporary issues and, 6, 8, 13, 14–15, 18–27, 35, 47–48, 51–52, 60–65, 85, 141–142, 210n3, 211n17; courage and (*see* courage); encouraging and equipping of, 7–8, 12, 184–186, 199–200; feelings of failure and, 190–192; female (*see* clergy, female); hesitant to preach prophetically, 5–8, 14–15, 18–27, 41, 141–142, 183–184, 211n17; in dialogue, 55, 65, 84, 128, 200; listening (*see* listening); naming who the church is, 139–140; navigating Purple Zone, 3–4, 6, 199–200; relationship with listeners, 53–57, 84, 119–121, 124, 216n3; research and survey about, 6–8, 14–15, 18–27, 35, 183–184, 210n3, 211n15, 211n16, 211n17; "too political," 29–31, 35–37. *See also* clergy; preaching; sermons

"preacher-as-teacher," 9, 42–43, 48, 179–180. *See also* Voelz, Richard

preaching: African American; black, 48–49 (*see also* church: African American); authoritarian, 53–55; collaborative/conversational, 9, 10, 46, 48, 53, 55, 84, 119–121, 126, 124–126, 139, 150, 156, 184, 217n20 (*see also* Roundtable Pulpit [McClure, John]); conversation, as, 48, 55, 86; conversation partners and, 51–53, 62; context and (*see* context: preaching and); controversial justice issues, 2, 3, 8, 10, 13–27, 65, 85, 141 (*see also* sermon(s): social issues); dialogical lens and (*see* "dialogical lens"); New Homiletic and (*see* homiletics: New Homiletic); pastoral v. prophetic; pastorally prophetic 42, 48–50, 53, 56, 76, 85–86, 94, 165–167, 180, 182, 184, 190–192, 199–200; politics and (*see* political, politics: preaching and; preachers and); prophetic; (*see* prophetic preaching); public issues and, 4–5, 13, 14, 20–26, 29, 33, 41, 42–46, 47, 49, 50, 51, 56, 57, 60–65, 67, 89–90, 120, 156–157, 184, 199; (*see also* "issues of public concern"); public theology, as (*see* public theology); research about, 6–8, 14–27, 183, 196–199, 209n1, 210n3, 211n15, 211n16, 211n17, 212n19; social issues (*see* sermon(s): social issues); "trivocal," 48–49 (*see also* Gilbert, Kenyatta). *See also* sermons; homiletics; proclamation

Preaching Controversial Justice Issues survey, viii, 13–27, 55, 100, 183, 198, 210n3, 211n15

presidential elections, 1, 14, 97, 150, 181–182, 200

principles, 8, 21, 29–35, 37 66, 69, 100–101, 116, 119–120, 158, 188; biblical, 60, 64, 69, 88, 99, 100, 111, 131; *Christ and Culture* and, 30–33; deliberative dialogue and, 101, 116, 119–120, 197; justice and, 49, 120 (*see also* justice); resistance to prophetic sermons and, 8, 21, 29–35, 188; separation of church and state, 33–35; Two Kingdoms doctrine, 33–35

238   Index

privilege: preacher in position of, 54–55, 84; socioeconomic, racial, 3, 6, 174–179
proclaiming, proclamation 6, 14, 25, 34, 41–42, 46, 47–49, 52, 54–55, 57, 68, 69, 86, 100, 119–120, 137, 139, 141, 146, 155, 167, 182, 184, 190, 210n14; prophetic, 41, 49, 55, 167, 182, 184, 210n14. See also homiletics; preaching; sermon-dialogue-sermon method or process
prophet(s) (including biblical), 9, 13–14, 16–17, 45, 48–50, 56, 60, 90, 141, 184, 186
"prophetic care," 11, 125, 180, 181–183, 190–191, 199. See also Andrews, Dale P. Prophetic Invitation to Dialogue sermon, 9–10, 71, 75–77, 82, 84, 85–96, 121, 124, 127, 131, 134, 137, 156–157, 180, 184–185, 192, 195, 197; examples of, 90–96, 144–146, 147–148, 150–151, 153, 160–161, 164, 167–171, 174
prophetic preaching, 3–11, 13–15, 19, 23, 25, 34, 36, 41–42, 44–45, 48–50, 52–53, 55–57, 59–71, 75, 85–96, 119–140, 141–158, 159–180, 181–200, 210n14; avoiding, 21–22, 29; Communal Prophetic Proclamation sermon (see sermon-dialogue-sermon method or process); definitions of, 18–19, 48–50; "Five Paths of" (see "Five Paths of Prophetic Preaching"); Jesus and (see Jesus Christ); justice and (see justice: preaching and); negative pushback of (see sermons: negative pushback to); pastoral versus (see preaching: pastoral v. prophetic; pastorally prophetic); Preaching About Controversial Justice Issues survey and, 18–19; Prophetic Invitation to Dialogue sermon (see sermon-dialogue-sermon method or process); "prophetic care" (see

"prophetic care"; Andrews, Dale P.); silencing, 23–25
Prophetic Preaching (Tisdale, Leonora Tubbs), 5, 6–8, 15, 18–19, 21–22, 41, 49–50, 53, 125, 210n14, 212n19
public issues (see "issues of public concern")
public policy, 5, 17, 19, 98, 100, 105, 106, 136, 207
public theology, 8, 9, 25, 51, 119, 159
public deliberation, dialogue, discourse, 4, 5, 8, 12, 19, 38, 40, 47, 75–77, 92, 99, 100, 101, 112, 194, 195. See also discourse
public square (see church, churches: public square and)
Purple Zone: love in, 96, 200 (see also love); author's background and experience in, vii–x, 2–4, 44–45, 98–99, 105, 189, 191–192; building bridges in, 181–200; clergy ministering in, 2, 6–8, 13–27, 85–88 (see also church(es); congregation(s); red-blue divide); conflict in (see conflict); definition of, 2, 4, 6; deliberative dialogue in, 97–118; examples of preaching in, 141–158, 159–180 (see also sermon-dialogue-sermon method or process); Five Paths of Prophetic Preaching in, 59–71; future research about, 196–199; homiletical foundations for, 47–57; Jesus in, 41 (see also Jesus Christ); laity in, 11 (see also laity, lay leaders); Lydia of Thyatira in, 73–75; mistakes and failures in, 3–4, 183, 189–192; overview of, 8–12, 184; preaching in, 7–12, 14, 17, 27, 32–33, 37–39, 41–43, 46, 48, 50–56, 73, 80, 83–84, 85–86, 89–92, 120, 139, 142, 192–196, 199–200 (see also preach, preaching; prophetic preaching; sermons; preparing congregation for, 43–45. See also

church(es); congregation(s): divided; red-blue divide

quietism, 25, 32, 34

race, racism, 3, 23, 32, 82, 84, 100, 117, 130, 151, 156, 181, 182, 211n15, 211n18
"red-blue divide," 1–4, 6, 11, 18, 23, 27, 39, 41, 43, 71, 74, 91, 159, 163, 199. *See also* political, politics
refugees. *See* immigration
relationships, 39, 100, 120, 141, 157; church and, 22, 27, 35–36, 42, 75, 78–81, 118, 151, 157, 161, 163, 164, 195; clergy-parishioners (also, pastoral), 8, 11–12, 19, 22, 25, 27, 30, 35–36, 56, 79–81, 160, 179, 184, 186, 188–190; conflict and, 79–81; deterioration of civility in, 2; equality and, 17, 56; God and humans, 39, 79–81, 120, 133; healed, healthy, healthier, 8, 11–12, 27, 75, 133, 151, 157, 185, 186; justice and, 17, 34–35, 40 (*see also* justice); preacher-listeners, 8, 11–12, 25, 30, 35–36, 54–56, 80, 125, 139, 160, 179, 186; Purple Zone and, 37, 190; ruptured, 11, 30, 36, 78; Ten Commandments and, 34; trust and (*see* trust)
religion and politics 16–17, 31–33, 51, 100, 182. *See also* political, politics
respect, respectful 3, 5, 8, 37, 39, 48, 57, 86, 102–104, 107, 109, 118, 122, 139, 147, 155–156, 184, 189, 196
rhetoric, rhetorical, 64, 66, 119, 121, 132; divisive, inflammatory, toxic, 5, 85, 112, 167, 183; techniques in preaching, 119, 125, 132, 158, 184, 217n20
Roundtable Pulpit (McClure, John), 119–121, 126–127
Rose, Lucy Atkinson, 54–57
Ruth and Naomi, 63, 128, 192–194

safe, safety, 36, 110, 118, 134, 139, 148–149, 151, 154–155, 171, 181–182, 186, 187, 188, 195–196, 198, 216n8, 219n6; church as place of, 101, 148–149, 193, 195, 198; public, 95, 132
Schade, Leah D., vii–x, 3, 59–60
science and faith, 61
"separation of church and state," 8, 29, 30, 33–35. *See also* church, state and; "Two Kingdoms"
sermon-dialogue-sermon method or process, ix, 8–12, 25, 27, 37, 41, 43, 73–84, 85–96, 97–118, 119–140, 183–184, 192, 195–199; case studies, examples, 141–158, 159–180; choosing topic for, 76–82; "cool," "warm," "hot" topics, 78–79; deliberative dialogue within (*see* deliberative dialogue); timeline for process in congregation, 75–76. *See also* Communal Prophetic Proclamation sermon; deliberative dialogue; Prophetic Invitation to dialogue sermon. sermon(s), 84, 86–87, 96, 124, 157, 185–192, 199–200, 211n15; conversational/collaborative, 54–57, 119–121, 125–126; dialogical lens and (*see* "dialogical lens"); environmental issues and, 59; examples, excerpts 38–39, 69–70, 90–96, 134–139, 144–156, 160–179 (*see also* sermon-dialogue-sermon method or process); listeners interrupting, 187, 219n6; negative push-back about, 4, 8, 13–14, 19–25, 29–31, 35–36, 38, 44–45, 103, 187–192; New Homiletic, 53–55; political, 8, 13–14, 29–30, 33, 36, 38–39, 211n16 (*see also* political, politics: sermons); prophetic 4, 9–11, 13–14, 18, 21, 31, 36, 45, 64, 86, 142 (*see also* preaching); Prophetic Invitation to Dialogue sermon (*see* sermon-dialogue-sermon method or process); rooting,

flowering, pollinating, leafing, fruiting in 4–5, 7, 13–14, 19–26, 29–30, 43–44, 47, 75, 83, 85, 90–96, 196, 211n16, 211n17 (*see also* Five Paths of Prophetic Preaching, social issues and); topical, 9, 83–84, 128, 211n16. *See also* Communal Prophetic Proclamation sermon; homiletics; preaching; proclamation; Prophetic Invitation to Dialogue sermon; sermon-dialogue-sermon method or process

sin, sinfulness, 32, 41, 45, 49, 50, 52, 67, 68, 80, 89, 90, 92–93, 125, 142, 145–146, 155, 182–183; systemic, 9, 14, 15, 17, 45, 49, 51, 61, 68, 89–90, 135, 143, 160, 163, 174, 182–183, 187

social issues. *See* "issues of public concern"

social justice. *See* justice

story, stories: biblical (*see* Bible; God; Jesus Christ); personal, 108, 115, 189, 191, 207. *See also* narrative

systemic sin. *See* sin, sinfulness: systemic

taboos, 19, 42, 43, 88, 94

taxes, 1, 47, 90–92; Jesus and, 41, 90–92, 142

theology, theological: ecological, 3, 167–173; deliberative dialogue and, 123, 127–128, 156, 165–166, 200; discernment and (*see* community, discernment of); justice and, 16–17, 75, 123; liberation theology, 52, 66; politics and, 29, 34, 37, 45, 51–53, 56–57, 141, 185; preaching and, 8, 10, 13, 26, 42, 45, 51–53, 56–57, 60–62, 64, 66, 75–76, 83–84, 85, 92, 94, 99, 119, 121, 123, 127–128, 131, 140, 141, 145, 152, 154, 156, 159, 165–166, 167–173, 184, 185, 193–194, 200; Lutheran (*see* Luther, Martin; Lutheran theology); public (*see* public theology)

"theology of conflict." *See* conflict, "theology of"

Tisdale, Leonora Tubbs, 5, 6–8, 15, 18–19, 21–22, 41, 49–50, 53, 125, 210n14, 212n19. *See also* Prophetic Preaching

topical preaching, topical sermons. *See* sermons, topical

transformation, transformational, transforming: church and, 10, 31, 37, 42, 46, 49, 52, 71, 80, 90, 98, 120, 133, 139, 173, 186, 190, 197; God/Christ and, 32, 41, 46, 49, 80, 88, 96, 120, 130, 141, 151, 173; preaching and, 42–43, 46, 49, 59, 64, 90, 94, 139, 180; social/cultural and, 31, 37, 46, 52, 59, 131, 139, 194

Trump, Donald, 121, 150, 182, 199

trust, 3, 25, 36–37, 96, 97, 145, 150–151, 188–189; clergy (preacher), parishioner and, 25, 29, 36–37, 47, 81, 84, 87, 109, 118, 119, 124–125, 153 156–158, 171, 184, 188, 212n19; God/Jesus/Holy Spirit and, ix, 40, 57, 75, 119, 134, 167, 189, 200

truth, 51, 87, 136, 137, 185; prophetic, 87, 184; speaking truth in love, 5–6, 75; speaking truth in preaching, 5–6, 56, 136, 184, 185; speaking truth to power, 40, 141

"Two Kingdoms," 8, 32, 33–35, 45. *See also* Lutheran doctrine; "separation of church and state"

values: competing, 6, 78, 101, 112, 115, 153–154, 165, 180; finding common, shared, core 8–10, 67, 89, 91, 99, 102, 104, 106, 107, 109–112, 114–116, 122–123, 127, 130–131, 137–139, 146–151, 154, 156, 161, 163–166, 175, 186, 193, 201; in deliberative dialogue, 102–118, 143, 147–148, 151, 153–154, 161, 164–165, 171–172, 175, 193, 203–207, 220n18; preaching about or informed by, 61, 63, 66–68, 76, 86, 89–91, 121, 127, 130–131, 137–139, 146–151, 154, 156, 157, 163–166, 171, 186

violence, 16, 68, 78, 108, 130, 137–139, 148, 189, 190; gender-based, 27, 130, 137–139, 217n21; gun, 19, 47, 82, 94–96, 118, 130; nonviolence, 37, 186; preaching about, 19, 82, 94–96, 130, 137–139; vision, envisioning: congregation's, 49, 121, 136, 149; of God's future, 18, 46, 49, 52, 92, 100, 120, 123, 133, 136, 179, 186; preaching setting forth, 136, 139, 163, 186

Voelz, Richard, ix, 9, 42–43, 179

vulnerable, "those most vulnerable," 14, 17, 59, 80, 105, 135, 137, 155, 192

vulnerability: feelings of, 36; preacher modeling and inviting, 57, 88, 109, 164, 186

white privilege, white supremacy, 23

wisdom, collective, 48–49, 55, 87, 95, 97, 107, 112, 115, 117, 119, 171

wonder, wondering: as invitation in dialogue, 110, 115, 116; community wondering together, 47, 110, 115, 116; sermon and, 88, 137, 139, 170, 177, 179. *See also* curiosity

Word of God, 6, 8, 44, 49, 51–52, 60, 101, 126, 173, 190, 200. *See also* Bible

worship, 13, 16–17, 19, 35, 39, 42, 56, 62, 73–74, 134, 174, 182, 186, 187, 200; Holy Communion, 171, 173

About the Author

Rev. Dr. Leah D. Schade is assistant professor of preaching and worship at Lexington Theological Seminary in Lexington, Kentucky. She is an ordained minister in the Evangelical Lutheran Church of America with twenty years of experience. She has pastored three different churches in suburban, urban, and rural settings with members spanning the red-blue political spectrum. Leah earned both her MDiv and PhD from the Lutheran Theological Seminary at Philadelphia (now United Lutheran Seminary) and is author of the book *Creation-Crisis Preaching: Ecology, Theology and the Pulpit* (2015). She has been an activist for environmental justice issues for over a decade.

Made in the USA
Monee, IL
23 February 2021